# A HISTORY OF THE WORLD IN

## SIXTEEN SHIPWRECKS

# A HISTORY
# OF THE WORLD IN
# *SIXTEEN*
# SHIPWRECKS

STEWART GORDON

*ForeEdge*

ForeEdge
An imprint of University Press of New England
www.upne.com
© 2015 Stewart Gordon
All rights reserved
Manufactured in the United States of America
Designed by Eric M. Brooks
Typeset in Bulmer by Passumpsic Publishing
Map by Patti Isaacs, Parrot Graphics

For permission to reproduce any of the material in this book,
contact Permissions, University Press of New England, One Court
Street, Suite 250, Lebanon NH 03766; or visit www.upne.com

ISBN: 978-1-61168-540-4
Library of Congress Cataloging-in-Publication Data
available upon request

5  4  3  2  1

# CONTENTS

# INTRODUCTION

Shipwrecks are a tragic but expected part of the human experience. Their numbers are staggering. A UNESCO estimate places three million shipwrecks in earth's oceans.[1] To this number must be added the ships lost on the world's lakes and rivers. Even this massive number is surely an underestimate, since scholars have no data on boats and ships in earlier periods for large parts of the world, such as the sea-lanes around India and Southeast Asia, the coast of China, South America, or the Caribbean.

We can be sure, however, that boats and ships are far older than any direct evidence of remains or shipwrecks. The forty-thousand-year-old human migration to Australia required some sort of boat or raft to cross the Torres Strait off the southern coast of New Guinea. The archaeological evidence from the earliest settlements on the York Peninsula suggests that a relatively large group, more than a thousand people, came at the same time. Even earlier craft would have been necessary to colonize the islands of Indonesia and reach New Guinea. Other, less ancient migrations also required watercraft; these include Sri Lanka, the Philippines, the Caribbean islands, and Ireland.

Additional evidence for very early ships comes from trade. Archaeologists have identified materials that come from only one place but have been excavated at sites reachable only across open water. Examples include greenstone from Scandinavia, flint from Sardinia, carnelian from India, and copper from southern France.

Of the millions of wrecks and the thousands of located wrecks, I have selected sixteen based on the following criteria:

1 The wreck represents a type of ship that had a significant impact on human history. In addition, some of the shipwrecks directly affected changes in design, construction, laws, or regulation.
2 Shipwrecks would come from around the globe and through history to the present. I especially wanted wrecks beyond the much-studied Mediterranean.
3 The shipwreck needed good archaeological and textual documentation, which describes the worlds in which the ship operated, such as

economics, migration, the movement of ideas, political rivalry, war, and environmental constraints.

The book does not, therefore, select only wrecks with a large number of casualties, those with especially rich cargo, or those that directly influenced maritime law or regulations. Rather, each chapter begins with the wrenching tragedy of the wreck and the excitement of the find, then moves to the design of the ship and wider questions. What was aboard the ship and why, where did it come from and where was it bound, who financed it, who sailed on it, and what we can infer about the surrounding society's contacts and interchanges. Some of the sixteen shipwrecks are well known, and others quite obscure.

In treating shipwrecks as a window into maritime and larger worlds, I have widened the traditional definition of a shipwreck from the destruction of a ship by storm or collision. This book includes ancient ships consciously buried, ships that sank following fire or explosion, ships lost in warfare, and the loss of boats that operated on rivers and lakes.

Overall, the book explores how small ancient local maritime worlds slowly merged into regional worlds and finally into our single unified, globalized maritime world. The viewpoint of the book is that a maritime world was—to borrow from ecology—a habitat, in which owners and builders struggled for "fitness." Shipbuilders judged local conditions (commodities, tides, surf, weather, seasons) and arrived at a variety of workable ship designs that used local materials and skills and seemed acceptably stable and safe, capable of carrying what was necessary, and cost-effective. Some ships were for open-ocean sailing, others for transport and fishing in estuaries and rivers, still others for specialized trade in a single commodity. If paddles or oars or a single sail proved adequate, given the terrors of water travel, a ship's configuration and materials might remain stable for centuries.

As in the world of nature, change was likely when boundaries between earlier regional maritime worlds were breached. For example, the design of a North Sea ship known as the cog came to influence ship design in the Mediterranean. The process was, however, patchy and piecemeal. Larger maritime regions sometimes devolved into smaller ones if empires collapsed.

I am particularly interested in the mental side of the gradual integration of various maritime worlds. For example, what constituted the mental toolbox of possible designs accessed by a shipbuilder? Did ships arriving from other places influence design, or did shipbuilders ignore them? How did ideas of ship design and function interact with larger political or economic trends? When possible, the chapters also discuss the cognitive geography of those involved with the maritime world of the shipwreck. What constituted the safe, known world? Where was travel considered easy or possible, rather than difficult or impossible? What goods were worth the effort, and why? Was there a spirit of adventure, pushing beyond the known world?

Globalization came slowly as various regional maritime worlds merged and traded people, commodities, and ideas. By the eighteenth century the maritime world was largely but not completely globalized. Ships sailed around the world, and battles were fought on several oceans simultaneously. Nevertheless, communication remained slow, and scheduled maritime travel had yet to appear. Few people crossed oceans except when required by employment, family obligations, or immigration.

The merger of the regional maritime worlds into a single global maritime world is a product of the twentieth century, considered in the last three chapters. The oil tanker and the cruise ship epitomize the trend toward a standard worldwide product, design, and schedule.

Shipwrecks are a feature of our modern world. Every year more than a dozen commercial carriers are lost at sea, though most go unnoticed. Several dozen more are severely damaged, but rescue operations save the crew, and oceangoing tugs save the ship. Let us, then, turn to the exciting and tragic stories of sixteen shipwrecks and their larger story of the creation of a single globalized maritime world.

––––––––––

Note: Throughout this book, "tons," as a defining feature of a ship, and "tonnage" refer not to dry weight or carrying capacity but to displacement, that is, the weight of water displaced by the ship. Carrying capacity (an unfortunate duplication of the term "tons") is identified by the definitive word "cargo" in the same sentence.

# A HISTORY OF THE WORLD IN

## SIXTEEN SHIPWRECKS

# DUFUNA DUGOUT

In May 1987, a Fulani herder in northeastern Nigeria was digging a new well. At a depth of sixteen feet he struck something hard and quickly realized that this was no rock, but something large, wooden, and likely old and important. First local, then state, and finally national officials visited the site just outside the village of Dufuna, located on the seasonally flooded plain of the small, often-dry Komadugu Gana River, about two hundred miles east of Kano.[1] Carbon dating of a wood fragment identified whatever was buried there as eight thousand years old. Nigeria did not, however, have the resources to fund an excavation. Fortunately, a local archaeologist named Abubakar Garba, from the University of Maiduguri, formed a partnership with a German team from the University of Frankfurt headed by Peter Breunig.[2]

In 1994 the team uncovered and photographed a fully intact boat, lying upside down. It is almost thirty feet long, carved from a single log a foot and a half in diameter, with sides and bottom two inches thick; it is missing only a few small pieces along the top edge. Elegantly designed, the boat features long rising tapers at both the bow and stern. It is made of African mahogany, likely either *Khaya grandiflora* or *Khaya senegalensis*, both of which grow in drier conditions than the typical rain forest habitat of the other two mahogany species. Mahogany is quite suitable for boats. It is dimensionally stable, survives well in water, and resists rot because the tree synthesizes and infuses phenol (carbolic acid) into its wood, which kills rot. The elegant design of the Dufuna boat suggests a long and well-developed boatbuilding tradition, not a recently acquired skill.

The boat was exposed and photographed. The team did not turn the boat over, so they could not see possible evidence of the use of fire or an adze in its construction. The Dufuna boat was initially reburied, to safeguard it until funds and facilities for full excavation and long-term preservation became available. The German-Nigerian team re-excavated the boat in 1998 and

Local men lift the Dufuna boat from the excavated pit.

PHOTO COURTESY PETER BREUNIG

moved it to a purpose-built conservation building in Darmaturu, the capital of Yorbe State. They placed the dugout in a vat of polyethylene glycol, the standard procedure for stabilizing ancient wood. The slow process by which PEG penetrates the wood and fills the cells is now complete, and as of 2014 the boat is ready for the gradual drying process, which must take place under carefully controlled conditions. The unstable political situation in Nigeria has prevented the team from beginning the drying process.[3]

Today, satellite photos show no agriculture and little settlement outside the floodplain of the Komadugu River. Both north and south of the river are miles upon miles of scrub desert, which in years with some rain supports herding. In the time of the Dufuna dugout, however, this region was a very different place. Lake Chad, now some two hundred miles to the east, was much larger, its shoreline perhaps only thirty miles east of the Dufuna site. It is even possible that the Dufuna site was a lagoon that connected to Lake Chad. It is not difficult to imagine the Dufuna boat's ordinary uses for fishing, crossing the Komadugu River, carrying gathered food plants, and visiting other settlements in the lagoons and on the shoreline of Lake Chad.

None of the excavated sites east of Lake Chad have yielded evidence of agriculture or domesticated animals. The Dufuna people likewise probably depended on fishing, hunting, and gathering. Equally likely the canoe would have carried men to war against rival groups in the region. Unfortunately, even though the site is well stratified by seasonal flooding, no artifacts or direct evidence of these activities have so far been discovered.[4]

## Dugouts in a Post–Ice Age World

Dated to about the same time period as the Dufuna canoe, similar dugout craft have been uncovered by archaeologists in Europe. For example, construction workers found a dugout in a peat bog near the town of Pesse in Holland. Currently housed in the Drents Museum near the find site, the canoe is about as unsophisticated a small boat as one can imagine. The builders merely hollowed out a Scotch pine log nine feet long and a foot and a half in diameter. There was no attempt to shape the bow or the stern. Several archaeologists doubted that such a crude craft could even be paddled. A reproduction of the Pesse dugout, however, proved to be both maneuverable and relatively stable.

Just as the Sahara was a very different place eight thousand years ago, so was Europe. Vast amounts of water had been tied up in the glaciers of the last ice age (at its maximum extent about twenty thousand years ago), which covered Holland, northern Germany, Scandinavia, and England. The sea level had dropped four hundred feet. As the glaciers retreated (about ten thousand years ago) they left behind newly cut lakes and much-changed river drainage. It was a time of marshes, bogs, and eventually large forests. Travel by river and across marshes probably spurred development of simple dugouts as humans recolonized the north European plain. Linden trees were suitable, common, and the most frequently used material for the oldest European dugouts. Archaeologists have excavated dugout boats across much of Europe in the period following the last ice age, for example in Stralsund, Germany (7,000 years old), Noyen-sur-Seine, France (7,000 years old), Lake Zurich, Switzerland (6,500 years old), and Arhaus, Denmark (5,000 years old).

In the north of what is today the United States, conditions were similar to post–ice age Europe: bogs, marshes, lakes, many rivers, and developing forests. The earliest finds of dugout canoes in North America date from the same period, roughly five to six thousand years ago.

The point of this discussion of various ancient dugout finds is that there was no diffusion of dugout technology from one broad region to another.[5] It now seems certain that the dugout was invented in many different places in response to local needs, such as fishing, migration, transport of materials, and coastal and river trade. Cultures experimented until they found the best available trees.[6] What tied these early boats into a "world" was not communication between peoples using them but common problems and solutions of material, production, design, and use.

## How to Make a Dugout

A small dugout requires a tall, straight tree with fifteen feet of usable trunk at least thirty inches in diameter. The fewer knots the better. Ecological conditions of deserts, Arctic regions, and high mountains rule out such trees. On the steppe and plains, dugouts could only appear if one of the few native trees proved suitable. Nevertheless, the rest of the world offered a variety of species suitable for dugouts. It seems logical to assume that experimentation over millennia arrived at the best local trees for dugout canoes. In eastern North America white pine found favor in the north, while cypress dominated the south. On the Pacific Coast, Sitka spruce, redwood, and Douglas fir worked. In Northern Europe, linden was the preferred wood. Tropical forests offered a plethora of tall straight trees that formed the overstory of the rain forest.

An understanding of why ancient dugout makers found these particular woods desirable requires a short discussion of the physics and chemistry of trees. Trees are essentially complicated vertical piping—that is, long pores move nutrients from the soil up, and other pores shunt energy down. Some trees have large pores (oak, for example), producing prominent grain when the wood is cut. Other trees, such as pine and maple, have tiny, almost invisible pores. Only the outside inch or two of a tree contains active pores, which move nutrients and energy. The entire trunk inside this active zone is dead and merely provides support for the branches and leaves of the crown of the tree.

The bonding material that joins the long vertical pores gives wood its strength. Heavier wood means stronger bonding material. Tight bonding between pores was particularly important for the two ends of the dugout. Tapering these two vulnerable areas left less bonded wood than the sides or bottom. If either end dried unevenly, the boat would split. Over millennia, boatbuilders must have experimented with locally available trees to find the few that were light enough and strong enough to serve as dugouts. They also discovered that a few trees, such as cypress and mahogany, had properties that resisted rot. The best dugout canoe, therefore, came from a big, straight tree with few lower branches (therefore, no knots), which contained relatively small pores, was strong enough to resist splitting in the fore and aft, but was not so heavy that the boat sat dangerously low in the water. Dugouts must be made from green, living wood. Dry, fallen logs have usually shrunk and checked (cracked along the grain) so badly that they could never be structurally sound or waterproof.

The first problem was how to fell the tree. A controlled burn at the base of the tree was much more efficient that trying to cut it down with flaked stone tools. Dugouts from across the world show traces of controlled burn, so the technique must have been invented in numerous cultures at different times and places. The canoe carvers probably learned early that once the narrow layer of green wood under the bark had been cut away, the old wood underneath would burn quite readily. The carvers would have kept the tree wet above the burn area.

Once felled, the tree was almost certainly worked before it was moved. A fifteen-foot section of freshly cut pine, thirty inches in diameter, weighs more than a ton. After the log's interior was burned and scraped away to a remaining two-inch wall, and a bow and stern shaped, the canoe would weigh only about two hundred pounds. Making the boat in a harder, denser wood than pine might add another fifty to seventy-five pounds to the finished weight. This weight would have been quite movable from the felling site to the water.

Turning a trunk into a dugout required only the simplest of tools. Repeated controlled burns followed by scraping gradually removed the heartwood, leaving the outermost few inches. This process can be done without even a hafted scraper or cutter. Relatively unsophisticated scrapers will do just fine. They need not even be of particularly hard stone. A clamshell or fire-hardened wood will suffice, as long as there is plenty of material nearby, as these relatively soft tools wear out quickly. A few sites of ancient dugout canoes have yielded not only boats but also the many clamshells used in hollowing them out. Cultures that possessed better tools, particularly metal tools, could fell the tree and hollow out the trunk for a dugout without fire. The sequence probably began with chopping down the tree with primitive

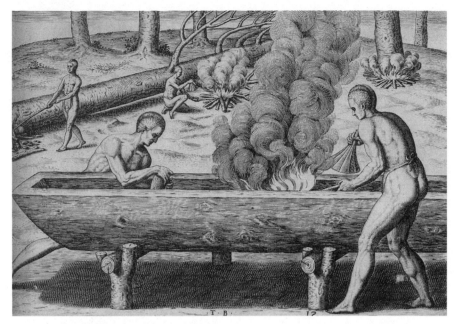

The burning of the inside of a dugout canoe by Native Americans
in sixteenth-century Virginia, from Theodore De Bry,
*Der Ander Theyl* (Manheim, 1590).

axes. Next the log was split with wedges. Lastly the dugout was hollowed out with chisels or adzes.[7]

Until recently, archaeologists had speculated that ancient dugouts would take months or even a year of work by a group of skilled boatbuilders. These archaeologists argued that such boats were a significant investment of a group's capital and therefore required some degree of social organization. Experimental archaeologists, in contrast, have used reproductions of ancient tools made from locally available materials to burn and scrape a serviceable craft from local trees. In several experiments in different countries they have found that a typical small dugout takes only the labor of a week or two by a small, relatively unskilled group.

## Limitations of Dugouts

Even optimal local wood dugouts had several intrinsic limitations. First, of course, was size. They could be no larger than locally available tree trunks.

Second, they were relatively heavy and not suitable for long portaging. They tended, therefore, to be made and used locally. In the larger picture, trade in such boats tended to follow rivers.

The third limitation was in the nature of solid wood, which tends to split along the grain if allowed to dry out. Areas where the wood is sheared across the grain, typical of the bow and stern of dugouts, are especially prone to splitting. Dugouts were best kept in the water. Dugout builders figured out that the safest place to store the boats against winter damage was on the bottom of a river or shallow bay, below the ice and away from winter storms. Several ancient archaeological sites in Europe have yielded boats filled with stones, still in winter storage after millennia.

Dugout builders faced yet another limitation: the round bottom of the boat, which made it relatively unstable and prone to capsizing. In many places around the ancient world, dugout builders realized that the hollowed-out tree could be opened with heat, wedges, and cross-braces, yielding a flatter, wider contour and a more stable boat. Such a process precluded a solid wood bow and stern. Dugout builders, therefore, generated a variety of designs, which attached supplemental wood to cover the opened log at the bow and stern. Unfortunately, the process of widening the dugout for stability did not solve another critical problem of design, the dugout's minimal height between the surface of the water and the edge of the log (known in maritime terminology as the "freeboard"). Waves of any size could throw water into the dugout. This was not a problem on rivers, marshes, small lakes, or close to shore, but open-water ventures required modified design. One solution was to add a plank at the top of the log to increase freeboard. Producing such a plank, however, required metal tools to cut and shape it. The second solution to low freeboard was to attach two hulls together, which produced a stable, seaworthy craft capable of long open-water voyages.[8] It is to the long history of the marvelous outrigger dugouts of the Pacific that we now turn.

### Dugouts of the Pacific

The history of dugouts of the Pacific begins on mainland Southeast Asia, whose colonization was an integral part of waves of early human migration from Africa into Asia. The timing and details of these migrations are much disputed. Archaeologists have found stone tools in several sites on mainland Southeast Asia, but the earliest direct evidence of modern humans is a recently found partial skull from a cave in Laos, dated between 58,000 and 43,000 BCE.[9]

The earliest direct evidence of modern humans in island Southeast Asia comes from human bones on the island of Palawan in the southern Philippines (43,000 BCE) and from another site in Borneo (40,000 BCE). With a lower sea level in this period, land bridges may have connected the mainland and some of what are now islands. There is, however, strong evidence of early open-water crossing from Southeast Asia to Australia. The remains of the first settlements of aboriginals on the Cape York Peninsula consistently date to about 48,000 BCE. These early explorers could only have come across the Torres Strait from New Guinea, traversing perhaps sixty miles of open water. None of these early sites, however, have yielded remains of boats or rafts, causing some archaeologists to speculate that a tsunami might have ripped a whole chunk of land, perhaps a matted mangrove swamp, off New Guinea and floated it across the Torres Strait. The sites on the north coast of Cape York suggest an initial population of around one thousand, making the mangrove/tsunami hypothesis extremely unlikely. Almost certainly those first migrants arrived by raft or boat.

## From Southeast Asia to the Pacific Islands

For the following millennia, three sorts of indirect evidence point to inter-island trade and migration from Southeast Asia to the Pacific islands. The first is the carbon dating of human remains, such as charcoal from cooking fires.[10] In theory carbon dating is simple. Earth's atmosphere contains fixed proportions of carbon 12, which is stable, and carbon 14, which decays at a known rate. A living plant takes up both isotopes, in accordance with their ratio in the atmosphere. Once a plant dies, however, the decaying carbon 14 cannot be replenished, and the proportion of carbon 14 to carbon 12 begins to decline. The ratio of carbon 12 to carbon 14 therefore provides an indirect measure of how long ago the plant died. In practice, there is a complication. Over the millennia the ratio of the two carbon isotopes in the atmosphere has shown some fluctuation; this problem has led scientists to develop other means of dating ancient plant material, such as thermo-luminescence.

The second sort of evidence comes from microanalysis of food grains and pollen from ancient settlement sites. Archaeologists focus on nonindigenous plants, which were likely brought by migrating humans. These grains and pollen are dated, like the charcoal of cooking fires, by carbon dating and thermo-luminescence.

The third sort of evidence depends on DNA analysis. Large-scale data on current human DNA from Southeast Asia and the Pacific suggest broad trends of migration, showing, for example, that the DNA of inhabitants of the westernmost Pacific island is closest to the DNA of current inhabitants of the eastern islands of Southeast Asia. DNA analysis of rats is also a useful marker of human migration. Rats cannot swim, so their movement from island to island necessarily involved transport, both conscious and inadvertent, by humans.[11] Fortunately, rat populations from different origins have distinctly, if slightly, different DNA.

The fourth sort of evidence consists of the origin stories handed down by native inhabitants of various islands and similarities between various island languages.

Though these four types of evidence by no means arrive at the same exact chronology, a rough consensus among archaeologists has emerged in the last decade. The evidence points to a common origin of the island Pacific peoples in the islands known as the Moluccas (south of the Philippines), which, along with New Guinea and the islands immediately east, had very early settlement. (As we have seen, the early settlement of Australia came from New Guinea.) This period of colonization was apparently followed by a long, long period without further exploration. Archaeologists have speculated that the numbers of humans were small, and the food supply was adequate.

The next period of migration was around 28,000 BCE. Settlers moved east from New Guinea and surrounding islands to the New Hebrides islands, Vanuatu and New Caledonia. A couple of centuries later they reached Fiji, Tonga, and Samoa. As in earlier periods we have no evidence of the craft that carried the settlers to their newly discovered islands. The likeliest candidates are dugouts or rafts. Even rudimentary depictions of these craft have not, so far, been found.

Once again, migration and new settlement stopped, this time for more than a thousand years. Only seven to eight hundred years ago new island exploration began once more. The evidence from rat DNA suggests that the new wave did not come from the previously settled islands, but may have come directly from Southeast Asia on a more northerly route to the Marshalls. In an explosion of long-distance exploration, these new settlers discovered and settled the islands of the central Pacific: Hawaii, the Christmas Islands, the Marquesas, the Society Islands, the Cook Islands, and New Zealand.

The early European explorers followed this migration by only three centuries, so that their observations are a useful window into the world of the Pacific island dugouts.[12] Expeditions produced drawings and descriptions of the craft. Ship captains brought home models, and a few returned with an entire dugout canoe. Many of the trade patterns existed well into the twentieth century and were recorded by officials and amateur anthropologists.

The first striking feature of the rapid migration to the middle Pacific islands (1200–1500 CE) is the many variations on the same basic dugout design. In Hawaii, for example, boatbuilders produced a range of craft, including small local vessels for fishing, medium-size outrigger canoes for trade and visitation within the Hawaiian chain, and huge double canoes for long-distance war and trade. The great double canoes were more than fifty feet long. Sturdy poles connected the two hulls and supported a platform for cargo or a retinue of nobles. The typical sail was a tall triangle, an inverted pyramid with a mast running down each long edge attached to a common base or stepping point in the boat. Paddles were oval.[13]

Across the islands everyone used either an outrigger or a doubled hull. Such an arrangement was far more stable and seaworthy than a single hull. Builders arrived at more than a dozen different layouts for lashing the poles to the two hulls or the hull and the outrigger. Small fishing craft had no provision for sail, but all oceangoing craft did. As in the craft of Hawaii, the sail was generally tall and narrow, tapering from the top of the mast to the deck (though craft from Tahiti inverted this pattern, with the triangle pointing upward). All builders utilized a panel along the top edge of the log (known in maritime terminology as a washstrake) to prevent waves washing over the boat's sides and shaped the washstrake into the rising fore and aft ends. Typically, builders "sewed" the washstrake, with heavy cord passing through holes in the hull and the washstrake. On islands without trees large enough to produce dugouts, builders made similar vessels by sewing together hulls from available wood. The carved fore and aft ends rose in a variety of profiles, some sharp, others more gradual. These variations were perhaps influenced by predominant wave patterns. A few islands carved the logs with a primitive keel. Carving and decoration, of course, varied from island to island. All were produced with simple tools of clamshell or stone.

These dugouts executed extraordinary trans-island voyages: fifteen hun-

The inverted triangle sail typical of Polynesian outrigger canoes.
Lithograph of painting by Louis Le Breton (1818–1866) in *Voyage*
*au pole sud et dans l'Oceanie . . . by the French ships* Astrolabe
*and* Zelee *under the command of Dumont D'Urville, 1842*
(Paris: Librairie des Sciences Naturelles [1841]–1853).

dred miles of open water from New Guinea to the Marshalls and another
fifteen hundred to Hawaii; more than two thousand miles from Hawaii to
the Marquesas, Tuamotu, and Tahiti. Two thousand miles southeast of the
Marquesas intrepid sailors discovered Easter Island.

A few Europeans recorded what they understood of native navigational
techniques. Pilots memorized a comprehensive knowledge of the stars, including visible stars in various portions of the Pacific at different seasons of
the year. By day navigation was by the sun. Pilots knew the position of sun-
rise and sunset at various times of year, in addition to predominant wave patterns, cloud formation over islands, and the migratory routes of birds. Birds
flew in a predictable pattern, and some rested on islands.[14]

The most famous voyages, retold in song and story, were of long distance
and discovery. The evidence from nineteenth-century European observers
suggests that shorter voyages, though less spectacular, supported self-contained trading, warfare, and visiting worlds within Oceania. Regular trade,
for example, connected the eastern coast of New Guinea with New Britain. Similar ties of trade and war connected Tonga, Samoa, and Fiji. The

most thoroughly studied of these inter-island networks connected a chain of small islands north of the far eastern end of New Guinea. When World War I began, Bronislaw Malinowski was researching indigenous cultures of New Guinea, but as an Austrian he faced imprisonment by the British colonial government. Instead he shifted his research east to the Trobriand Islands, then a German colony. During the war he produced his now-classic ethnography on the *kula*, a system of feasting and gifting, which formed the basis of the inter-island culture.[15]

## The End of the Dugout World

If the ancient rise of dugouts represented local invention, tools, and materials, then the rapid decline of dugouts was a truly worldwide phenomenon. European colonial power reached to the ends of the earth, and with it came new boat designs and the iron and steel tools to realize them. By the early nineteenth century, saws became trade items in the Pacific islands and made possible the cutting of planks and frames. Steel hammers and iron nails connected the planks to the frame. By the middle of the nineteenth century, planked boats had replaced virtually all large oceangoing dugouts in Oceania, the west coast of America and Canada, and throughout Southeast Asia.[16] Smaller dugouts were still produced for fishing and river transport in tropical South America, Africa, and Southeast Asia. Through the twentieth century even these smaller dugouts were largely replaced by designs using planks, frames, and nails.

A sad story of this period comes from Samoa. In the second half of the nineteenth century, traders from Germany, Britain, and the United States established plantations for cacao, rubber, and coconut on the islands. Though the Germans had the largest holdings and dominated trade, all three powers supported various chiefs and local factions.

In 1885 one of the largest chiefs of Samoa commissioned construction of an enormous double-hulled long-distance dugout canoe as a state present to the kaiser of Germany, hoping it would cement German support for his faction and rule. The dugout was constructed from two huge first-growth logs from the coastal forests of North America, which had washed ashore on the main island. Photographs of its launch suggest that it was at least sixty feet long and show it carrying more than fifty men. It proved too big to ship to Germany.

Shortly after the canoe's launch, Samoa descended into full civil war. Germany, Britain, and the United States not only armed local rival factions but landed their own troops. By 1889 all three powers had warships in Apia harbor, but a major storm destroyed all the foreign ships before war could begin. The dugout slowly fell to pieces on the beach in Samoa and proved to be the last such craft ever built.[17]

Today, a few dozen boats and models are housed in anthropology museums across the world. Many ancient dugouts are no longer suitable for exhibition. Without proper preservation either permanently in water or through PEG treatment, ancient dugouts deteriorate rapidly to split and misshapen logs. Nevertheless, dugouts remain essential for fishing and transportation in a few locations, such as Dominica in the Caribbean, the Orinoco River in Venezuela, and some islands in western Oceania.

## And a Beginning

About fifty years ago a revival of outrigger craft began in Hawaii. Clubs formed, and racing competitions developed. Eventually, outrigger racing became the designated state sport. Now high schools and clubs sponsor teams and competitions in various categories: single, four-person, and six-person hulls, in divisions by age and gender. Races include both sprints and long-distance open-water races. The sport has spread, with racing organizations on the east and west coasts of the United States and in Canada, Hong Kong, and Australia. The vast majority of teams race in outrigger canoes of fiberglass, but a few teams build and race traditional wood outriggers in a special category.

In 1986 Ben Finney and his crew sailed a replica outrigger canoe from Hawaii across three thousand miles of open water to Tahiti, using only traditional navigation methods. The voyage was the culmination of two decades of research and experimentation. Finney was an American anthropologist who had studied Hawaiian surfing for his master's thesis in the 1950s and dreamed of re-creating the great transoceanic canoes. His first attempt was the *Nalahia* (1968), which provided much practical information on building and sailing these vessels. The Polynesian Voyaging Society (which Finney founded) brought together those who still had traditional knowledge and others with resources and energy to build a traditional double-hulled dugout, named the *Hokule'a*. The inaugural traverse to Tahiti was followed by many long-distance voyages throughout Polynesia, including French Polynesia, the Cook Islands, Tonga, and New Zealand. Most of the voyages were performed without modern navigation tools.

The dugout tradition has also not entirely disappeared from other areas that long ago produced the craft. Museums have found that creating a dugout is an engaging educational community activity. Dugouts have recently been built from trees that were felled and hollowed out by controlled burns and scraping in, for example, upstate New York, Florida, and several locations in Europe. Both instructions for making a dugout and videos of dugouts made by individuals and groups of friends appear regularly on the Internet.

The dugout's eight-to-ten-thousand-year history suggests not a single place of invention but many. Cultures in Africa, Asia, the Americas, and Europe creatively experimented with local trees and the tools they knew to fashion something they needed. The world of these early dugouts was local: crossing a river, fishing, transporting gathered food, bringing men to local wars. In most of the world the dugout canoe remained within a local maritime or riverine setting.

Change was, however, coming in the form of the Neolithic Revolution. The development of agriculture, pottery, and the resulting stratified societies looked profoundly different from the local worlds of the early dugout canoes. The revolution appeared independently in Mesopotamia, China, India, Japan, and the Americas. It is to ancient Egypt, one of these early agricultural societies and its maritime world, that we now turn.

# 2
# KHUFU BARGE

In November 1952, the Antiquities Department of Egypt began removal of nearly sixty feet of rubble and debris from the base of the southern face of the Great Pyramid of Giza. Such routine work had proceeded for more than a decade, revealing an original pavement and surrounding wall at the base of the pyramid. The rubbish removal on the southern face was, however, to be anything but routine.

Underneath a wall exposed by the removal of debris was a strange layer composed of charcoal and compressed earth. As workers dug into the layer, they struck a massive limestone block. Over the next two excavation seasons they exposed two parallel rows of forty blocks covering some sort of chamber that had been cut into the living rock. Seams between the blocks had been sealed with pure white gypsum and had every appearance of still being sealed after four thousand years.

In May 1954, workers chipped a small hole through one of the limestone blocks. Inside could be seen a steering oar, boards, columns, and remains of rope. Through the following fall and winter the great covering blocks, about fourteen tons each, were winched up by hand and moved to the courtyard. Even early in the work it was obvious that the chamber contained a large disassembled boat.

The announcement of the find of an ancient buried royal boat traveled quickly around the world, but the decades-long struggle to preserve and reconstruct the boat had barely begun. In the early years conditions were difficult, at best. Workers first built a shed on the site and shelves for storing pieces of the boat, then built a hanging platform for photographing layers and a railed scaffold for removing timbers. It was well into 1957 before the more than twelve hundred boat pieces were lifted, photographed, numbered, and placed in the storage shed.[1]

No climate or humidity control was possible, and some pieces desiccated quickly in the dry Cairo air. The principal restorer, Ahmad Youssof Moustafa, and Dr. Zaky Iskander, director of the chemical laboratory, experimented with various techniques to stabilize the wood.[2] Years passed as one problem followed another. New wood had to be laid painstakingly into timbers and planks to make the ends sound and reassembly possible. Missing sections of wood were filled with a wood fiber and animal glue composite and stained to match the existing color. In some cases molds were constructed to build a piece up to its proper dimensions. Sometimes a long piece of new wood was set into a damaged piece to provide structural strength.

Ahmad Youssof Moustafa attempted the first assembly of the boat between November 1957 and August 1958, starting with the heavy bottom timbers and using holes, marks, and curvature to place pieces. The boat would be disassembled and reassembled four more times over the next thirteen years. The second reconstruction correctly placed all the interior framing and support pieces. The third repaired damage to disassembled pieces from both drought and a flood in the assembly shed. The third attempted reconstruction established that virtually every hull plank had to be re-bent so that its contour fit the various inner supports. This process entailed pouring boiling water over the plank every five to ten minutes during careful pressure-bending that took as much as three weeks. In the fourth reconstruction virtually everything fit together, even the devilishly complicated placing of the supports for the wood deck structure.

Unfortunately, it was not until the fourth reconstruction that anyone on the team noticed that most of the pieces were, in fact, inscribed with hieroglyphs that coded their placement, both in general and specifically adjacent to another piece. Matching hieroglyphs convinced the team that their placements had been correct. Only a handful of small pieces were swapped to their correct spot. The fifth reconstruction made minor adjustments to the curvature of planks and settled how the boat would be supported. The Khufu boat finally went on public display in March 1982, twenty-eight years after its discovery. Today's modern museum next to the Great Pyramid incorporates the original vault, with the reconstructed boat filling the second floor.[3]

What sort of a boat does a visitor see in the museum in the shadow of the Great Pyramid? It is long and narrow, just over 140 feet long and only 30 feet wide in the beam. The bottom of the hull rakes upward from the center to tall vertical posts fore and aft. An elegant "house," consisting of support poles and panels, sits on the deck. The darkened planks fit so well

The reconstructed Khufu boat in its modern museum, Cairo, Egypt.

together that its date, c. 2600 BCE, seems impossible. For most visitors the boat is striking, perhaps beautiful, but probably worth only a few minutes in a crowded schedule.

For maritime archaeologists, however, the boat has been a treasure of information on the millennia-old tradition of boatbuilding in Egypt. Many of the critical features are not visible from the outside, but buried in the structure below the deck. The Khufu boat was sewn together, not nailed. Though many cultures independently invented this technique, Egyptian sewn boats are unlike any other on earth.[4] Sewn boats in other parts of the world feature laced cords through holes on both sides of a seam between two planks, much as one might sew together two pieces of stiff cloth. Egyptian boatbuilders, in contrast, laced cords in groups across a series of planks. They did not drill holes clear through their planks. Instead, they drilled pairs of angled holes that met partway through the plank, which allowed the cords to pass into and out of the plank on the inside surface. Planks also had complementary edge notches to prevent them from sliding longitudinally. Internal framing was lashed to the planks and supported the deck and the superstructure on the deck. Rather than caulking in the joints between the planks of the hull, the Khufu boat used internal battens sewn to the adjoining planks.

Long, narrow boats or ships have a common problem: the ends droop. This condition, technically known as "hogging," results from greater buoyancy amidships than fore and aft. Uncorrected hogging is particularly dangerous in heavy seas, which push the drooping bow down into the water. Until the period of steel ships in the late nineteenth century, maritime designers invented only one solution to hogging—a "hogging truss." It consisted of a heavy cable or chain attached to the prow, passing up and over a sturdy post amidships, and connecting to the stern. Tightening the cable or chain lifted the bow and stern relative to the middle of the ship. Ancient Nile vessels must have "hogged," for many of the earliest drawings show a hogging truss supporting the bow and stern.

The Egyptians never developed either iron smelting or iron tools, in spite of iron-smelting technology appearing relatively early in sub-Saharan Africa. The use of lashing and the various forms of wood dowels, pegs, and mortises in the Khufu boat is completely consistent with a general lack of nails throughout the culture. The only iron items excavated have been small knives or bowls, all fabricated from iron meteorites.

### The River World of the Khufu Boat

Why were ancient Egyptian kings buried with and in boats as opposed to, say, carts or large amounts of weapons? To look down on Egypt from space—a view available only to the god Ra in his sun boat—is immediately to understand why boats were central to ancient Egypt. For three hundred miles a green ribbon of fertile land flanks the Nile on both sides. The transition to desert brown is abrupt and complete. Every aspect of the wealth and splendor of ancient Egypt depended on the life-giving, crop-growing waters of the Nile.

Bureaucrats from the earliest dynasties observed the Nile. Each summer the river mysteriously rose and overflowed its banks, flooding the surrounding fields with mineral-rich silt from some unknown place far, far upstream. This yearly rise was recorded on rocks and riverside buildings from the earliest of Egypt's dynasties.[5] Too little rise meant drought and starvation. Too much rise meant flooding, with whole villages washed away, followed by months of waterborne disease and death. After the rise, crucial work had to be done, such as clearing irrigation channels, repairing irrigation equipment, preparing the fields, and planting crops. Government officials reestablished village and field boundaries and fixed taxes.

Speculation went on for millennia about possible natural and supernatural causes for the rise. It was not until the late nineteenth century that European explorers provided observations that solved the riddle of the Nile's rise. A vast monsoon pattern dominates the yearly pattern of Africa's weather. Onshore easterly winds in early June bring clouds and moisture from the Atlantic to the heart of the continent. Heavy rain falls in the Nile's upland watersheds, in current-day Kenya, Uganda, and Tanzania. This additional rainfall feeds the rise of life-giving waters to the lower Nile.[6]

Not only was the Nile the source of all prosperity for dynasty after dynasty, it was the crucial artery connecting north and south. The Nile Delta has always been enormously productive.[7] Its grain fed upstream capitals of successive kingdoms for thousands of years. Especially useful for this transportation were the prevailing winds, which blew from north to south, opposite the flow of the Nile. Grain could thus be moved upriver by sail power most of the year.

The long, gentle drop from the area of Aswan four hundred miles to the Nile Delta meant that building stone and temporary laborers could be transported downstream with relative ease. The few roads in the whole region ran east and west, either connecting the Nile and oasis towns or the Nile and the Red Sea.[8]

### The World of Egyptian Boats

The earliest representations of Nile craft are a few scattered images that date to about 4500 BCE, a period known as Badari. More frequent are images from the next millennium, which show flat-bottomed boats with high tapered ends, deckhouses, and rowers. These crude drawings lack the detail to answer even the most basic questions regarding shipbuilding construction or materials.[9]

In 1991 David O'Connor, then assistant curator of Egyptology at the museum of the University of Pennsylvania, led a team that discovered, in the ancient city of Abydos, twelve parallel burials of fifty-to-sixty-foot boats dating to Dynasty I or II, that is, roughly one thousand years before the Khufu boat. It was a sensational find, and the news flashed around the globe. Stories appeared in the following months not only in the papers of London and New York, but, for example, in the *San Diego Times*, the *Salt Lake Tribune*, the *Montreal Gazette*, and the *St. Petersburg Times*.

The team unearthed one of the boats. Here was concrete evidence of ancient Egyptian boatbuilding, not crude drawings and speculation. First, these were wood boats, not reed or other materials. Second, they were "sewn," uncannily like the construction of the thousand-year-later Khufu boat. Third, the Abydos boats were likely used, rather than built only as funerary vehicles; O'Connor thought these were working boats, which had been dragged to the site almost seven miles from the Nile and set upright. Fourth, the Abydos boats show a sophistication in design and construction that can only be a result of many centuries of prior boatbuilding and experimentation.

The construction of the associated burial vaults likewise showed considerable sophistication. Brickwork was built underneath to support the hulls. The burial was most likely inside the boat, though no direct observation proved this. The boat was then filled with mud bricks, so that nothing of the deck supports, deck, or superstructure remained, if indeed there ever was a deck.[10] After the team's limited excavation, the unearthed hull of the first boat was reburied, and the others were not disturbed further.

The site is crucial for understanding the larger significance of these boat burials. Abydos was the funerary center for the early Egyptian dynasties, centering on the god Osiris. It is today chockablock with tombs, temples, and cult shrines that span thirty-five hundred years, intensively studied and extensively excavated. (David O'Connor began digging in Abydos twenty-five years before the boat burial discoveries.) Through dozens of scholarly papers and books, archaeologists have arrived at a consensus that Abydos and its funeral beliefs and architecture were the precursors to the boat burials and pyramids a millennium later at Giza.[11]

Just as there were boat burials long before the Khufu boat, the tradition continued long after it. In 1894, archaeologist Jacques de Morgan unearthed three boats in a single vault next to a pyramid at Dashur, about thirty miles upriver from Cairo. The pyramid and boats were associated with Senwosret III of the Middle Kingdom (c. 1850 BCE), almost eight hundred years after the Khufu boat. Morgan reported three more craft buried about one hundred yards south of the first group, for a total of six. Two are in the Cairo Museum; one is in the Field Museum in Chicago; the fourth is in the Carnegie Museum in Pittsburgh. The whereabouts of two boats are unknown.

Like the Khufu boat, all of the Dashur boats are constructed of expensive cedar imported from what is today Lebanon. Documents of the time of Senwosret III include accounts for materials and labor for construction of such boats. They are all about the same proportions as the Khufu boat, a length-to-width ratio of 4 to 1. A similar mortise-and-tenon system connects the edges of hull planks. All have a high upturned bow and stern. All the Dashur boats have the same sewn joints as earlier boats, though the modern reconstruction (done early in the twentieth century) replaced the lashing and cordage with dovetail wood joints of considerably poorer workmanship. The Chicago boat shows ancient repairs, clear evidence that it was used, rather than constructed for funerary use.

It is important to emphasize, however, that royal funerary boats were only a tiny fraction of the boats on the ancient Nile. More than 150 types of boats appear in Egyptian hieroglyphics. Some are pictured in wall murals and identified as fishing boats or transport barges; but in reality scholars can translate few hieroglyphs that represent types of boats into craft of distinctive sizes or uses.

The wall paintings, carvings, and texts detail the commodities moving on the Nile: stone for the great walls and monuments; basic grains for food; cloth for the rich and poor; wood for buildings, sarcophagi, and furniture; glue to make furniture and sacred objects; even laborers shipped to constructions sites. Boats also carried animal skins, used for water carrying, and pottery, both functional and sacred. Metals, including the magical and revered copper and gold, moved by boat. Boats transported the luxury items of wealthy houses: ebony, ivory, carved wood panels, pigments to paint walls, glass for vessels and beads and other jewelry, incense to burn, makeup for the eyes, ostrich eggs as vessels, seashells for bracelets, and scented oils for the body in life and death. The feathers for the royal sunshades probably came down the Nile.

Two excavations have aided in understanding the working boats of ancient Egypt. The first is Wadi Gawasis, a Red Sea port active in the same period as the Khufu boat, but even more active in the Middle Kingdom (1991–1688 BCE), several centuries after the Khufu boat. In the 1990s archaeologists located seven long, narrow, cavelike rooms cut into the coral above the beach. Some of the rooms showed evidence of ceramics production or large-scale baking. Three rooms were devoted to repairing hull planks and timbers from boats. The likeliest explanation for the massive amount of cordage found in one of the caves is that boats were built on the lower Nile, came up the Nile, were disassembled by cutting the cordage, carried 150 miles over the mountains, and reassembled on the Red Sea shore for seagoing expeditions.

The hull planking found in the caves is smaller and thicker than the long, elegant planking of the Khufu boat. Local woods, especially acacia and sycamore, were found, along with some cedar, the expensive imported timber of the Khufu boat. Wood, regardless of species, was expensive enough that timbers were routinely reworked and reused. Fortunately, worn-out ship timbers were recycled into supports for ramps up to the caves, and planking was recycled into flooring. These timbers and planks have distinctive wormholes produced only by saltwater worms, proof of seafaring.[12]

Besides Wadi Gawasis, archaeologists have found a second site at which ship timbers were recycled to build ramps. The site, known as Lisht, is about forty miles upriver from Cairo. The timbers date from c. 1950 BCE, that is, within the active period of Wadi Gawasis and perhaps five hundred years after the Khufu boat. The timbers are from working cargo carriers, rather than royal barges. These boats were shorter and stockier than the Khufu boat. The planking is smaller in size, thicker than that of the Khufu boat, and made from local acacia, not cedar. The internal structure of these cargo boats would have been much stronger than the Khufu boat, featuring a heavy beam that runs fore and aft and rests on notched floor timbers. These working boats were built to take the stresses of moving large stone blocks or obelisks.[13] At the site archaeologists found a ship model that confirms the basic shape and configuration suggested by the timbers.[14]

The conclusion from the Wadi Gawasis and Lisht sites is that Egyptians used the same basic designs and construction techniques for millennia for both royal boats and working boats. Working boats merely had smaller and thicker planks and heavier internal structure. Egyptian boatbuilding was, thus, a largely self-contained world that centered on the Nile River. The importance of boats is suggested by the tomb invocation of a man named Rekmire, who was a close associate to one of the Egyptian kings.

> I was the heart of the Lord, the
> ears and eyes of my Sovereign.
> I was his skipper, and knew not
> slumber by night or day.

Whether I stood or sat, my heart
was set upon prow rope
and stern rope, and the sounding pole.[15]


## A World of Trade, or Not?

How important and extensive were trade and exchange in ancient Egypt?
It seems a simple enough question, but archaeologists, anthropologists, so-
ciologists, historians, and economists have been arguing this question—
often with considerable heat—for more than two centuries. Ranged against
each other are one tradition that is broadly anti-market and another that has
been equally broadly pro-market.

The anti-market tradition has its roots in German, French, and English
Romanticism of the early nineteenth century. Reacting against the Industrial
Revolution happening around them, these artists, writers, and philosophers
believed that markets, which treated goods merely as items for cash sale,
were intrinsically evil. Markets destroyed the bonds between members of
communities, generally substituted grubbing for money for old and important folk cultures, broke up common land for sale to private owners, and created vast, ugly cities whose major function was to exploit poor people who
had been driven off the land.

Central to the anti-market viewpoint is the idea that markets and market-
focused economies were a recent phenomenon, beginning no earlier than
the nineteenth century even in the industrializing societies of Europe. Evidence of markets and trade at the center of any other society of an earlier
time was simply incorrect. This viewpoint concluded that the logic and rules
of market transactions, therefore, had no significant role in either ancient
cultures (Mesopotamia, ancient China, the Indus Valley, or the Mayans) or
"premodern" cultures anywhere in the modern world (traditional Africa,
Southeast Asia, Polynesia, the tribal cultures of India). Therefore, peoples
of the ancient and recent past and modern-day "primitives" were people
who lived out their lives free from the oppression and alienation of market
forces.[16]

Ranged against this anti-market viewpoint is an equally long-standing
pro-market viewpoint, which holds that market analysis is suitable for all
times and places: wherever they are, people have always understood and
operated on notions of profit, the exchange value of labor, risk, and choice

about how to spend and use their resources. The origins of this mode of thinking date back to David Ricardo and Adam Smith in eighteenth-century England. Its twentieth-century proponents include, of course, Milton Friedman and the Chicago school of economics. The output of this now-dominant viewpoint includes tens of thousands of studies of "rational choice" behavior. Its influence extends from policy studies of self-regulating markets to arguments for schools-of-choice.

Egyptologists have, by and large, been in the anti-market camp. This is understandable, as the obvious evidence—wall murals, massive architecture, inscriptions recounting the great deeds of kings in war and peace, records of tribute and taxes, royal sponsorship of overseas expeditions—suggests hardly any role for markets. The biblical book of Exodus reinforces the picture of a supremely powerful pharaoh commanding all he ruled.

Only in the last few decades have scholars found new evidence of markets and trade in many places in the ancient world. The first major discovery of ancient markets was in Babylon. Thousands of cuneiform inscriptions on clay tablets showed that not only did prices fluctuate, but buyers were attuned to rates of return and costs of credit. In Egypt the many finds of imported cedar from Lebanon, both for nonroyal coffins and for working boats, suggested that a market must have existed for this expensive import.

Scientific analysis has also added tantalizing suggestions of a market mentality. "Knockoffs" were apparently common across the ancient Eastern Mediterranean and also in Egypt. Scientific analysis has found that much "Egyptian" faience found in the Eastern Mediterranean is, in fact, not the expensive imported glazed pottery but instead cheaper locally produced copies. Similarly, several of the "Egyptian" stone vases found in Syria turn out to be, in fact, crafted of local stone. Conversely, in Egypt, lesser local woods were grained and painted to look like more expensive imported woods in furniture, boxes, and sarcophagi. While jewelry often set Egyptian carnelian with expensive imported turquoise from Iran and lapis lazuli from Afghanistan, cheaper jewelry substituted glass paste for the expensive imported stones.[17]

Collectively, this evidence suggests something much more interesting than basic exchange of commodities or a trade controlled and managed by kings. Locally made knockoffs of expensive imports suggest that buyers were well aware of the prestige value of the expensive imports. So, indeed, were local artisans. They experimented with, produced, and marketed cheaper, fashionable copies. A "knockoff" trade requires a sophisticated set of market estimations by both buyers and sellers. Would the lower price of the local copy justify the risk of observers (perhaps friends, family, fellow officeholders) recognizing the copy? From the viewpoint of the artisan, were the copies good enough and cheap enough to tempt buyers? Were they up-to-date enough in fashion? Here we have long-ago precursors of the knockoffs of our own time—Rolex watches, Prada shoes, Gucci bags—and intuitively understand the economic decisions of ancient Egyptians and the active market thinking those decisions imply.

In the ancient world of the Mediterranean, the Middle East, and the east coast of Africa, markets likely operated side by side with nonmarket means of acquiring resources, such as colonization, conquest and extraction, tribute, embassies, and temporary and slave labor.

## The Meaning of Boats: Supernatural Journeys

So why did ancient Egyptians place full-size boats and boat models in their tombs? Egyptologists have not arrived at a definitive answer, beyond broad agreement that the tombs required enormous amounts of money and labor and generally consisted of everything a person might need in the afterlife. Depictions on the walls of tombs of pleasant oases and palm trees expressed the hope that this would be the permanent home of the deceased. Perhaps boats, boat models, and boat pictures in tombs have a simple, mundane explanation. A boat—like grain, clothes, and servants—was simply something that the deceased would need in the afterlife, which, as described by various ancient Egyptian texts, seems much like Egypt itself. Many tombs, for example, have yielded small human terra-cotta figures in groups. Inscriptions identify these figures as substitutes for the deceased in the expected yearly, impressed labor of clearing canals and building monuments. A boat would thus be an enjoyable, perhaps even necessary, way to sail up and down the Nile of the afterlife.

Scholars, however, suspect that there is much more to boat burials than pleasant after-death transportation. Ancient Egyptians believed that the deceased embarked on a journey, which was fraught with dangerous demons and omens. The priestly guides to this journey, including the famous *Book of the Dead*, suggest the best routes to take and incantations to recite at crucial junctures. The guides also describe several means of travel, such as

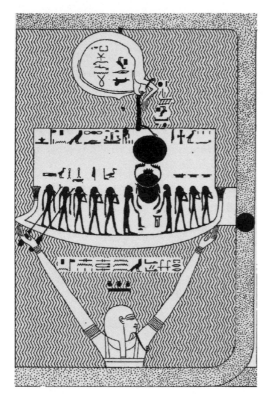

The god Ra and his sun boat, from E. Wallace Budge, *Egyptian Ideas of the Future Life* (London: K. Paul, Trench, Trübner and Co., Ltd., 1900).

ascending on the back of a goose, falcon, or other bird, riding a waft of incense, and climbing a ladder. The most common vehicle is a boat, both in texts about the death journey and pictures representing the journey.[18]

At a deeper level, much of the ancient Egyptian belief system was based on polar opposites: earth/sky; the Nile lands/the western lands of the deceased; god/man; family solidarity/family warfare. Success in navigating these opposites required a vehicle that could travel between the opposites safely and also live with both opposites simultaneously. The correct vehicle and the correct prayers allowed the voyager to both fully understand the opposites and encompass them at the same time.

The most visible god enacting just such a journey was Ra, who traveled across the sky each day in his sun boat, and traversed the dark and dangerous underworld at night, only to reemerge at dawn. Perhaps a buried boat allowed the deceased to go along with Ra on this glorious journey. It is likely, however, that the core ideas of a dangerous journey after death and the importance of the proper vehicle long pre-date the cult of Ra. The recent finds of boat burials at Abydos pre-date by centuries the emergence of Ra as a major god. At this long, long historical distance from ancient Egypt we will, however, probably never know exactly what the boat burials meant to ancient Egyptians.

## The End of the Nile World

Ancient Egypt was a regional riverine world, larger than the local worlds of the early dugout canoes, but smaller than the trans-Mediterranean world developing beyond the Nile. For more than two thousand years, ecology, economics, and politics reinforced its boundaries. The ribbon of arable land created by the Nile defined what was worth fighting over. And, indeed, the characteristic pattern of politics and warfare included periods when a government controlled the Nile from the delta to the cataracts, alternating with periods when rebellious local officials or invading Nubians from the south controlled portions of the river. No one thought the deserts to the east or the west of the Nile were worth controlling. The yearly rhythm of the Nile's rise flooded fields adjacent to the river with precious water and even more precious dissolved nutrients. The rise also required a social structure capable of organizing large amounts of local labor for several months each year to clear the irrigation channels, repair irrigation equipment, and reestablish field boundaries.

Boats were essential to such a bounded riverine world. They brought the stone from the south to build the great cities, temples, tombs, and walls of the north, and the flax from the fields of the middle reaches of the river to the looms of the cities. They transported the grain that fed the capital cities. Boats brought invading armies from Nubia, just as they brought reinforcements from the north to oppose them. The middle reaches of the river were the site of many ferocious, bloody battles. Pharaohs sailed on the Nile, as did officials to their postings. Even the belief system reinforced this bounded riverine world, as characterized by Ra and his sun boat.

A series of conquests changed crucial elements of this pattern, beginning with two centuries of control by the Nubians (a people from southern Egypt and Sudan), followed by the successful invasion of the Assyrians in 671 BCE, which reduced Egypt to a province of the Assyrian Empire. Next came the Persians (525 BCE), who made Egypt a province of their empire. Alexander the Great conquered Egypt in 332 BCE and incorporated it into his empire.

Finally, Cleopatra, installed as queen by Julius Caesar and supported by Mark Antony, surrendered Egypt to the Roman armies of Octavian in 31 BCE. Egypt would be ruled by the Roman Empire for the next six hundred years.

Each of these conquests shifted the largely self-contained world of the Nile and Egypt toward integration into larger economic and political worlds. After Alexander established of the new port city of Alexandria in the delta, the grain of the Nile no longer stayed in the world of the Nile. Roman officials collected it, stored it, and oversaw the loading of the grain in a yearly fleet bound for Rome. Egyptian wheat allowed Rome to grow far larger than the meager food supply in its own region of Italy. As the gods of ancient Egypt faded in importance, it was no longer Ra's majestic sun boat or the royal boat of Khufu that constituted Egypt's future, but rather the Mediterranean grain ships from Rome that crowded the port of Alexandria.

# 3

# ULUBURUN SHIPWRECK

In the mid-1950s a photographer and journalist named Peter Throckmorton arrived on the west coast of Turkey, chasing a rumor that a large Greek sculpture had washed ashore. He met a local ship captain, who claimed to know the location of several ancient wrecks. In 1958 Throckmorton persuaded the Explorers Club in New York to mount a preliminary search, which indeed located an ancient ship off a promontory named Cape Gelidonya. The University of Pennsylvania mounted an expedition in 1960 to document the ship and bring up artifacts. The Cape Gelidonya wreck was, at the time, the oldest shipwreck ever located (c. 1200 BCE) and became one of the foundational sites that developed the basic techniques of underwater archaeology, including gridding, specialized lighting and photography, the use of balloons to raise objects, and the rhythm of daily dives. The team brought up wine jars, metal ingots, and ceramics.[1]

After their spectacular success at Cape Gelidonya, Turkish and American members of the excavation team reasonably expected to find other ancient shipwrecks in the same area. They fanned out along the coast, interviewing local sponge divers and showing them pictures of how an ancient shipwreck might look. Over many years, they talked with virtually every sponge diver then active on the Turkish coast. Two decades passed with no results.

In 1982 a new young sponge diver sketched for his captain "four-handed" metal ingots he had seen on a steep underwater slope less than fifty miles west of the Gelidonya site, off a cape called Uluburun. The captain immediately recognized the ingots as similar to drawings and photos that the Gelidonya team had shown him. The diver contacted the Museum of Underwater Archaeology at Bodrum (a major Turkish coastal city two hundred miles to the west of the new site). The hunt was on. The next dive season, the Institute of Nautical Archaeology and Bodrum Museum found the wreck on a steep slope about 150 feet down. They recovered one of many large copper ingots,

"Four-handled" copper ingots from the
Uluburun shipwreck, Bodrum Museum, Turkey.
PHOTO COURTESY OF MARTIN BAHMANN, WIKIMEDIA COMMONS

a tin ingot, several terra-cotta pieces, and an amphora, as examples of the ship's contents.

The Institute of Nautical Archaeology organized the first full expedition in 1984. Team members lived for months either aboard the dive ship, sharing its sixty-foot length with compressors, oxygen tanks, a full darkroom, freshwater maker, a repair shop, and hoses, or in temporary shelters on the rocky, barren coast. The team established a rhythm of morning and late-afternoon dives, completing more than thirteen hundred dives in the 1984 season. They measured the wreck site (roughly thirty feet by fifty-four feet), established location grids over both the steeply sloping seafloor and two gullies that cut into it, photographed pieces in situ, and began lifting objects to the surface. Only the upper portion of the wreck was excavated the first season. What at first appeared to be lumpy rocks littered this portion of the site. These turned out to be cargo solidified together into masses, which required hammer and chisel to break them free. The objects in the southern gully were merely buried in sand and easier to excavate. At the end of the dive season, thousands of objects still remained on the bottom. The team dumped tons of sand onto the wreck to prevent looting.

The trading ship had lain undisturbed for more than three thousand years and was a veritable catalog of the trade and cultures of the Eastern Mediterranean of the time. The first dive season yielded extraordinarily important material: elephant and hippopotamus ivory, a silver bracelet, amber jewelry, faience jewelry, a drinking cup, seals, copper and tin ingots, glass (beads, figures, and cobalt-blue ingots), lead fishing weights, stone balance-scale weights, bronze weapons, a gold chalice, medallions and a pectoral (a worked sheet of gold that covered the bare chest), bronze finger-cymbals, bronze tools, and stone ship anchors. In addition, the team brought up a variety of ceramic storage vessels, lamps, and bowls typical of ancient Greece, Cyprus, and Syria. Beneath the ballast stones were some remaining ship's timbers.

At this early stage of the excavation many basic questions remained unanswered, such as which end was the bow and which was the stern. Though some amphorae (cone-shaped storage vessels) contained readily identifiable materials, such as yellow lead, glass beads, or olive pits, others had unidentified resins or seeds. Many of the ceramic objects required cleaning before archaeologists could even speculate on similarities to other Mediterranean pieces of the period. It was not yet possible to separate much of the material into trade goods, ship's stores, or personal possessions. The original arrangement of the cargo awaited study of photographs and drawings.

The 1986 dive season (June–August) consisted of almost three thousand dives on the wreck, many farther down the slope than earlier explorations. The results were, once again, extraordinary. Divers brought up bulk silver and gold, ship anchors, cast and worked gold pendants, cylinder seals (with which people "signed" documents or secured trade goods) and seal blanks (not yet cut with an individual's signs), more beads (one of rock crystal and others of types not seen before at the site), bronze tools, more hippopotamus teeth, bronze fishhooks, the matching finger cymbal to the two found in 1985, another drinking cup in the shape of a ram's head, and a broken ostrich egg. A quite significant find consisted of two matching rectangular wood panels, originally hinged together, each with a rectangular recess and surrounding lip. The piece's original function was to hold wax in both recesses, into which scribes carved messages, tallies, or administrative orders. Equally important was a gold scarab (a signature seal in the shape of a beetle) inscribed with the name of Nefertiti, the reigning queen of Egypt at the time, found among a group of Egyptian rings, seals, and scarabs.

## A Ship of the Eastern Mediterranean

What sort of a ship was the Uluburun wreck? Under ballast stones the divers found a few remaining planks attached to a short section of the keel. Other shattered pieces of the ship appeared under rows of copper ingots. The recovered material did, however, yield significant information on the ship's construction. The planks were edge-joined, with no evidence of internal framing. Egyptian boats were also built this way, but the Uluburun wreck was very different from Egyptian vessels. As we have seen in chapter 2, Egyptian boats were sewn together with a unique pattern of rope ties, which marched across the planks. None of this stitching is present on the Uluburun planks. In contrast, deep, almost continuous mortises, like long slots, were cut in the lateral edges of the planks. The shipwrights then fitted broad tenons into the mortises and secured them with pegs, which passed through both the mortised planks and the interior tenon, preventing adjacent planks from separating or shifting. The Uluburun ship is the earliest known maritime use of these pegged mortise-and-tenon joints. The boat was open, with no evidence of deck or cargo holds. Analysis of the wood revealed that the keel was of fir, the tenons and pegs of oak, and the planks of cedar, most likely from Lebanon. As we have seen in chapter 2, Lebanese cedar was also the wood of choice for expensive royal boats in Egypt.

The ship certainly came from the Eastern Mediterranean, most likely from either Cyprus or coastal Syria/Palestine. The wreck yielded cymbals of a Near Eastern type, unknown in the Aegean, and many balance weights conforming to standards in the Near East. All twenty-four ship's anchors conform to designs typical of Syria/Palestine.[2]

The visual record in Egypt may be somewhat helpful in understanding what the Uluburun ship might have looked like. Much evidence comes from a mural in the tomb of Kenamun, an Egyptian official who served under Amenhotep III (ruled 1386–1349 BCE) and, therefore, died only a few decades before the Uluburun wreck. The wall painting depicts ships sailing, in port, and unloading. Unfortunately, Egyptologists have identified many features of the scenes as merely stylized depictions of ships, identical to other paintings in other tombs. Several scholars believe the ships to be, in fact, Egyptian.[3] The ships are, however, very similar to one portrayed in a contemporary tomb with an accompanying wall text that states that the person coming off the ship came from Syria/Palestine for medical treatment.

Replica of the Uluburun ship, Bodrum Museum, Turkey.
PHOTO COURTESY OF MARTIN BAHMANN, WIKIMEDIA COMMONS

So, combining all the admittedly fragmentary evidence, what might the Uluburun ship have looked like? It was apparently a sailed ship, not rowed, as there are no oarlocks on the few remaining planks. Existing pieces of the keel at bow and stern suggest a crescent shape with high bow and stern. The Uluburun ship was built of Lebanese cypress with oak for joints and pegs. Wickerwork screens likely ran along the highest plank of the open hull. The ship did not have a hogging truss (described in chapter 2) typical of Egyptian vessels.

Direct evidence from the keel suggests that a mast was placed amidships. A simple terra-cotta ship model found in Enkomi on the east coast of Greece of approximately the right period suggests several additional features of the Uluburun ship. The sail was likely low and wide. The massive spar supporting the sail curved downward at both ends. Steering was by means of two large steering oars, one on each side of the stern. A crow's nest topped the mast.[4] The excavators believe the Uluburun ship to have been about forty-five feet long, with a carrying capacity of about fourteen tons of cargo.[5] The ship would have been good in a following wind, but the large, heavy sail would have made tacking into the wind laborious and dangerous. It is understandable why ships of this design stayed close to the shore whenever possible, probably seeking shelter in stormy conditions.

It seems possible to place the Uluburun wreck within a shipbuilding world that most directly linked Cyprus, the Syria/Palestine coast, and the west coast of Turkey. This shipbuilding tradition shared few features with Egypt but more with Crete, the Greek islands, and the Peloponnesus.

## From Where, To Where, and When?

Quite remarkably, given the absence of any documents that mention the Uluburun ship, clever scientific research on material from the wreck has built a strong case for both the ship's last port of call and the date of its last voyage. The data on the last port of call begins with one of the seemingly least important of the Uluburun finds, the bones of a mouse trapped in a food storage jar. Researchers managed to extract DNA from the mouse bones. It turns out that mouse DNA varies in subtle but distinct ways among the various ports and coasts of the Eastern Mediterranean. The Uluburun mouse DNA matches that of mice in the area of Ugarit (northern coastal Syria) and no other port, suggesting that one of the ports of the Syrian coast was the ship's last port of call.[6] (The reader might recall from chapter 1 that rat DNA was important evidence in establishing the pattern of colonization of the Pacific islands. We should not underestimate rodent information.)

The dating of the ship also required careful research, based on examination of many ancient samples of wood from the region. Trees grow more in wetter years and less in drier years, yielding, over the life of the tree, a distinctive pattern of rings. It has proved possible to assemble from thousands of tree samples from the Eastern Mediterranean long timelines of distinctive patterns, to which a newly unearthed building post, ship timber, or piece of furniture can be matched. The crucial Uluburun data came from an unlikely source. To protect the hull from abrasion by the copper ingots, they were stacked on freshly cut branches. Comparing the tree rings of these young branches proved more accurate than using the larger trees of the ship's planks. By this method the Uluburun shipwreck was originally dated to 1306 BCE, though a recent and more thorough Anatolian tree ring timeline has placed the wreck between 1334 and 1323 BCE.[7]

## Contours of Exchange

Texts from the Eastern Mediterranean in various languages from the period of the Uluburun wreck describe similar ships with equally diverse and valuable cargoes. The Egyptian pharaoh Thutmose II (ruled c. 1479–1425) celebrated his capture of two merchant ships from Syria/Palestine in 1450 BCE with the inscription "now there was a seizing of two ships . . . loaded with everything, with male and female slaves, copper, emery, and every good thing, and his majesty proceeded southward to Egypt."[8]

Texts in Ugaritic (from coastal Syria) from the period of the Uluburun wreck contain a variety of references to long-distance trade. One mentions a ship lost on a voyage to Egypt; another refers to the loss of a ship laden with copper. A third text mentions the taxes due from a ship, which had traveled to Greece and traded there.[9] Overall, the texts suggest a thriving trade in relatively high-value goods, such as copper, slaves, and specialty woods, all of which connected Egypt, the coast of Syria/Palestine, the coast of Turkey, Cyprus, Crete, and Mycenae in Greece. Let us now turn to some specific goods aboard the Uluburun shipwreck and how they complicate and stretch this image of a self-contained maritime world of the Eastern Mediterranean.

## The Commodities aboard the Uluburun Wreck

At the very bottom of the ship and resting in neat rows on cut branches to protect the hull were ten tons of copper, cast into large ingots in two well-known shapes: 354 "four-handled" (also known as oxhide) ingots, and 121 "bun" ingots.[10] Copper was one of two essential components of bronze (tin, also found in the wreck, being the other). Without copper there would have been no bronze tools or weapons and no Bronze Age. Where it came from and how it was produced are discussed below.

Archaeologists have excavated "four-handled" copper ingots like those from the Uluburun wreck in a broad band from Sardinia (where fifty ingots were found) on east through Sicily (one ingot), Greece (twenty-two ingots), and Crete (thirty-seven ingots), to Cyprus (twenty ingots). The ingots found on the Uluburun ship, and the Cape Gelidonya wreck located only fifty miles west on the Turkish coast, constitute about two-thirds of all known four-handled copper ingots. Taken as a whole, the Mediterranean ingots vary in thickness, taper, and length of the handles. Weights vary from ten kilograms (22 pounds) to thirty-seven kilograms (81.5 pounds). The earliest of these copper ingots (c. 1600–1500 BCE) lack "handles." The addition of handles might simply have been to ease carrying the heavy, bulky ingots. Incised marks on many of the ingots belong to no known script and have stubbornly resisted deciphering.[11] Production of this sort of ingot likely ceased about 1200 BCE.

Before turning to the origin of the copper ingots of the Uluburun shipwreck, it is necessary briefly to consider the earliest techniques for the production of copper. Around 9000 BCE the first evidence appears in Iran and Anatolia of the working of copper. In a relatively simple process not requiring a furnace, native copper was heated in flat pans to remove impurities and later reheated to work and form. The earliest cast copper objects date from this period. In the sixth millennium BCE a much more sophisticated process was discovered. When the copper was heated to over 1,000 degrees Fahrenheit, impurities in the ore melted together and formed a lumpy slag, which could be skimmed off the molten surface. This process, known as smelting, yielded a copper with more residual iron than native copper. Archaeologists examining unearthed crucibles and slag can trace the rapid spread of the new process across many copper-producing sites in the Middle East, the Eastern Mediterranean, and Egypt. The new technique required not only high temperatures, but control of air and the gases above the melting copper ore. Charcoal was essential to produce high heat, but it also drew oxygen out of the copper oxide, forming carbon monoxide gas. Adding external air turned the carbon monoxide into more oxygen-trapping carbon dioxide. Such conditions could only be produced in a smelting furnace, rather than the earlier open pan. The early smelting furnaces were carefully sited below the lip of a hill to catch prevailing winds. The artisan smelters used blowpipes when the winds failed.[12]

By the time of the Uluburun shipwreck, sites across Iran, the Middle East, Egypt, and the Mediterranean had been producing copper for thousands of years. Removing impurities was so elemental to the process that it might seem impossible to identify the source of copper aboard. Fortunately, sophisticated science came to the rescue. With highly sensitive assay methods, scientists discovered that copper ore from each mining site leaves a distinctive fingerprint of trace elements, even through the process of smelting and refining. Three sorts of trace element analyses have proved accurate enough to differentiate the origin of a copper ingot or artifact. One relies on differing proportions of isotopes of lead in the refined copper (based mainly on the geologic age of the copper). The second uses proportions of tellurium and selenium for the same purpose. The third analyzes the proportions of trace silver and gold in the copper. When used together, these tests are particularly good at ruling out sources that decisively do not match the trace element fingerprint. All three methods, however, require a large number of ore samples from each ancient mining area to calibrate the distinctive fingerprint of the area. Only with analysis of many such samples is it possible to establish the parameters of variability of the trace elements within a copper mining area.[13]

Trace element analysis has cut through some uncertainty about the origin of the copper ingots aboard the Uluburun wreck and at other archaeological sites in the Mediterranean. It shows that Cyprus was the origin of the copper ore that was smelted into ingots found in Sardinia, Greece, and Cyprus, as well as the few ingots tested from the Uluburun shipwreck. This sort of analysis cannot, however, establish where the ingots were actually smelted, since it is possible, even likely, that copper ore was traded to smelting sites quite distant from the mine.

The copper ingot trade is not, therefore, a simple story of exports from Cyprus to the nearby Mediterranean world. The earliest copper ingots were discovered not in Cyprus but in Crete and date from the high Minoan period (1580–1500 BCE), two centuries before the Uluburun wreck. Trace element analysis shows that these ingots were neither from Cyprus nor from any known source in the Mediterranean region or Turkey. Archaeologists will have to look farther afield for the source, perhaps to Iran, Afghanistan, Uzbekistan, or Tajikistan.[14] In addition, one of the analyzed ingots from the Uluburun wreck also does not match trace elements from any known sources. Further complicating the picture is the fact that the only known mold for such ingots was found not on Cyprus but a hundred miles east on the coast of Syria.

Taken together, this scientific research suggests that Cyprus displaced earlier sources of copper. Its copper ore was processed both on the island and the nearby Syrian coast and carried west in ships like the ones wrecked at Uluburun and Cape Gelidonya. From the Turkish coast the ships headed west to Mycenae in Greece and, perhaps, on to Sardinia. A single find of a four-handled copper ingot just off Sozòpol in the Black Sea about fifty miles north of Istanbul raises the possibility that the copper ingot trade included the Black Sea.[15] Archaeologists have excavated four-handled copper ingots in southern Germany, suggestive of some sort of carrying trade over the Alps.[16]

Some of the goods aboard the Uluburun shipwreck even further stretch the notion of an enclosed Eastern Mediterranean trading world.[17] Consider, for example, the jointed wood writing boards found at the wreck site. Archaeologists have excavated similar receptacles for incised wax letters and accounts in Old Kingdom Egypt (2686–2181 BCE), and they are mentioned in Middle Assyrian (sixteenth to tenth century BCE) and Babylonian texts, which document the use of wood letter-boards throughout the area of present-day Iraq. The vast majority of the references to wood letter-boards, however, come from the Hittite Empire (at its height around 1350 BCE), which included almost all of modern-day Turkey and Syria. It is possible to envision a cultural world of the wood writing board that stretched from the Nile River more than a thousand miles eastward to the Tigris-Euphrates Valley.[18]

Also aboard the Uluburun wreck were several examples of a drinking vessel known in ancient Greek as a rhyton. The word is associated with an even older Indo-European word meaning "flow." The rhyton was perhaps originally used to dip water or wine out of a large container in order to drink. Subsequent designs were in the shape of animals or animal heads, with a stream of wine coming out of the mouth.[19] Such vessels in the shape of a bull or bull's head, fish, octopuses, and beetles have been found on Crete in the ruins of Minoan sanctuaries.[20] Mainland Greek finds include rhyta in the shape of rams, hounds, boar, deer, and goats.[21] In the period of the Uluburun shipwreck, however, the rhyton was also used for feasting, in the area of present-day Iran. If one could define a "rhyton zone," it would have to stretch from the Eastern Mediterranean fifteen hundred miles eastward to central Iran. Such cultural zones were anything but stable. The rhyton was a common drinking and feasting vessel much later in Rome, and the object traveled with Roman conquest and became localized in what is now Germany, France, and England. The rhyton also traveled along the Silk Road, appearing early in Central Asia and reaching China, at least as early as the Tang dynasty (618–907 CE). There it joined a centuries-older indigenous wine-horn tradition.[22]

The glass aboard the Uluburun wreck both reinforces the picture of an active Eastern Mediterranean trading world and supports the assumption of an even broader trading world. Divers recovered three sorts of glass: thou-

Glass ingot from the
Uluburun shipwreck,
Bodrum Museum, Turkey.
PHOTO COURTESY OF MARTIN
BAHMANN, WIKIMEDIA COMMONS

sands of beads, several cast figures, and 175 glass ingots, ranging in weight from 3.3 pounds to 5.5 pounds (the lighter ingots had been worn by wave and sand action). The ingots were primarily cobalt blue and turquoise, but a few were purple and amber.[23]

The grinding of glass into decorative beads, the melting of colored glass powders into faience jewelry, and the pouring of molten glass into molds to make figurines were widely practiced in the Eastern Mediterranean at the time.[24] Primary production of glass ingots, however, required more specialized knowledge and more sophisticated technology than secondary casting. George Bass, who led the initial Uluburun excavations, in his early analysis suggested that the ingots came from Syria/Palestine, though no known primary glassworks had been located. He conceded, however, that the ingots seemed identical to those from the Nile Delta.[25]

Subsequent research has in fact shown that the glass ingots from the Uluburun wreck are in every way identical to those produced in the Nile Delta. Archaeologists have now excavated an ancient glassworks at Qantir in the Nile Delta where the Uluburun ingots were likely produced. The specialized technological process began with a relatively low-temperature firing of plant ash and crushed quartz, which produced a powdered material. The remaining plant ash had to be washed from the powder. The next phase of production was a relatively high-temperature firing in a crucible with colorant minerals. At the Qantir site, the evidence suggests that individual workshops specialized in specific colors of glass. The shape and size of the crucibles found at Qantir match the ingots from the Uluburun wreck.[26] Colored glass ingots from this Egyptian source were traded across the Eastern Mediterranean and formed the basis for the colored castings of figures sacred and profane, decorations, beads, and other jewelry.

The materials used in coloring the glass, such as cobalt, copper oxide, iron, and gold, suggest connections to a wider world. They, in fact, came from as far away as Persia, Afghanistan, and Africa. Not only had the Qantir craftsmen figured out which minerals and additives produced which colors; they also figured out where the minerals came from and established a stable enough supply chain to produce a steady output of a variety of colored ingots.

It is worth noting the sheer variety and quantity of organic cargo aboard the Uluburun shipwreck. Cheryl Ward, one of the excavators, summarized the plant material as follows:

> So far, Ulu Burun samples have produced almonds, acorns, pine nuts, pine cone fragments, wild pistachio nutlets, olives and olive stones, pomegranate and fig seeds and fruit fragments, and grape seeds of two types. . . . Also recorded are coriander, nigella (black cumin) and sumac seeds, charred barley in the husk and charred wheat, rachis and chaff fragments from barley and other grasses, several kinds of small grass seeds, at least three types of pulses and seeds from more than forty different weeds and other plants.[27]

The wreck yielded 120 large jars that once held a ton of terebinth, an aromatic tree resin from Syria/Palestine, which was either burned for the scent or used in perfumes. Another jar held a multitude of olive stones larger than most olive stones of the period. Olives were not widely cultivated at the time of the Uluburun wreck, and those found may well have been cultivated specifically for eating, rather than oil. Both terebinth and olives were commercial items of elite lifestyle, rather like the African blackwood, hippopotamus teeth, and ivory found aboard.

So, too, were pomegranates elements of elite lifestyle. Aboard the Uluburun wreck, the remains of pomegranates—seeds and bits of skin—turned up in more than a quarter of the sediments in jars.[28] The pomegranate was no mere fruit but carried complex associations with the passage to the afterlife, as well as romantic and sexual meanings. In the Eastern Mediterranean the fruit appears on tombs, painted on fine ceramics, carved in ivory, represented in faience, cast in imported glass and bronze, and even worked from gold sheet. The geographic spread of these images in the Eastern Mediterranean includes Egypt, the cities of Crete, Cyprus, and Syria/Palestine, and Mycenae and Athens. The symbolic status of the pomegranate is suggested by two of the Uluburun finds—small ivory finials in the shape of pomegranates. The twelfth-century BCE Turin papyrus gives this poetic voice to the pomegranate tree: "My seeds shine like the teeth of my mistress, the shape of my fruit is round like her breasts. I'm her favorite."[29]

At the time of the Uluburun wreck the pomegranate, native to the Caspian Sea area, had been cultivated for millennia, but was grown nowhere in the Eastern Mediterranean. Fresh pomegranates were thus a high-value, elite food traveling to wealthy cities and elite tables aboard the Uluburun ship. In the larger picture, the movement of expensive fresh fruit suggests a predictability of demand and a backflow of information of tastes and markets that, on the face of it, seems astonishing for a period more than three thousand years ago.

The Uluburun wreck carried mainly high-value raw materials for the expression of a shared elite lifestyle across much of the Eastern Mediterranean: elephant and hippopotamus ivory, copper, tin, and glass in ingot form, ostrich eggs, African blackwood, pomegranates, olives, and tree resins for perfumes. Some of the goods came long distances, such as resins from southern Arabia, lapis lazuli from Afghanistan, and ostrich eggs from sub-Saharan Africa. While archaeologists have quite a good idea that the ship came from the coast of Syria/Palestine, they can only speculate as to where it was going. Minoan Crete is unlikely; its fabulous palaces had been destroyed more than a century earlier. The more likely destination was the wealthy city of Mycenae on the Peloponnesian Peninsula of Greece. Archaeologists have found a good number of artifacts from Egypt, Syria/Palestine, Mesopotamia, Cyprus, and Anatolia in and around Mycenae.[30] From Mycenae the ship might have been bound for Egypt, though the direct route from Syria to Egypt would have been much shorter and safer.

It is important to emphasize two features of this Eastern Mediterranean world. First, in spite of trade connections, it contained profoundly different cultures, such as Egypt, Mycenae, and the Hittite kingdom. The copper, tin, and glass aboard the Uluburun wreck was likely turned into a variety of different objects in different places. As we have seen, however, the entire region did share some elite objects, such as the drinking vessel known later as the rhyton. Second, demand connected to supply sources far beyond the Eastern Mediterranean, reaching into Asia and Africa. Political boundaries in no sense matched trade or economic boundaries. It is worth noting, however, that the Eastern Mediterranean world barely connected, via supply or demand, with the western Mediterranean, and not at all to most of Europe.[31]

## The End of the Uluburun World

This interconnected trading world, which brought elegant materials for beautiful and powerful objects, fresh pomegranates, drinking cups for banqueting and metals for statues, weapons, and tools, was not long to survive. Within two centuries of the Uluburun wreck many of these glittering capitals and the kingdoms that supported them were gone.[32] Ugarit on coastal Syria, and the cities of Cyprus and Mycenae, were attacked and destroyed by the mysterious "Sea Peoples." A few documents of the time mention them, but none describes them, so theories are rampant: they came from the north of Greece in waves of migration, they came from Central Asia, or they were native to the Syrian coast and rose against their overlords.

All we actually have are the facts of near-simultaneous decline and destruction, much of which seems to have little to do with "Sea Peoples." The Hittite capital, Hattusha, about 150 miles east of Ankara and far from the sea, was burned in 1160 BCE. Troy was destroyed, rebuilt, and destroyed again. Archaeologists have speculated that the new iron weapons coming into use throughout the Middle East and the Eastern Mediterranean were so lethal that defeated armies were utterly destroyed and sacked cites never recovered. Like other theories of the sudden decline of this world, the "iron weapon" theory has been roundly criticized.

The end of the world of the Uluburun wreck also likely had natural causes. Pollen analysis suggests that the whole region became much drier, and drought was common. This reality may be the time referred to in the biblical story of Exodus from Egypt, with its years of good harvest and the years of famine. Drought and famine would have stressed, if not doomed, kingdoms around the Mediterranean. Still, it is important to remember that Egypt and Assyria survived as major kingdoms. So did some smaller cities, such as Phaistos on Crete. But not until three centuries after the Uluburun wreck would begin the long, slow development of the city-states of classical Greece.

# 4

# SUTTON HOO BURIAL

Sixty miles northeast of London the River Deben flows south off the Suffolk plateau into the North Sea. It rises and falls with the tides a full ten miles upstream. In 1939 this unlikely and unprepossessing bit of rural England produced headlines around the world.

A Mrs. Edith Pretty owned an estate that included several miles of the eastern bank of the Deben, the steep palisades above the floodplain and the plateau above the river. In the summer of 1938 she funded an amateur excavation of one of several ancient burial mounds on the estate. The mounds were well known. A document of the seventeenth century mentions them, and all maps of the region from the seventeenth century onward accurately place them on the edge of the plateau overlooking the palisades and floodplain of the River Deben. Robbers had looted some of the mounds centuries earlier. In the nineteenth century the owners of the estate planted the plateau and floodplain in mixed hardwood and conifers, as shown in maps and illustrations of the time, so that the mounds no longer dominated the landscape.

Mrs. Pretty's interest in archaeology stemmed from a trip to Egypt. She was thus heir to several generations of English men and women whose passion for archaeology began when viewing the ongoing excavations in the Valley of the Kings. Mrs. Pretty shared a cognitive geography, a fascination with Egypt, with like-minded professional and amateur Egyptologists from England, France, Germany, and around the world. Ruins were just one feature of the globalization of the past that she was about to experience personally.

She hired a local archaeologist named Basil Brown. He first surveyed the site and numbered each identifiable mound from one to fifteen. His formal dig began with Mrs. Pretty's gardener and gamekeeper opening a trench into the side of Mound 3. Brown's records are meticulous, and his methods were admirable. After uncovering what remained of the burial in Mound 3, Brown, the gardener, and the gamekeeper moved on to Mounds 2 and 4. By the end of the summer, the excavations yielded only small bits of carved bone, fragments of incised metal foil, some iron nails, a bit of luxury textile, and a couple of shield bosses. The finds were exciting enough that Mrs. Pretty decided to continue excavations the following year, though clearly robbers had long before removed the important objects.

Excavation resumed in the summer of 1939. Basil Brown and his team (the gardener and the gamekeeper) opened a trench into Mound 1, the largest on the site. Brown first encountered a single iron rivet, telltale evidence of a ship burial. Within a few hours the workers uncovered the extreme end of a ship, which was filled with sand. Brown realized that the wood of the ship was gone, but a full impression of the ship remained in the surrounding clay. Weeks of hard labor followed as he gradually emptied the first forty feet of the hull, yellow stains in the sand caused by rusting rivets alerting Brown when he approached the sides of the ship. It became clear that robbers had abandoned their pit a mere six inches above the burial.

The apparent size of the ship, the delicacy of the sand covering the clay ship impression, and the possibility of an intact grave demanded professional expertise. The curator of the local Ipswich Museum called in an expert from the Archaeological Department of the Ordinance Survey, who assembled a small team of archaeologists from London. Through June, Brown's team removed the sand from the remainder of the ship, and on July 10 they began bringing up a hoard of priceless artifacts of the seventh century from the burial at the center of the ship.

In spite of the imminent outbreak of World War II (only two months later), the Sutton Hoo hoard was rightly characterized as one of the greatest archaeological finds of the twentieth century. The *Times* story was about as excited as *Times* stories were at that time: "The magnificence of the gold and silver treasure from the seventh-century ship burial at Sutton Hoo was even greater than one had expected. Particularly fine was the silver, including six extremely shapely shallow bowls, in almost perfect preservation."[1]

The story quickly reached America, with coverage in newspapers in Boston, New York, and Washington, D.C. In a month both the Billings, Montana, *Gazette* and the Hindustan *Times* had stories on the Sutton Hoo hoard. A few months later, coverage spread to less likely venues, such as a full-page feature in *La Prensa*, a Spanish-language newspaper from San Antonio.[2]

The Sutton Hoo hoard had several adventures before it finally settled into its permanent home. A local hearing decided on the basis of arcane early medieval law that the find was not "treasure trove" and therefore belonged to Mrs. Pretty, not the government. Mrs. Pretty, aware that she had neither the expertise nor the money to restore the pieces properly, gave it all to the British Museum. The hoard, however, got caught up in the imperatives of war. Along with tens of thousands of other artifacts, the Sutton Hoo pieces were crated and trucked away from London to safe storage in the countryside.

For decades after the Sutton Hoo discovery, British archaeologists and historians emphasized the Anglo-Saxon nature of the burial. They expected to locate further ship burials at Sutton Hoo and in other mounds in England. These expectations have gone largely unfulfilled.[3] More than a half century of research has shown that the world of ship burials was not somehow English but stretched from Denmark, Sweden, and Norway to the Orkneys, the Isle of Man, and Scotland. Shared ship construction, metalwork, and artistic motifs suggest that Sutton Hoo was intimately part of this larger maritime world of the northern seas, whether the buried warlord was Scandinavian or born in England.[4]

## The Shipbuilding World of the Sutton Hoo Burial

The evidence from ship burials and other shipwrecks from the period of roughly 600 CE to 1000 CE strongly suggests a unique shipbuilding tradition that began in Scandinavia and spread across the Baltic and the North Sea, eventually encompassing what is today the British Isles, Ireland, and Greenland. What were the core features of this sort of boat, as impressed into the clay of the Sutton Hoo burial? A new ship began with its keel, slightly curved through most of the length of the ship and steeply curving upward at the bow and stern. Shipwrights then nailed a long wood strip, usually of oak, on each side of the keel. Subsequent strips overlapped and were nailed to the previously placed strip. The boat rose, strip by strip, with no internal support (technically termed "clinker-built" construction). The shipwright added crossties when the relatively flat bottom turned upward to form the sides. The earliest of these boats lacked sails and were rowed, mainly along rivers and coasts. A seventh-century stone carving from the Jutland peninsula of Denmark shows that by the time of the Sutton Hoo burial (645 CE), boatbuilders were experimenting with sails.[5] Within a century shipwrights developed various mast-to-boat attachments. Most involved strengthening and interconnecting crossties. Later developments in the Viking period (c. 750–1000 CE) included shifting the steering oar from the side to the stern, sometimes adding a weather deck to create a drier hold for cargo, and improvements in sail shape and in methods to move, increase, and decrease sail.[6]

The "Viking-style" boat had its good points. Rowing made it fast and maneuverable. The boats were supple and tended to flex and ride waves. The same crew both rowed and fought. More than a century of annual invasions of England by Vikings from Scandinavia is proof enough of the boat's success in open-water sailing. Construction could be scaled up from small fishing vessels to great naval longboats. Some boats were designed wider, with more freeboard and a deck to accommodate cargo, animals, and settlers. Once the Roman Empire retreated from Northern Europe, these boats transported Angles, Saxons, Jutes, and Scandinavian settlers to England, Scotland, Wales, Ireland, the Orkneys, Iceland, Greenland, and Newfoundland.[7]

The boat also had its drawbacks. Many versions were more suited to war and looting than trade. High-value loot, such as gold, silver, weapons, and slaves, was not spoiled by contact with seawater and could be fitted among the rowers. But rowers took up most of the boats' space, and there was no place to keep trade goods dry.[8] In a naval engagement, the boat was really only suitable for grappling and hand-to-hand combat. Both Vikings and their foes much preferred land battles. The problem of low freeboard was never really solved, and the boats could be swamped in heavy seas. There was no protection for the crew in bad weather.

### The Culture of Ship Burials

The Sutton Hoo burial made headlines around the world not because of its boat design but because of the extraordinary treasure that came from the collapsed wooden burial platform, objects the lord might want or need when his ship arrived in the afterworld. Common domestic items included iron-bound wooden buckets, an iron chain, a lamp, a cauldron, a bronze bowl, and a small pottery bottle. The acidic soil, which had eaten away the wood of the ship, had also destroyed all but tiny scraps of the fabrics and skins in the burial vault. Microanalysis of the scraps has identified blue and yellow dyes, fine linen weave, and patterned weaves of wall hangings. Toward the center of the burial were the luxury items: a large silver dish and a fluted silver bowl, burl walnut cups, inlaid bone combs, silver buckles, silver-trimmed drinking

The Sutton Hoo helmet, British Museum, London.

horns, the gold fittings of a purse, gold and garnet fabric clasps. The remains of a lyre and a tall iron stand were found near the west wall of the burial. Most famous of all are the weapons and armor at the center of the burial: a pattern-welded gold-decorated sword, gold and garnet fittings for the scabbard and sword belt, an iron ax-hammer, the coat of mail, and an iron helmet with a silver and gold decoration.

Archaeologists have found close parallels to the Sutton Hoo treasure in Scandinavia. Several burials there have yielded helmets strikingly similar in shape and coverage of head, face, and neck, with identical decoration, down to details of bushy eyebrows and the motif of dancing hunters with spears. The bosses on the shield at Sutton Hoo are strikingly similar to such bosses found in Sweden from the same period.

Some of the buried artifacts at Sutton Hoo thus overlap the common shipbuilding world of Scandinavia, the Baltic, the North Sea, and the Atlantic. Other pieces of the Sutton Hoo treasure, however, go far beyond this world. Style, decoration, and inscriptions place the crafting of a large silver tray, a fluted silver bowl, a nest of eight silver bowls, and two silver spoons to the Byzantine Empire (with its capital at Constantinople—present-day Istanbul). The large silver tray is stamped with the symbol of the reign of Anastasius I (491–518 CE). It was thus well over a century old by the time it was buried at Sutton Hoo. The tray had traveled more than fifteen hundred miles even by the most direct routes. More likely the tray was traded from the Caspian Sea region up the Dnieper River, past Kiev and Novgorod, into Scandinavia and across the North Sea to England. Records from the Byzantium area only mention Norse arriving at Constantinople in the 700s, decades after the Sutton Hoo burial. Nevertheless, a hand-to-hand trade likely brought high-value goods along the route long before any single group traversed its entire length.

From about 750 to about 1000 the shallow draft of the Viking boats made the river route from Scandinavia to Constantinople as feasible and profitable as any route to Western Europe. The Vikings traded amber and slaves captured in Poland for silver and gold in Constantinople. The routes were in such regular use that archaeologists have located a number of Norse settlements and burial mounds along them. The earliest Norse artifacts located in these sites date from first decades of the 800s. Two large hoards of coins from Islamic Baghdad are associated with the Norse river sites.

In a time of very low literacy, any eyewitness account of a ship burial is quite unlikely. And yet—against all odds—one exists. In 921 the caliph of Baghdad sent a diplomatic mission to a nomadic chieftain named Almish, who encamped with his flocks and followers on the Volga River in what is now Georgia. The intrepid ambassador, Ahmad ibn Fadlan, had to circumvent the hostile Byzantine Empire, traveling by caravan first east to Bukhara, then north and west to Kwarazim, where he spent a long and very cold winter; but he finally arrived at Almish's camp. Though the mission was an utter diplomatic failure, Ibn Fadlan was a keen observer of customs and practices while he was more or less a prisoner in Almish's camp. He saw Vikings stop often enough at Almish's camp that his memoir details what they ate and drank and their religious offerings to permanently erected icons.

Late in his memoir Ibn Fadlan described the funeral of a boat captain. The ritual took place over several days. First, the body was laid out in a temporary shelter. His companions divided his wealth into three parts: one for his family, one for the preparation of the costly funeral garments, and one for the sacrificed animals and the drink for the day of the funeral. Ibn Fadlan's memoir describes the events in graphic detail.

> I went to the river where his boat was and, indeed, it had already been taken out of the water. . . . Then the boat was dragged up until it was placed on top of the wooden platform. . . . They then came with a bed [*sarir*], put it on the boat and covered it with quilted mattresses of Byzantine brocade, as well as with cushions of Byzantine brocade. . . . They had placed alcohol [*nabidh*], fruit, and a three-stringed lute in the grave with him. . . . They dressed him in trousers, leggings, a tunic, and a brocaded caftan with gold buttons. On his head they placed a cap made of brocade sable fur. . . . They seated him on the quilted mattress and propped him up with the cushions. . . . They then brought all his weapons and laid them at this side. [With elaborate ritual a slave girl gave away her silver anklets and bracelets, was ritually killed and laid next to her master.] The nearest relative then appeared, took a piece of wood [and] . . . set fire to the wood that was stacked under the ship. . . . And truly an hour did not pass before the boat, the wood, and the girl and her master had become ash dust. They then built on the site of the ship they had drawn out of the river, something resembling a round hill, and raised in the center of it a large pine wood post.[9]

Except for the burning of the boat, this ceremony on the Volga River seems uncannily like what might have happened at Sutton Hoo, though it took place two thousand miles away and three centuries later. The great chief's body, surrounded by his weapons and wealth and sacrificed animals, reclined on a brocade-covered platform in the center of his boat. After the ceremony the great chief's followers raised a mound over the burial.

Byzantine bowls found in the Sutton Hoo burial and the similarity of Ibn Fadlan's description of a ship burial on the lower Volga River to that of Sutton Hoo suggest a vast cultural world of Scandinavian raiding, trading, and settlement in the period from 650 to 1000. Its western boundary encompassed the north coast of Europe, England, Scotland, Wales, the northern islands (such as the Orkneys), Iceland, Greenland, Newfoundland. Viking raids and settlement also included coastal Spain and Sicily in the Mediterranean. To the south of Scandinavia, Viking raids and trade followed the Volga and the Dnieper to the Caspian and Black Seas. Raid and trade went hand in hand. The raids yielded high-value slaves, who could be sold in any of the well-known markets, such as in France, Italy, and Constantinople.

Let us consider just three of the many complex interchanges that marked this vast cultural world. The first is chess. Invented in India sometime before the sixth century, the game was carried westward. A seventh-century Persian romance describes the chess battlefield:

> The sage has invented a battlefield, in the midst of which the king takes up his station. To the left and right of him the army is disposed, the foot-soldiers occupying the rank in front. At the king's side stands this sagacious counselor advising him on the strategy to be carried out during the battle. In the two directions the elephants are posted with their faces turned toward where the conflicts is. Beyond them are stationed the war-horses, on which are mounted two resourceful riders, and fighting alongside them to the left and right are turrets ready for the fray.[10]

Also in the seventh century, one of the Prophet Muhammad's earliest converts played chess in the town square of Medina. The game was so popular in Constantinople that the Orthodox Christian Church banned it on the grounds that it promoted gambling (680 CE).

The earliest chess piece so far discovered in Europe comes from Scandinavia. The active trade in slaves and amber to Constantinople brought chess to the Viking homeland several centuries before it arrived in southern Europe via Muslim Spain. Chess had been played in Scandinavia for more than three centuries before the carving of the magnificent twelfth-century chess pieces now in the British Museum, which were found on Lewis in the Outer Hebrides.[11]

The second story of the broad Viking cultural world is, literally, more tasty than chess and is about cardamom, a spice native to India. Arab traders regularly shipped it (along with pepper and cinnamon) from the Malabar Coast of India to Aden, then to Cairo. Yearly, Constantinople merchants sent a fleet to Cairo to buy tropical medicines and spices. By the time that the Vikings arrived in Constantinople, this trade was centuries old.[12] Viking traders in Constantinople encountered cardamom and brought it home. Their wives must have loved it because to this day cardamom is one of the most popular tastes in Scandinavian baking, sauces, and as a flavoring for aquavit.

The third story of the Viking cultural world is that of amber. This mysterious material is both hard and warm to the touch, both clear and golden. It can be transparent and hold a tiny treasure inside—an insect or a leaf. Amber is now known to be fossilized tree sap and is actually found anywhere there are forests with resinous trees. Amber can be millions of years old or relatively recently fossilized.

Until about twenty year ago the only successful test identifying amber's place of origin required the destruction of a fairly large sample and chemical analysis of the burned powder. Advances in spectrometry now permit nondestructive analysis of trace element markers that identify place of origin. The test is quick and inexpensive, which makes practical the analysis of large numbers of amber samples.

Spectrographic analysis of many thousands of amber samples from the Middle East has yielded astonishingly long trading patterns. Baltic amber was traded to the Middle East in the Neolithic period (c. 10,500–4,500 BCE) and possibly even earlier. In this long perspective it no longer seems surprising that the Vikings carried amber for trade to Constantinople or Baghdad. They were merely traversing the whole route of what had been a hand-to-hand trade for millennia.[13]

## The End of the Viking Ship

The world of Viking raids was actually a fragile balance of economic factors. Relatively few warriors were full-time, professional soldiers. Most were farmers who took up raiding in hopes of either acquiring capital for more farmland or gaining a new place to settle with better land and climate.

At the beginning of the Viking period (c. 750 CE), Scandinavian society consisted of many small farmers, who could perhaps afford to send a son on a raid as a kind of entrepreneurial investment. By the end of the period (c. 1000), Scandinavian society had become much more hierarchical. A few rich families owned the land, which was worked by labor that was bound to it and thus unavailable for raiding. In Western Europe, which had been heavily raided, equally important changes made raids less profitable. Kings had consolidated their lands at the expense of local warlords. One effect was to limit the ability of local warlords to buy off the raiders or, conversely, ally with them in attacking a neighbor. The second effect of kingly consolidation was to put enough resources in the hands of the king to enable him to keep full-time professional armies capable of manning forts and protecting coasts, cities, and towns. Raiding a protected coast with fortifications was considerably more dangerous and costly than merely swooping down on a coastal village and seizing the population and its wealth. Viking-style ships would, however, remain the dominant ships of war, built or hired by kings, until about 1200, when, as we shall see in chapter 8, a ship known as a cog superseded them for trade and war.

## Sutton Hoo Today

After World War II the British Museum's treasures returned from various hiding places in the countryside, and restoration of the Sutton Hoo hoard began. Some of the silver required only reshaping and cleaning. A magnificent gold-embellished helmet was in hundreds of fragments, which had to be placed and fit on a support armature. Most of the restorations were completed in the 1950s, but some took even longer. Scholars examining the edges of the many fragments of the helmet under high magnification discovered in 1968 that several of the pieces were incorrectly placed. Over several months the helmet was correctly reassembled.

Research at the site continues. Between 1965 and 1971 the British Museum funded further excavations, which mainly established facts about Mound 1, such as the structure of the mound and its relation to the ship. Archaeologists also explored a portion of the site now known as the cemetery, discovering Neolithic graves that preceded the ship burial by more than ten thousand years. Between 1983 and 1991 the British Museum sponsored a third archaeological exploration, which focused on several unexcavated mounds, the areas between them, and the relation of the cemetery to the surrounding landscape.[14]

Today there is a small museum at the Sutton Hoo site, which holds a drinking cup and several pottery finds. The centerpiece of the museum is a replica of the ship in which the warlord was buried, built based on photographs of the impression of the boat in the soil. The replica shows that the Sutton Hoo boat was rather different from many other later Viking boats known from excavated wrecks and ship burials. The Sutton Hoo boat is wider than expected ("beamier"), but still with little freeboard. A boat of this contour would be in such peril of swamping in heavy seas that scholars have suggested that it operated only on rivers. This hypothesis is plausible, since Viking groups, it is now known, later traveled long distances on the rivers of Russia and what is now Georgia and may well have built specialized boats for these operations.

Boatwrights built the first replica of a Viking ship in 1883, long before the Sutton Hoo find, and it successfully sailed from Scandinavia to America. More than a hundred replicas have been built since, from small river vessels to full longboats. Some are private, but others take tourists on journeys of varying length.[15]

In the larger picture, the most lasting heritage of Sutton Hoo and the centuries of Scandinavian shipbuilding is less romantic and glamorous than the boats and the treasure of the ship burials. It is the heritage of ordinary people who made a perilous journey and settled far from home. Over the last decade DNA studies of historical immigration and settlement have become far more accurate. Researchers have now identified many distinct genetic markers of historic populations and have developed better sampling and methods to identify later migrations. For example, an ongoing project at Leicester seeks DNA markers in men living in areas with many Scandinavian place names and possessing identifiable Scandinavian surnames found in the earliest land registers (generally from about five hundred years after the Viking settlements). The results suggest that Scandinavian immigrants were, in the Viking period, perhaps the majority population in this area of England.[16] Studies show similar results for portions of Ireland and the Isle of Man. Here is the strongest proof of a unified world based around the Scandinavian boats.

Two wider conclusions can be drawn from the worlds related to the Sutton Hoo ship burial. First, the regional maritime world of the Sutton Hoo burial and Viking longboats was much larger than the Eastern Mediterranean world of the Uluburun shipwreck. At its peak, several centuries after the Sutton Hoo burial, the Viking maritime world included war and trade on the north littoral of Europe, in addition to the Mediterranean, Russia, the Caucasus, Constantinople, and settlements in Iceland, Greenland, and briefly in North America. Secondly, the merger and globalization of maritime worlds by the Vikings would not last. The decline was swift. By the eleventh century, the silver mines in the Black Sea region were exhausted, and the Vikings simply stopped coming. At the same time their explorations to distant Greenland and North America ceased, and with the exception of conquering Sicily in the Mediterranean, their world shrank to the British Isles and the northern littoral of Europe.

In April 2014 the new Early Medieval Gallery opened at the British Museum, with the Sutton Hoo hoard as its centerpiece. In a large, airy, high-ceilinged room, the great finds are displayed: the extraordinary garnet-and-gold shoulder clasps, the heavy scepter with carved heads at the top and bottom, the silver drinking vessels and the silver and bronze serving vessels. At the distant end of the room the gold war helmet is finally revealed.[17] The effect is uncannily like coming face to face with the owner of all the beautiful objects. While the new display offers many objects, which connect the Sutton Hoo burial to wider worlds of Scandinavian raiders, traders, and settlers, the power of the helmet makes this world personal. "Here is my world, the rewards and the dangers. Be part of it if you dare."

# 5

# INTAN SHIPWRECK

In 1996, the appearance of a cache of antique ceramics in antique shops in Jakarta, Indonesia, alerted government authorities that a wreck had been located. The pattern was familiar to the police. Subsequent investigation showed that seabirds actually identified the wreck. The seabed is flat and featureless for many miles around the site, forty-five miles north of the coast of Java. Local fishermen knew that fish colonize anything that sticks up from the flat seabed and provides cover. The fishermen, therefore, seek concentrations of diving birds, assuming fish are below. By now, fishermen also know that a favorable habitat for fish may well be a wreck, its artifacts worth far more than prosaic fish. Fishermen sold information of the site to looters.

The wreck lay seventy-five feet below the surface, the most extreme depth possible for dive equipment owned by the looters. The extreme depth substantially slowed looting and allowed time for the Indonesian navy to locate the dive ship and arrest the looters. The government shipwreck committee sanctioned a local salvage company in partnership with a Singapore-based excavation company to undertake a full archaeological expedition. The site was named Intan after a modern village on the coast. Nothing prepared the team for the astonishing hoard they were about to uncover. The team gridded the site and, racing against the approaching stormy season, brought up more than twenty-seven hundred historically important artifacts.[1] The pottery and the silver dated the find to around 1000 CE.

At a historical distance of more than a thousand years, it is impossible to know for certain what caused the shipwreck. Unlike the Uluburun wreck, foundering on rocks can be ruled out; the seafloor is flat, featureless clay. The most likely cause of the disaster was a sudden storm, which either swamped or broke the ship. The unknown sailors and merchants were 150 miles from their port in western Java. Recent research techniques allow us to understand many features of the lives of those aboard and follow the goods to their origins, some as far away as the Middle East.

## Southeast Asian Ship Design and Navigation

The Intan wreck was a ship of Southeast Asian timber and design, about ninety feet long and twenty-five feet across, perhaps three hundred tons, with a V-shaped keel rather than the flat bottom typical of Egyptian or Chinese ships. As with Egyptian ships, the builders used no iron, though of course there is nothing to suggest that Southeast Asian shipbuilders somehow knew about Egyptian ships. Both Southeast Asian and Egyptian shipbuilders arrived at similar solutions, based on locally available materials and technology.[2] The details of construction are, moreover, completely different from Egyptian design.

Southeast Asian shipbuilders first carved a keel, then carved and stacked curved planks to form the hull. Wood dowels on the edges joined the stacked planks. On the inside of these planks, shipbuilders left matched projections, which were then drilled. Cross members (thwarts) rested on and were lashed to these projections with palm fiber rope. Vertical lashing between the thwarts kept the planks tight. These ships usually had three or four sails and a large rudder about three-quarters of the way aft along one side.[3] Folktales of the Bugis, oceangoing Southeast Asian traders, suggest that there were hundreds, if not thousands, of such ships plying the islands and mainland ports of Southeast Asia in the tenth century. These ships used local materials in a light, elegant design, which allowed the ships to flex and not break in heavy seas, as noted by early European explorers, centuries after the Intan wreck.[4]

The site of the wreck would have been unknown at the time, and the cargo lay on the clay bottom of the Java Sea for a thousand years. Torpedo worms ate the exposed timbers. The cargo spilled out; the heaviest stayed close, and lighter objects drifted farther away.

It is likely that the goods were loaded at an entrepôt in Sumatra, probably Palembang, and bound across more than four hundred miles of open ocean to a port on the north coast of Java. By the tenth century, navigational technology had been refined; routes and ports became more numerous. Among other objects of the Intan wreck, divers found a compass bowl. This technological breakthrough came from China but had spread throughout

Bas relief of ship on the Borobudur Buddhist monument of Java of the
same period as the Intan wreck. The many differences between this ship and the
evidence from the wreck suggest different sorts of ships plied these waters.

PHOTO BY THE AUTHOR

Southeast Asia and along the shipping lanes to India. The compass consisted of a natural fragment of magnetite, the magnetized form of iron, which
was mounted on a small wooden disk. This lightweight apparatus was then
floated on water in a special bowl with incised markings on the inner surface.
Like a modern compass, the magnetite always pointed to magnetic north so
that sailors could set their course from the incised lines on the bowl. The
compass was common enough. There was one aboard the wrecked ship, an
otherwise undistinguished cargo carrier.[5]

## A Cargo of Tin

In the hold of the ship were thousands of pounds of tin, in similar-size,
marked, squat pyramid-shaped ingots from the Kedah region of the western
Malay Peninsula. At the time of the Intan wreck, tin was mined much like
gold. Tin-bearing ore was ground by hand and washed. The heavy tin oxide
settled to the bottom of sluices. Miners also panned for tin pebbles in rivers.
From either source, the tin oxide was then smelted into ingots. The tin ingots of the shipwreck were bound for Java, which was devoid of the metal.

(The reader might recall that tin ingots were also found in the hold of the Uluburun shipwreck of the Eastern Mediterranean, dating more than two thousand years before the Intan shipwreck.)

Tin was valuable as the crucial additional component to copper in bronze, a metal in extraordinarily wide use in Southeast Asia at the time of the shipwreck. Bronze was cast into statues and religious objects, simple domestic objects such as mortars and door hinges, jewelry, and weapons. Bronze coinage with high tin content was minted in India and the Middle East in addition to Southeast Asia. At the time of the Intan shipwreck, Arabs in the Middle East knew about tin from Kedah in mainland Southeast Asia (today in Malaysia). Abu Dalaf, the geographer, in 940 CE wrote, "In the entire world there does not exist a tin mine as this one in Kalah [Kedah]."[6]

The Intan ship carried many items made from tin alloys. Two separate batches of mirrors lay on the seafloor. One, of lower quality with an indistinct image, was characteristically Indonesian in design. The other, with a much higher quality image, was of Chinese origin. Tin was an important component of both. The Chinese mirrors were 25 percent tin, alloyed with copper and lead.[7] This mixture yielded a brittle metal that took a lustrous, reflective polish and yielded a superior image. It is likely that Malay tin was shipped to China in ingot form, melted into this special alloy, and cast into high-value items such as mirrors, some of which were then reexported to Southeast Asia.[8]

There were a number of large kingdoms in tenth-century Southeast Asia. On the mainland were four: Pagan, just emerging in upper Burma; Angkor in Cambodia; Champa in southern Vietnam; and, slightly later, Dai Viet in northern Vietnam.[9] These kingdoms were based on intensive rice cultivation and increasing population in areas close to the capitals, and were places of sophistication and courtly ritual.[10]

The island kingdoms of the period produced some extraordinary monuments. The most famous is Borobudur, now a world heritage Buddhist site on Java. In the ninth century, royal patrons financed the reconfiguring of an existing 115-foot-high hill into a massive, stone-faced shrine. Steep steps lead to walkways around the hill at higher and higher levels. Installed along the base and the walkways are 2,672 stone panels, carved in deep relief, which picture earthly life below and heavenly life above. The monument also has 504 life-size stone sculptures of the Buddha. On one panel at Borobudur, a sophisticated court woman is pictured using just the sort of mirror found in

Chinese mirror found on the Intan shipwreck.

the shipwreck to apply makeup and comb her hair.[11] She wears elaborate jewelry similar in style to the more than thirty gold rings, plus numerous gold earrings, pendants, and beads, found at the wreck site. Tin and gold were essential to the expression of courtly culture throughout Southeast Asia in this period.

The Chinese and Sumatran versions of hand mirrors imply a sophisticated and differentiated market. The Sumatran mirrors, less shiny and decorated with local motifs, presumably found their way to less wealthy buyers. Manufacturers, even in distant China, had to have enough information to make mirrors that would be desirable in Java.[12]

The tin trade involved much more than simply mining and smelting. Tin and the bronze it formed with copper were too valuable to throw away when items broke or wore out. The sheer human labor in each pound of bronze meant that recycling was an economic imperative.[13] Broken objects from all over the Asian world were remelted into ingots and recast into new objects, perhaps again and again over centuries. (Recall that one of the copper in-gots in the Uluburun shipwreck could not be matched to any known source of copper. Perhaps it was a composite, recycled from copper from several sources.) En route to remanufacture was a hoard of scrap brass, an alloy of copper and zinc, in the hold of the Intan wreck. The recycling and recasting of objects make it difficult to know whether any metal object from that time was from far away or locally made.

## A Buddhist and Hindu World

A Buddhist statue found on the shipwreck embodied a very long tradition. By the tenth century, Buddhist and Hindu objects and ideas had moved along the trade routes into Southeast Asia for at least five hundred years, together with the establishment of monasteries, shrines, and rest houses in Myanmar, Indonesia, Thailand, Vietnam, Cambodia, and Laos.[14] By the tenth century, the time of the Intan wreck, the great kingdoms of Southeast Asia had a distinctly Buddhist or Hindu cast. Kings in Southeast Asia found in Buddhism a new vision of kingship that transcended ethnic loyalties and chains of institutions that promoted trade.[15]

Southeast Asia was connected to all branches of Buddhism at the time.[16] The salvage divers brought up a hoard of ritual objects associated with Vaj-rayana or Tantric Buddhism: bells and the distinctive spear-shaped scep-ter. This form of Buddhism was well developed in eastern India but also strong in Southeast Asia in the tenth century, competing for patronage with other, more established Buddhist sects. This was the time that Vajrayana Buddhism also moved into Tibet. Patrons commissioned exactly this sort of scepter on several panels of the ninth-century Buddhist monument of Boro-budur in central Java.[17]

Other artifacts aboard the ship seem connected to forms of ritual from India: a bronze lion's head finial, a bronze lotus bud, ceremonial spears, vessels, and trays. The most striking of these objects is a set of incised and carved brass hinges and door decoration. The wood has rotted, but the scale of the brass fittings is far too large for a house.[18] The doors were probably intended for a well-endowed religious site on Java. Various Hindu and Bud-dhist sects were in competition for royal patronage and followers.

At the time of the Intan shipwreck, Buddhism had already spread along both maritime and land routes. Its institutions and teachings far transcended

Inscribed Chinese silver
found on the Intan shipwreck.
PHOTO COURTESY OF
MICHAEL FLECKER

any empire or kingdom. Its monks traveled far for learning and in pursuit of texts. The cognitive geography of monks in China included the Silk Road, India, and the kingdoms of Southeast Asia.

## Silver, Iron, and Beads

Ingots of silver were also found on the seabed with the inscription "Sword office high grade silver of 52 liang certified by officer Chen Xun." Unlike the tin, which was concentrated close to the center of the wreck site, the silver was found in many sectors of the underwater grid, suggesting that it was not a single hoard; perhaps several traders on board kept a few ingots.[19] One wonders about the importance of official Chinese stamping of the silver ingots. Could local traders have read the text? Did they care? It is possible that the answer to both questions is yes.

A second form of silver, the dirham coin from the Islamic world, entered Southeast Asia with Arab traders about two centuries before, and by the time of the Intan wreck Muslim traders had established small resident communities and built mosques in ports along the sea routes. Gradually, Muslim clerics and jurists moved to these ports to serve congregations. The dirham seems to have been readily understood and accepted as currency, even

Glass "eye" beads from the Intan shipwreck, manufactured in Iran.

though local traders surely did not know Arabic. We should recognize the skill and sophistication of local traders. Their cognitive geography—their expectations about places near and far—encompassed a world of precious metals that stretched from China to the Middle East.

The iron aboard—ingots, cooking pots, and spearheads—was also Chinese. China at the time had a highly efficient two-stage smelting process that far outclassed local manufacture in iron-producing areas of Southeast Asia. Archaeologists have found Chinese cast-iron cooking pots in most precolonial-era shipwrecks in Southeast Asia and many sites on land.[20] Java, for example, produced no iron. For many centuries after the Intan shipwreck it simply imported what it needed, in spite of some iron ore deposits on the island.[21] (It is perhaps no surprise that the Intan ship used no iron fittings.)

The divers brought up more than 245 glass beads, similar in size and style. The chemical composition of the glass and the colors suggest an origin in Iran, rather than China or India, the only other glass manufacturing regions at the time.[22] Glassmaking had been entirely lost in Europe after the fall of Rome and would not be recovered for more than two centuries after the Intan wreck. The Intan beads are especially interesting because they are "eye" beads. One method of manufacture was to form molten glass into a small globe. While the globe was still soft, the glass worker pushed several small drops of another color of glass into the surface, creating dots. He finished the bead by pushing a tiny droplet of yet another color into the center of each dot. The base color of the beads found in the wreck was green or blue or, in a few cases, brown. The dots were white with blue centers.

"Eye" beads of this type from around the time of the shipwreck have been found in several archaeological sites in Thailand.[23] They are particularly common in archaeological sites near Kedah, the region of the Malay Peninsula associated with tin. These well-traveled eye beads were apparently one of the objects purchased with the profits from tin and the tin trade and used in warding off the "evil eye," the existence of which was an extraordinarily widespread cultural belief across Europe and Asia.

The bead trade, like the tin trade, was quite complex and already long established at the time of the shipwreck. Beads are among the earliest foreign items found in Southeast Asian archaeological digs. Distinctive carnelian stone beads from India have been excavated at sites that date before the Common Era.[24] Throughout the millennium before the shipwreck, such beads show up in most digs of capital cities and many more-prosaic sites. There is good archaeological evidence that centers in Southeast Asia were, by the tenth century, making glass beads, even eye beads. These manufacturing centers, however, could only melt imported glass to make beads; they were unable to make the glass itself. Evidence from the shipwreck supports this viewpoint. Not far from the beads, the divers found many pieces of glassware, only a few still intact. When the archaeological team tried to assemble the vessels, it became clear that most of the glass had been shipped as broken pieces, raw material for the bead works of Southeast Asia.

## Bones and People

The divers working on the Intan wreck found forty-four human bones. When a small ship sinks, the crew and passengers usually try to escape; the bodies of those who do not are generally carried far away from the site of the wreck by currents. Why didn't these unfortunate people get off the boat as it sank? Perhaps they were just asleep belowdecks; but it is equally likely they were slaves, imprisoned below. Slavery, in many forms and for many purposes, was common. Slavery in Southeast Asia encompassed an extraordinary variety of legal and practical relationships between owner and bondsman or bondswoman—in households, businesses, armies, and courts. Like pilgrims, traders, and ambassadors, slaves moved in large numbers throughout the Asian world.

Of other people on board, there are only hints. The divers found many well-used sharpening stones that probably belonged to sailors who passed the time sharpening their swords and knives or tools. In Southeast Asia, as on both coasts of India, there was little distinction between a sailor and a pirate. All were armed, and the main difference depended on who owned the cargo or the ship. Piracy was such a continuing problem that it even shows up in some Southeast Asian inscriptions contemporary to the shipwreck.[25] Some well-used cooking pots, a fishhook, and three mortars and pestles are other traces of the crew.

Small hoards of coins and multiple sets of scales and weights make it almost certain that traders were aboard the Intan wreck. Java, the apparent destination of the Intan ship, was well set up to distribute imported items. Though it had no large cities, the towns and villages of the island had regular markets on designated days. Inscriptions from the period list traders, items of trade, and the kinds of taxes paid. Some groups of professional traders worked more than one circuit and several towns. (Agricultural taxes were paid in cash, suggesting that enough local currency circulated to buy imports.) These regional traders brought Chinese iron cooking pots and everyday ceramics deep into the interior of the island. Like other places in the Asian world, local entrepreneurs produced cheaper copies of foreign imports. Local Javanese pottery closely followed Chinese styles.[26] Once again we should not underestimate the attraction of fashion and the lure of the exotic, such as Chinese ceramics. The lure was strong enough that local potters made copies of Chinese ceramics and traders carried them all over the island. Even far from sophisticated courts in small towns and villages people shared a desire for Chinese ceramics and their copies.

What about balance of payments? Suppose the ship had not gone down; what might it have carried back to the entrepôt and perhaps on to other ports to pay for the ceramics, silk, tin, cotton, and other items? Chinese government documents of the time describe an almost insatiable demand for Southeast Asia's many varieties of aromatic resins and woods. Government officials were so concerned at the drain of Chinese silver to pay for these forest products that they suggested development of ceramics to sell in Southeast Asia. The large quantity of simple ceramics on board the shipwreck suggests that this policy was not only implemented but also successful.[27]

Aromatics were essential commodities across the Asian world. Such resins and woods were the basis for the incense required in China and India for religious and domestic ceremonies at home, in court, in temples, and in graveyards. Aromatics from Southeast Asia were important components of drugs and medicines of the time, as well as perfumes and oils for the body. They were high-value trade commodities all the way to the Middle East and filled the censers of the churches of Europe. At the shipwreck site, the only suggestion of this important trade was twenty-four small pieces of benzoin, a Southeast Asian tree resin widely used in Buddhist monastic and home ritual.[28] There may have been other aromatics, but ocean currents probably carried away these lightweight objects.[29]

The important conclusion here is that the Intan wreck carried a variety of goods: luxury and prosaic, religious and secular. Demand from China for Southeast Asian aromatics reached deep into the hinterland forests, affecting people far removed from elegant courts or urban centers. In those interior markets we should not discount the appeal of Chinese ceramics or locally manufactured copies. The lure of these ceramics gives hints of a cognitive geography, even in the interior, that included awareness of a wider world. The ports easily absorbed Muslim traders.

The worlds of the Intan wreck did not follow the contours of empires or religions. Incense from Buddhist and Hindu Southeast Asia moved easily to the Muslim Middle East and Confucian China. Trade goods were integral to the practice of religion. The high-value doors on board suggest the prosperity, strength, and vitality of the Buddhist monastic orders in island Southeast Asia of the time. The Vajrayana Buddhist ritual objects suggest a new sect on the move. Islam was new and growing along the very same routes. The shipwreck has revealed the complexity, commerce, and connections of a Southeast Asian world of about the year 1000 CE.

# 6

# MAIMONIDES WRECK

In the tenth century a man named Buzurg ibn Shahriyar lived in the port city of Hormuz at the mouth of the Persian Gulf. He might have been a sea captain, but more likely he was an avid listener to the stories of sailors who came to his port. In the library at Istanbul remains the only known copy of Buzurg's collection of 123 sea stories, titled *'Aja'ib al-Hind* (*The Book of the Marvels of India*). Many of the stories concern storms and adverse winds that blow a ship far off course; the ship is frequently destroyed either by the storm or the rocky coast of some strange and magical land. Some of the stories, however, have no fantastic islands, but are prosaic accounts of the terrors of ocean travel in the tenth-century Indian Ocean. Here we let Buzurg ibn Shahriyar tell a story "as told to me by a merchant":

> I sailed from Siraf [at the midpoint of the eastern shore of the Persian Gulf], he informed me, in the year 306 [918 CE], upon a ship which was going to Dhimour [near current-day Mumbai]. We were accompanied by a ship, belonging to Abd-Allah, son of Djanid, and another which came from Seba. The three vessels were, all of them, large craft and well known at sea; their captains also enjoyed a considerable reputation in the world of sailors. The passengers they carried, merchants, pilots, crew, and others, numbered twelve hundred souls. Their cargo, in provisions and merchandise, was of an incalculable value. After eleven days' sailing we came within sight of the eminences of the coast of Sendan, Tana, and Dhimour. Never before, it was generally said, had the voyage been accomplished in so short a space of time. We were in high spirits and congratulated one another on such a fortunate crossing. We were out of any danger, we thought, and would touch land during the morrow morning; our sails were unfurled; when a sudden squall got up, accompanied with lightning, thunder, and rain. "Best throw the

cargo overboard" advised the pilots and sailors. But (the captain of the vessel), Ahmed, opposed this suggestion. "Nothing shall be thrown overboard," he declared, "till I have given up all hope and am quite sure that our doom is imminent."

[The storm raged for five days; the merchants pleaded to be allowed to throw the cargo overboard; the captain steadily refused. By the time the captain relented, the goods were so water-soaked and heavy that they could not be hoisted overboard.]

Our danger was pressing, and we launched the long-boat, some thirty-three men entering it. Ahmed was begged to come, too, but he answered, "I won't leave the ship. The ship has a better chance than the long-boat. If it sinks I shall sink with it."

[Those in the long-boat survived five days without food or water and considered eating the son of one of the traders.]

Happily, that very same hour, we sighted land, and soon could distinguish it clearly. The long-boat was borne ashore, touched land, split, and filled with water. We had not the strength to move or rise.

[Two local men came by, dragged the men out of the boat and helped them to a nearby village, where they received water, food, and clothing.]

As for those souls who had stayed on the three ships, not a soul of them was saved, but only those who had put out in the long-boat.[1]

The saved and the dead are clear enough in Buzurg's shipwreck story, but he writes nothing of the effect of the shipwreck on the families of sailors or traders. Fortunately, some detailed documents from the Indian Ocean about two hundred years later suggest the devastating emotional and economic effects of a trader's death at sea.

In the spring of 1167 David Maimonides, the younger brother of the not-yet-famous philosopher Moses Maimonides, headed upriver on the Nile from Cairo to further the family fortunes. The previous two decades had been turbulent and difficult for the Maimonides family. The Almohads, a fanatical group of Muslims from North Africa, had captured the family's native city, Cordoba (in Spain), in 1148 and demanded that Jews convert or leave. The Maimonides family managed to put off expulsion for a decade but finally emigrated in 1159. They found the restrictions on Jews too burdensome at Fez (Morocco), the economy too depressed in Palestine, but relative freedom and prosperity in Cairo. The father died soon after the family arrived, but David, by trading gems, supported an unmarried sister and his brother Moses, who studied Jewish religious and philosophical texts.

David decided he needed to get closer to the source of the gems to make larger profits. After a routine boat trip up the Nile to Qus (about two hundred miles above Cairo) David joined a caravan headed east to the Red Sea, which entailed two weeks of hard traveling across a barren landscape and mountains.[2] Bandits attacked a caravan only slightly behind his and robbed one of his friends.[3] David, however, arrived safely at Aydhab, a prominent port on the Red Sea, only to discover to his dismay that no gems were for sale. Over the strenuous objections in letters from his older brother, David decided to push on by ship to India, source of the gems he sought.

Scholars have managed to decipher and translate David's last letter, though it is badly deteriorated. The younger Maimonides implored Moses to reassure the family: "And, please calm the heart of the little one and her sister; do not frighten them and let them not despair, for crying to God for what has passed is a vain prayer. . . . Anyway, what has passed is past, and I am sure this letter will reach you at a time when I, God willing, shall have already made most of the way."[4]

David sailed with at least four young Jewish traders that he mentioned in his letter. Somewhere in the Indian Ocean between Aden and India David's ship went down, with no survivors. With him went virtually all the family wealth, leaving the elder brother with a small child and a widow. The actual site of the shipwreck remains unmarked and unknown to this day. Moses was distraught. His pain is still evident in a letter written eight years later.

> On the day that I received that terrible news I fell ill and remained in bed for about a year, suffering from a sore boil, fever, and depression, and was almost given up. About eight years have passed, but I am still mourning and unable to accept consolation. And how should I console myself? He grew up on my knees, he was my brother, he was my student; he traded in the markets and I could safely sit at home. He was well versed in the Talmud and the Bible, and knew (Hebrew) grammar very well, and my joy in life was to look at him. Now, all joy is gone. He has passed away and left me disturbed in my mind in a foreign country. Whenever I see his handwriting or one of his letters, my heart turns upside down and my grief awakens again.[5]

Eight and a half centuries later we know the intimate details of David Maimonides's hopes and his brother's inconsolable grief because of a belief of Jews at the time, namely that a letter or document that contained any form of the word "God" could not be destroyed. It could not be buried, burned, or shredded.[6] One solution was a building, called a geniza, that had no door and no windows, merely a ladder leading up to a large slot in one wall. Members of a congregation wishing to dispose of unneeded documents that contained some form of the word God threw them through the slot. For hundreds of years members of the congregation to which the Maimonides family belonged filled its geniza with tens of thousands of documents. They remained intact because of Egypt's dry climate.[7]

## A World of Sewn Ships

What sort of a ship carried the young traders to their deaths in May 1167? Texts of the time describe three distinctive features of an Indian Ocean cargo carrier. First, the ship was not nailed like European ships but sewn together with coconut-husk rope. The boundaries of this world stretched from the Philippines in far eastern Southeast Asia more than six thousand miles around India to the east coast of Africa. Second, a triangular (lateen) mainsail was mounted along the length of the ship.[8] The only way that such ships could make headway against an unfavorable wind was actually sailing backward during frequent turns. The third distinctive feature of Indian Ocean sewn ships was, therefore, a tapered bow and stern, which allowed the ship to sail both forward and backward, as necessary.

The literature from the time of David's journey yields only a single reference to size, about seventy-five feet, but scholars do not know whether this was a large, small, or average boat.[9] European observers in later centuries saw no evidence of a deck, so David's ship was almost certainly open and was steered by a side rudder. The earliest evidence for a stern rudder is a century later, in the middle of the 1200s, which—perhaps coincidentally and perhaps not—is exactly the same time that the stern rudder appeared in Europe.

Lateen-rigged ships (much later termed "dhows") of the Indian Ocean mainly hugged the coasts of western India, Arabia, and East Africa. They also sank with alarming regularity, but often in shallow coastal water. In David Maimonides's last letter he wrote of two traders known to him and his

Arab dhow built many centuries after the sinking of the
ship carrying David Maimonides but likely similar in design.
Scottish Mission lantern slide (1875).

brother. One remained in "Dahlak, since the ship in which he traveled foundered, but he was saved and absolutely nothing of his baggage was lost." The other was in a boat that sank "and only their dinars [gold coins] remained with them." David perhaps hoped that this news would hearten this brother that even if the ship sank he would likely survive.

## Winds and Monsoons

As novices, David Maimonides and his young companions probably did not understand the risks of traveling to India at the wrong time of year. Monsoon winds gave the Indian Ocean route a profoundly fixed yearly pattern. Across Asia from November through February wind flowed off a massive high pressure system centered on the steppes connecting Europe and Central Asia. The prevailing Indian Ocean winds, therefore, blew south and west. These steady and predictable winds allowed ships easy passage from the ports of the Arabian Peninsula to the east coast of Africa, as well as to the west coast of India. From early June to September a massive low pressure system, centered on the Himalayan region, produced steady flows to the north and east in the Indian Ocean, reversing the November–February pattern.[10] June through September was, thus, the ideal period for bringing goods from Africa and India to the Middle East. Knowledgeable captains used these prevailing winds in two ways. One group loaded their vessels in Indian ports in June, sailed to an Arabian port, such as Aden, Mocha, or Kish, sold their cargoes, and returned to India when the winds reversed in November. Another group of captains, making use of the same the wind pattern, loaded goods from Africa and sailed to Arabian ports, returning in November to Africa laden with Indian goods. Merchants in the Arabian ports warehoused, bought, and sold the African and Indian goods.

From March to May winds on the Indian Ocean were too light and variable for safe passage anywhere. Sadly, this is precisely the time that David and his friends set off for India.

## Spices, Medicines, and Paper

David Maimonides sought India for gems, but his young companions on the ship might well have entered the Malabar spice trade, which was large in scale and profitable. Indian spices were in regular use across a broad swath of Asia, Egypt, and North Africa, and—in much smaller quantities—in Europe.[11] For example, a thirteenth-century recipe for meat patties (*isfîriyâ*) from Muslim Spain uses several Indian spices: "Take some red meat and pound as before. Put it in some water and add some sour dough dissolved with as much egg as the meat will take, and salt, pepper, saffron, cumin, and coriander seed, and knead it all together. Then put a pan with fresh oil on the fire, and when the oil has boiled, add a spoon of isfîriya and pour it in the frying pan carefully so that it forms thin cakes. Then make a sauce for it."[12] Note the use of coriander, pepper, and cumin from Malabar. Black pepper was the core of the trade, both as flavoring and medicine. Arab and Indian traders had shipped it to Rome in the heyday of the Roman Empire. For example, it was pepper, three thousand pounds of it, that Alaric I, king of the Visigoths, demanded and obtained as part of his ransom of Rome in 408 CE.[13]

Today we think of spices as pleasant flavorings for food, but in the time of David Maimonides they were equally important as medicines, forming important parts of the pharmacopoeia of a vast world that included Asia, North Africa, and Europe. Ibn Sīnā (Avicenna, 980–1037), in his well-known *Canon of Medicine*, listed more than thirty-six tropical plants among his remedies. Turmeric, for example, which is now mainly used to flavor Indian curries, has strong antibacterial properties; applying it to a wound prevented putrefaction.[14]

The thousands of letters between Jewish traders preserved in the Cairo Geniza suggest the critical importance of paper to their lives and livelihoods. Jewish and Muslim traders succeeded or failed based on timely long-distance information. Paper technology had passed down the Silk Road from China into the Middle East with the Abbasid dynasty, probably about 750 CE. With royal support at Baghdad, the process was reinvented to suit local conditions. Chinese paper required tropical plants that did not grow in the Middle East. It was soon discovered that linen and cotton fibers produced a supple, smooth paper. Within a century there was a flourishing paper market and many paper mills in Baghdad. Paper quickly moved beyond government use and was taken up by merchants and wealthy individuals. The earliest surviving paper document from the Middle East is an official Jewish letter from Baghdad to Egypt.[15]

Other capitals such as Damascus and Fustat[16] soon competed with Baghdad, offering alternate sizes and compositions of paper. Paper made possible the hundreds of thousands of volumes of the Baghdad imperial library, the circulation of these texts to multiple capitals in the Middle East, Persia, Central Asia, and Spain, and the letters and ledgers that form the Cairo Geniza archives. As the fifteenth-century historian Ibn Khaldun put it in his *Muqaddimah*, "Thus, paper was used for government documents and diplomas. Afterwards, people used paper in sheets for government and scholarly writings, and the manufacture reached a considerable degree of excellence."[17]

It is perhaps also worth noting where paper did not take hold. Both India and Europe saw paper, probably understood what it could do, and rejected it. India stayed with palm-leaf manuscripts and records until the arrival of the Portuguese in the sixteenth century. Scholars have speculated that since literacy was confined to Brahmins, there was an intrinsic conservative attitude that favored palm-leaf books. The answer may be even simpler. Older Indian taxation and revenue systems did not require extensive record-keeping. The king's representative and the farmer merely divided the grain on the threshing floor (known as *batai*). The European rejection of paper is simpler and well documented. The Catholic Church banned paper for financial reasons. It held extensive flocks and made substantial income from turning its sheep into sheepskins for writing documents and books.[18]

## Trading Partnerships

The structure of Jewish trading practices consisted of personal one-to-one partnerships between traders in different locations. Often these relationships grew naturally from an apprenticeship that a young trader's family arranged with a senior trader. One example can illustrate the network and the process. In the 1120s the head of the Jewish traders in Aden (at the time a very important port on the south coast of Arabia near the mouth of the Red Sea) received a twenty-two-year-old apprentice named Ibrahim bin Yiju. He carried a letter of introduction—on paper—from his father to the senior trader, a fellow Tunisian Jew. For three years Ibrahim labored in the senior trader's warehouse, keeping accounts and writing letters. When the senior trader decided that Ibrahim was ready to become a junior partner, he provided him with capital and sent him to the spice-growing lands of coastal India, known as Malabar. Both men expected to exchange letters regularly about market conditions, trading opportunities, the comings and goings of mutual friends, and family information. The senior partner expected to give trading advice to his younger partner.

The expectations and trust, however, ran much deeper than merely an exchange of information. Traders dispatched goods to their partners in distant cities with instructions as to how they were to be divided, to whom they were to be sent, where they were to be sold, what price was acceptable, what was to be purchased, how these return goods were to be packed, and where they were to be sent. Let us consider in some detail a single letter (dated 1139, just three decades before David Maimonides set off for India), sent to Ibrahim in Malabar by one of his partners in Aden. Ibrahim had sent spices to the Aden partner with instructions to sell them for whatever the market dictated and send him the proceeds of the sale in gold.

> I sent you five mann [about ten pounds] of good silk on my account . . . it was reported . . . that it was selling well in Malabar. Therefore, I thought that it was preferable to send, instead of gold, merchandise which might bring some profit. Thus, kindly sell it for me at whatever price God, the exalted, assigns and send it to me in any ship, without any responsibility for any risk on land or sea. If there is the opportunity to buy betel-nut or cardamom, kindly do so, but you, my master, need no instructions, for you are competent.[19]

Note several features of these transactions. First, the Aden partner purchased and sent a quantity of silk rather than only gold, as Ibrahim presumably instructed. There was no written "contract," and both partners were free to take opportunities as they saw them.[20] Second, the Aden partner justified the substitution of silk for gold based on market information about Malabar, which arrived at Aden. Other geniza letters bear out that there was regular detailed information flowing back and forth between India and Aden. Third, and perhaps most striking, the Aden partner charged nothing for the work he did for Ibrahim. Likewise, Ibrahim did not charge a fee for handling the partner's silk in Malabar or finding profitable goods to send to Aden. Ibrahim and the Aden-based trader were truly partners. Neither was a paid agent of the other.

Trader partners built confidence in each other through small presents, listed in the final section of the sample letter. The Aden partner sent to Ibrahim items described in the self-effacing style of these letters as "what has no importance or value"—a bottle of sugar and a hide from Abyssinia inscribed with Ibrahim's name. A partner in a sophisticated place like Aden also sent household items difficult to obtain in India. In this letter the Aden partner tells Ibrahim that he has dispatched an iron frying pan and glassware for his household use, "sixty-eight goblets, ten bowls, and five cups," in addition to "five green bottles in their baskets." The partner even dispatched preferred foods. Wheat, which would have been a staple for Ibrahim, was unavailable on the southwest coast of India, which was (and still is) a land of coconuts, fish, and rice.

Partnerships, by themselves, did not reduce risk, since each individual trader risked his (or his family's) money. Nevertheless, the India traders and their Mediterranean counterparts developed many strategies and tactics to reduce risk. Some of the biggest traders formed temporary alliances to invest jointly in building and stocking a boat. They knew they had a new boat and could pick the captain they wanted. All traders dealt in a variety of goods, to cover unknown fluctuations in distant markets. Traders always divided their goods into several parcels and dispatched them with various ships. They exchanged information on reliable ship captains and tried to get their goods aboard their ships. Traders "containerized" shipments to reduce theft in handling. The largest parcel had a standard weight of about five hundred pounds. A variety of goods—spices, medicines, cloth, even gems—would be sewn into separate bags, sealed, and labeled. The bags would then be combined to the five-hundred-pound size, and a heavy cloth sewn around the lot. Sewn to the outside were instructions about delivery to a designated trader. Each bag inside the five-hundred-pound parcel had instructions where the receiving trader was to send it. Before dispatching goods, traders wrote several copies of a letter, sent on different ships, to their consignee, describing in detail what was coming.[21]

The important point here is that had David Maimonides reached India, he almost certainly would have sought trading partners in Cairo and Baghdad to sell his gems rather than undertaking a risky ocean crossing year after year.[22] His letters to his partners would have had the same sorts of greetings and the same small presents as a spice trader's, and it is entirely possible that he would have branched out into spice trading if the opportunity presented itself. The trading world between Cairo and Malabar was so well established that he would surely have been tempted.

## Jews in a World of Islam

Jewish traders were always a minority in both the Indian Ocean trade and the Mediterranean trade. There has been much scholarly dispute on two important questions. The first is how similar were their practices, culture, organization, and legal system to the larger Islamic society in which they lived and worked. The second related question is how autonomous and self-governing were Jewish partnerships, groups of Jewish traders, or the Jewish community as a whole.

On the question of the similarities of Jewish culture to Muslim culture there is broad scholarly consensus that Jewish traders looked and lived much like their Muslim counterparts. They wore the same long flowing robes and turban.[23] There was no residential segregation in Muslim cities. In Malabar, for example, the houses of all traders clustered close to the harbor. Many traders lived over their warehouses. Among Muslims and Jews dietary habits were also similar, both eschewing pork and preferring wheat, but otherwise adapting to local cuisine. Many traders in both communities left wives and family in Cairo or Aden and bought concubines in Malabar. Traders in both communities had trusted, highly regarded male slaves who traveled and conducted business for them in distant places. Like Muslim traders Jews rarely ventured inland and never set up their own spice plantations. They were content to advance money to local dealers and receive the crop after the harvest.

Traders in both communities preferred to settle disputes by negotiation, rarely turning to their respective religious courts. The Cairo Geniza documents mention some formal trading co-ventures between Muslims and Jews.

Despite the cultural similarities there were, however, marked differences between the two communities. The Jews entered only the Malabar trade, not the larger Indian Ocean trade. There is no evidence that they competed with Yemenis for the lucrative trade on the east coast of Africa. Jews, thus, never traded in slaves or ivory. Jews also, with a tiny number of exceptions, did not own ships and never became ship captains. They were content to move their goods on Arab, Tamil, or Ethiopian-owned ships.

Both the Jewish and Muslim communities had long-standing geographic and sectarian divisions. In Islam, divisions were both sectarian and geographic. The Sunni-Shia divide went back to bloody wars in the first century of Islam (and continue today). Other divisions followed the rise and fall of dynasties, the interpretation of the correct Islamic path, and differed from Morocco to Egypt to the Middle East and Central Asia. The sectarian divisions separating Jewish communities are less known but were just as passionately felt and discussed, though no wars were fought between sects. Tunisian, Baghdadi, Palestinian, or Egyptian Jews preferred to form partnerships and marry others from their home kingdom.[24] Recall Moses Maimonides's letter from Cairo that David's death left him in "a disturbed state in a foreign country."

Now let us consider the issue of the degree of autonomy of Jewish traders. Based on relatively few but intact samples of the geniza letters, some scholars concluded that Jewish traders operated in networks overseen by a Jewish "head trader" and had little contact with or oversight by any government, whether a Muslim government at Aden or a Hindu government on the Malabar Coast.[25] Scholars with the necessary language skills have more recently examined the relevant documents of these governments and concluded that earlier scholars who relied solely on the Cairo Geniza documents were simply wrong. Governments, from the Middle East to India, were deeply involved in recording, taxing, and often controlling the sale of goods both coming to and going from their ports.[26] On the Malabar Coast, kingdoms competed for the long-distance spice export trade to Aden and Cairo, and governments took steps to make their port attractive, by, for example, lowering taxes and building storage facilities and mosques. A few even provided armed escorts to protect trading ships from pirates.[27]

## War and Politics

The larger political and military situation in Europe and the Mediterranean is the backdrop of the Maimonides family's flight from Spain and David's venture in Egypt. In the early decades of the 1100s, crusader armies fought in Palestine and established kingdoms over much of the coast of what is today Israel and Lebanon. The holy wars hardened attitudes toward non-Christians in Europe and made it difficult for Jews to work there. Anti-Semitism was rampant. Waves of warfare in Syria (present-day Israel, Palestine, Jordan, Syria, and Lebanon) sharply depressed trade. The situation on the Mediterranean was equally grim. War fleets from Venice and Genoa attacked Muslim shipping and port cities. The core business of the Jewish merchants retreated to the safety of Egypt, where they operated as middlemen in various phases of the collection and cleaning of flax and its production into cloth.

Some Jewish traders, both refugees from Europe and those resident around the Mediterranean, turned away from the religious conflicts toward the opportunities of the spice trade from India.[28] Thus, the restless search of the Maimonides family for a place to live and safely conduct their business was part of a much larger movement of Jews out of Europe to the Muslim lands of North Africa and the Middle East. Cairo, Damascus, Baghdad, and Tunis all gained substantial Jewish populations in this period. In today's era of conflict between Jews and Muslims, it is perhaps worth remembering that it was not always so. Muslim kingdoms and Muslim cities were the refuge of Jews when anti-Semitism forced them out of Europe.[29]

A few Jewish traders, however, found means to work in both the Mediterranean and the Indian Ocean. Ibrahim, the recipient of our sample letter, for example, saw an opportunity among the skilled metalworkers of the Malabar Coast. He set up a metalworks but not for new production. From his widespread contacts he received damaged and worn metal items: lamps, dishes, and candelabras from as far away as Spain. With them came instructions for the new items: "I am sending you a broken ewer and a deep wash basin weighing seven pounds less a quarter. Please make me a ewer of the same measure from its bronze as it is good bronze. The weight of the ewer should be five pounds exactly."[30] Here is an example in the twelfth century of international outsourcing and recycling that carried goods thousands of miles and relied on skilled Indian metalworkers.

# The End of the Trading World
## of the Geniza Documents

After the loss of his brother in the shipwreck on the Indian Ocean, Moses Maimonides was forced to become a practicing physician to provide an income for his family. He went on, however, to become a towering figure in Jewish law and biblical commentary and eventually found a viable living as a court physician for the Muslim king Saladin and his family. He corresponded on questions of faith and practices across the Mediterranean world.

Only a couple of centuries after the shipwreck that took the life of David Maimonides, Jewish traders largely lost the spice trade to better-financed Muslim combines from Cairo. A Jewish presence on the Malabar Coast, however, remained until just a few decades ago. At Cochin the old synagogue supported a congregation, and a scattering of Jews continued in the spice trade.

The design and construction techniques of traditional Indian Ocean sailing vessels lasted for centuries. The yearly monsoon voyages continued to interconnect Africa, the Middle East, and Africa. The attacks of the Portuguese, trying to enforce their system of exclusive charters of all oceangoing craft, altered but did not end the dhow trade. Local Gujarati traders built faster boats and often eluded Portuguese patrols.[31] Until the 1980s these locally built ships made yearly crossings from Gujarat on the west coast of India to the east coast of Africa and back.[32] They were eventually supplanted by locally built wooden tramp steamers, which carry low-value bulk goods, such as sugar and charcoal, from India to Africa.

We might draw a few conclusions from the wreck described by Buzurg ibn Shahriyar and the ship carrying David Maimonides. The story related by Buzurg was from a trader whose world included the Persian Gulf and the coast of India. The trading world of David Maimonides was larger, including the Mediterranean, Egypt, and India. Note that the east coast of Africa formed no part of the world of either trader. This is not to imply that Muslims generally had a smaller worldview or more bounded trade. Quite to the contrary; though a sprinkling of Jews found their way to China, it was primarily Arab traders who, from before the time of Buzurg until long after Maimonides, had explored the sea-lanes to China, settling in major port cities along the way. In fact, the Mediterranean, the Indian Ocean, and Southeast Asia as separate regions were moving steadily toward maritime integration.

Second, both Jewish and Arab traders demonstrated that neither networks nor ventures conformed to the boundaries of a single empire or kingdom. Like other traders, both presumed that they could work in a Hindu or a Muslim kingdom. Third, the back-and-forth flow of information, which for previous periods we could only infer from different colors of the same cloth sold in different places, or copies of manufactured goods, becomes explicit in the twelfth-century Cairo Geniza documents. Traders sought and received timely market information and personal information to strengthen the emotional and practical bonds of their network.

Suppose that a trader was cast away on the bleak shore of Gujarat. How might he have recovered and returned to Siraf to tell someone like Buzurg ibn Shahriyar his story? The geniza documents suggest that it was a trader's network, which rescued him and bankrolled him to continue as a trader. For example, on the Gujarat coast pirates seized the ship of a well-connected trader from Cairo named Judah bin Joseph ha-Kohen, seized all his goods and money, and forced ashore the passengers and crew. He must have somehow written to members of his trading group, but we only have the response of a ship captain who worked with the group:

> In all circumstances, please come quickly to Mangalore and do not tarry, for I am waiting here in Mangalore and — if God wills — we shall embark on our way home as soon as possible. It is better for you to travel from Mangalore with me than to travel in the ships of foreign people. Please remember that there is no difference between us, my money is yours, it is just the same.
>
> And again, my lord, do not take to heart what you have lost; you have, praise be to God, plenty to have recourse to and be compensated with. When life is saved, nothing else matters.[33]

# 7
# KUBLAI KHAN'S FLEET

On October 19, 1274, a massive Mongol war fleet sailed into Hakata, Japan's most important harbor for overseas trade.[1] Chinese records of the time claim a thousand ships and more than twenty-three thousand soldiers, though modern scholars believe that the actual numbers of both ships and soldiers were considerably smaller. To the beat of huge war drums the Mongols and their allied Korean troops came ashore in small landing craft. News of the imminent invasion had well preceded the fleet's actual arrival, and a substantial force of samurai, at least six thousand, awaited them.[2]

Hand-to-hand combat began on the beach. Both sides took heavy casualties. Japanese sources claim that two thousand samurai died on the beach and in the pine grove adjoining the shore. The Mongol forces gradually pushed the samurai back into Hakata town. Fighting continued in the streets and alleys. By nightfall, the invading troops had taken and burned the port. The defending samurai regrouped in the hills above the town.

Through the early hours of night the commanders of the Mongol/Korean force debated tactics. One faction favored an immediate night attack to press their advantage. Other commanders argued that the troops were exhausted and needed sleep. Finally, it was decided to continue the battle in the morning, and the troops returned to their ships. In the morning, however, the fleet was gone from Hakata Bay. Japanese sources report that a strong, "divine" wind blew the ships out of the harbor and into the sea.

The likeliest scenario is that the fleet simply sailed away, its commanders aware of problems that the Japanese were not. The fleet was low on arrows, having used large numbers in taking two strategic islands on the way to Hakata. The commanders perhaps also wanted to reconsider their strategy. Struggling ashore and fighting hand to hand on a beach and in trees was probably the least favorable terrain for Mongol troops. They were superb cavalry, trained for plains battles, massed arrow attacks, and group maneuvers, but largely untrained in hand-to-hand sword fighting on foot, and avoided this sort of battle whenever possible.[3]

The results of the first battle of Hakata were perhaps satisfactory to the great Mongol ruler Kublai Khan, Genghis Khan's grandson.[4] His strategy was straightforward: conquer all China and supplant the Song dynasty. By and large, the war was going well. Mongol armies had pushed the Song into far southern China. The destruction of Hakata meant that the Song would gain no revenue from trade with Japan.

This first battle of Hakata, however, produced no shipwrecks. Even the Japanese sources concede that only a few of the Mongol ships were beached by the mysterious wind that blew the fleet back to "their lands."

Much had changed between the first invasion attempt in 1274 and the second invasion in 1281. Mongol armies had pursued the remaining Song forces into South China, defeated them, and captured and executed the last emperor.[5] Kublai Khan was, indeed, ruler of a united China, with all the resources and the problems that entailed. He founded a new dynasty, the Yuan, and moved his capital from Karakorum, deep in Mongolia, to Beijing, the better to rule his new conquests.[6]

Kublai Khan sent envoys to Japan, in 1279, demanding surrender. The *bakufu*, head of the alliance of Japanese nobles, had the envoys executed on the beach at Hakata. Kublai Khan and the king of Korea conferred and agreed the invasion force to conquer Japan would consist of one hundred thousand troops. The king of Korea agreed to construct an enormous fleet, which would carry Mongol and Korean troops across the Korea Strait to Hakata.[7] Kublai Khan ordered a second fleet constructed on the Chinese coast, which would carry Chinese troops to join the Koreans and Mongols at Iki Island off Japan's west coast.

For more than a year, in both Korea and south China forests were stripped for the ships and harsh taxes levied to equip them. The Koreans, eager to engage, sailed in early May 1281, knowing that the Chinese fleet was not ready. The samurai had constructed a stone wall along the beach at Hakata, which halted the invading force. In heavy fighting the samurai drove the Mongols and Koreans back to their boats. A stalemate set in, the samurai holding the beach and the port and the Mongols and Koreans holding the harbor. The samurai attacked the fleet in small boats, sometimes boarding, sometimes pushing fire-rafts to burn the invader's ships. The attacks eventually forced the invading fleet into a compact defensive circle in the bay.[8]

The samurai Suenaga facing Mongols, by Mōko Shūrai Ekotoba
(1293 CE), Museum of the Imperial Collections, Tokyo Imperial Palace.

The Chinese fleet eventually did arrive but could not assist in the stale-mate at Hakata. Instead, the Chinese attacked inland from Imari Bay, thirty miles south of Hakata. Samurai fought the Chinese soldiers in the inland hills, finally pushing them back to their ships. In the end a typhoon destroyed both fleets, which were at anchor through the height of the typhoon season.[9] The fierce storm piled ship upon ship, driving them onto the rocky shore. Casualty estimates are, of course, speculative but run upward of fifty thousand men. Some thirty thousand Chinese soldiers were captured and enslaved. Both Chinese and Japanese sources agree that the second battle of Hakata Bay littered the bottom with wreckage.[10]

## The Mongols at War

The two opponents at Hakata Bay had quite different military and political backgrounds. Fifty years earlier Genghis Khan had reorganized bands of steppe cavalry into the most successful rapid strike force the world had ever seen. The important changes were in organization, discipline, and ideology. Genghis Khan reassigned the men of family and ethnic units into mixed units, thereby promoting loyalty to the larger Mongol goals rather than narrow family concerns. The units were arranged on a decimal system, with commanders over one hundred, a thousand, and ten thousand men. Cavalry practiced daily and honed their skills in frequent large hunts. Genghis Khan also enforced discipline on the welter of ethnicities that constituted his army. For example, looting after battle was prohibited on pain of death. The military goal was to annihilate the opposing force, and looting disrupted the process. Genghis Khan promulgated and practiced his belief in "world conquest"—his forces were destined to defeat all opposition and rule the entire world.[11] This ideology is perhaps best exemplified by a letter from Guyuk, grandson of Genghis Khan, to Pope Urban IV. The pope, in an official letter, proposed an alliance between the European kings and the Mongols against Muslims, as their common foe. Guyuk replied:

> Thanks to the power of the Eternal Heaven, all lands have been given to us from sunrise to sunset. How could anyone act other than in accordance with the commands of Heaven? Now your own upright heart must tell you: "We will become subject to you, and will place our powers at your disposal." You in person, at the head of the monarchs, all of you, without exception, must come to tender us service and pay us homage; then only will we recognize your submission. But if you do not obey the commands of Heaven, and run counter to our orders, we shall know that you are our foe.[12]

Mongol forces were mounted cavalry and used a short reverse-curve bow, which could be shot from horseback. With both hands occupied with the bow and arrow, Mongol cavalry had to control their horses with their knees, commands every horse knew and every horseman practiced from childhood onward. The reverse-curve bow was of composite materials, including wood, horn, and steel. It was enormously powerful, capable of penetrating armor at 150 yards. The preferred tactics of Mongol cavalry therefore avoided charges into well-entrenched positions. They much preferred tactics that included massed arrow attacks from outside the range of enemy weapons; the feigned retreat, which drew the enemy into ambush; or large-scale flanking movements, which resulted in attacking the enemy on three sides. These maneuvers depended on careful tactical coordination, usually by means of large signal flags. Mongol armies were, therefore, at their best in plains battles, with room to maneuver their horses and sweep in large formations.

Commanders of opposing forces quickly learned that they would likely lose a plains battle to Genghis Khan. Those who could, retreated to fortified positions. Genghis Khan's first siege was in 1218 at Otrar, a typical Silk

Road fortified town in what is now southern Kazakhstan. After establishing friendly relations with the king of the region, Genghis Khan equipped and financed a large caravan of Muslim traders to buy luxuries on the Silk Road and bring them for sale to his capital. Four hundred and fifty Muslim traders purchased silks, satins, carpets, and gems. When the returning caravan halted at Otrar, the governor of Otrar seized the goods and animals and executed the traders. In the colorful language of the *Secret History of the Mongols* (written shortly after Genghis Khan's death),

> The control of repose and tranquility was removed, and the whirlwind of anger cast dust into the eyes of patience and clemency while the fire of wrath flared up with such a flame that it drove the water from his eyes and could be quenched only by the shedding of blood. In this fever Cheingiz-Khan went alone to the summit of a hill, bared his head, turned his face toward the south and for three days and nights offered up prayer, saying: "I was not author of this trouble; grant me strength to extract vengeance."[13]

Genghis Khan divided his army, half attacking in the north of the kingdom to tie down the king's forces, the other half investing Otrar, which had been reinforced with thousands of royal troops. Genghis Khan had no clever siege engines, no catapults or trebuchets, only tenacity. The army formed "several circles around the citadel," fought the sallies from the city, and maintained the siege for five months. In desperation some of the town's troops rode out and offered service to Genghis Khan. He saw their action as dishonorable and executed them as his troops poured through the undefended gate. "All the guilty and innocent of Otrar, both the wearers of the veil and those that donned kulah and turban, were driven forth from the town like a flock of sheep, and the Mongols looted whatever goods and wares were there to be found."[14] The Mongol troops eventually fought their way into the citadel and captured the offending governor alive. He was executed by pouring molten silver down his throat, just punishment for his greed.

Though the Mongols are famous for their sweeping cavalry strategies, a majority of Genghis Khan's battles were actually fought against a fortified hill, palisade, or town.[15] The Mongols quickly copied from their opponents a weapon of war new to them, the trebuchet, which utilized a heavy counterweight's force multiplied by a long lever arm and an equally long flexible sling. Invented either in Europe or the Muslim West (though perhaps an improvement of an earlier Chinese catapult), the trebuchet hurled a heavy stone (generally more than 150 pounds) with enormous force, capable of knocking down men and horses like bowling pins and equally capable of crashing through gates and walls. Genghis Khan recruited and gave military appointments to Muslim technicians capable of building such a weapon.

Less than two decades later Mongol siege engines from the West and the technicians to build them had moved across all Asia and were attacking fortified cities in China. Only three years after Otrar, the Mongols were using siege engines on the eastern front in their campaign against the fortified cities of northern China.[16] Thus, it is no surprise that the Mongols took great, fortified cities. Baghdad, one of the largest cities in Asia at the time, fell to the Mongols in 1258 (fifteen years before Kublai Khan attacked Japan).[17] It is likely that the great Mongol fleet that attacked Hakata Bay carried siege engines such as the trebuchet in anticipation of attacking forts and fortified cities.

Mongol armies generally suffered defeats in only two circumstances. First, highly trained professional soldiers who knew Mongol strategy and tactics occasionally simply outperformed them. The Mamluks, full-time, trained slave-soldiers, were just such a force and defeated the Mongols in Egypt. Second, problems of adverse terrain limited the effectiveness of Mongol cavalry. Mountains were a serious problem for the Mongols. Horsemen could not wheel and move in large units. Ambush lurked in every defile. Even in defeat the enemy could disappear into the mountains, eliminating the Mongol tactic of annihilating the opposing army. Massed arrow attacks did little against mountain fortresses, which were also almost impossible to surround. Troops from the fortresses could often defend agricultural land nearby, which provided the fortress with food. The combination of mountains, fortresses, and resolute resistance, for example, made the conquest of Sichuan, a southwestern province of China, slow, difficult, and costly. Mongols fought in the mountains of Sichuan virtually every year for more than three decades before conquering it.[18]

China's coastal plain was equally difficult terrain for Mongol armies. Canals crisscrossed it, and the rice fields were flooded much of the year. Large-scale cavalry movements were impossible. Fortified cities were frequent and were connected by boat more than road. The Mongols had to adapt, and they did, incorporating Chinese and Korean leaders and infantry who knew how to fight in this watery terrain, so different from the dry steppe of the

Mongol homelands. Mongol armies traveled by boat and learned siege techniques. They recruited artisans to build the powerful Chinese trebuchet. Chinese troops used gunpowder weapons extensively for the first time.[19]

## Samurai Warriors

On the beach at Hakata Bay were six thousand of the most highly trained, most professional, and best-equipped troops the Mongols ever faced. Samurai were the elite product of an entire social and economic system, just as were the Mongols. Within the fragmented Japanese political system, wars between elite families were frequent, and formal training in schools of the martial arts was mandatory for elite men (and a few elite women). A nineteenth-century text of one of these schools well illustrates the focus and rigor of samurai training. Students learned, for example, unarmed fighting, grappling, short sword fighting, quick sword drawing, stick fighting, dagger technique, the use of rope, and crossing rivers in armor on horseback.[20] The training was as much mental as physical:

> Because the beginner does not know how to stand with the sword in his hands or anything else, in his mind there is not a thing to be attached to. When he is attacked, without any deliberation he tries to fend off the attack. But gradually he is taught many things, he is instructed how to hold the sword, where to concentrate his mind and other things. So his mind will be attached to those things and when he attempts to attack his opponent, his movements will be awkward. However, as days, months and years pass, due to innumerable trainings, everything, as he stands, as he holds the sword will lose consciousness, in the end getting back to the state of mind he had in the beginning, when he did not know anything.[21]

The samurai code of honor preferred single combat, which was almost certainly a detriment in their first encounter with the Mongols. Samurai quickly learned that Mongols were quite content to fire massed arrows at any opponent who sought single combat. The samurai also learned that their superior sword skills made up for lesser numbers in close combat. A recent scholarly book has persuasively argued that the samurai needed no "divine wind" to drive off the Mongol ships. They repelled the invasion based on their skills, armor, and training.[22]

# Shipbuilding in the China Sea

What sort of ships brought the Mongol invasion fleet from Korea to Japan? The evidence is meager but suggests that Korean long-distance trade ships were the likeliest carriers. The decorative back of a lady's mirror from the period shows such a Korean ship, sails reefed, in roiling seas. Recovered timbers and planks of actual vessels show that these craft had an almost flat bottom. Shipbuilders attached successive planks of pine with overlapping edges and mortise-and-tenon joints. Elm was used for pegs to lock the mortise and tenons in place. Oak was used for a heavy yoke, which was set amidships and served as a sturdy cross member to stabilize the hull. Cross planks of oak were fitted low in the hull for the same purpose. Another layer of heavy oak crossbeams joined the upper planks of the two sides of the hull. The pattern of crossbeam support passing through the planks was apparently unique to Korea.[23] Xu Jing, a Chinese emissary to the court of Korea, noted that the Korean ships were different from contemporary Chinese craft.

Both Chinese and Korean long-distance ships had a stern rudder, a large mast set amidships, and a smaller foresail. Sails were rectangular and reinforced with battens. Chinese and Korean ships used a windlass to raise the heavy anchor (as the scene on the Korean mirror shows). Korean ships had a planked deck, but it is unknown whether the space below the deck was divided into holds, as was typical of Chinese ships of the period. The mirror scene shows piled goods on deck and commodious cabins for the rich merchants who owned the goods. Korean sources assert that seventy people could comfortably sail on these ships. The current state of the archaeological, textual, and visual evidence does not permit even a speculation on the size and tonnage of these craft.

About the Chinese ships, which formed the second fleet attacking Japan, we have good material evidence. In 1974, Chinese archaeologists excavated a hull from the mud off Quanzhou Bay. The ship was amazingly intact from the waterline down. Coinage aboard dated the ship to 1272, only two years before Kublai Khan's first attack on Hakata Bay. The ship was 113 feet long, with a beam of 32 feet, drew only 10 feet of water, and displaced about 375 tons. Unlike stereotypical Chinese ships with flat bottoms and ends, the Quanzhou ship had a keel, was V-shaped in section, and had sharp prow. Twelve bulkheads divided the hull, which also had stepping for three masts. A flat transom carried the rudder, rather than a sternpost. Iron nails secured the overlapping planking. The cargo of incense wood, pepper, and hematite suggests that this was a long-distance goods carrier, returning from Southeast Asia. Such a ship could have been impressed to carry troops to Japan.[24]

In the last three decades Japanese archaeologists have been searching Hakata Bay for the physical remains of the battle of 1281. Tantalizing evidence has turned up, such as Chinese- and Korean-style anchors, Chinese ceramics, disc-shaped articulated armor, and weapons typical of Mongol fighters. Various scans of the bottom of the bay have revealed clumps of timbers, which are likely the remains of a ship or the mixed remains of several ships. Much of the timber is smaller than that used in big Korean trade ships, which suggests that the Mongols also commandeered coastal craft and probably even flat-bottomed river craft.[25]

Archaeologists in 2013 located a section of an intact hull. Ultrasound scans revealed a thirty-six-foot section of keel with adjoining planking under only three feet of sediment just off the shore in Hakata harbor. Ceramics, stone anchors, and other artifacts surround the wreck. For now, it remains buried, awaiting future excavation.[26]

In a larger geopolitical perspective, Japan, Korea, and the east coast of China formed a complex a maritime world, which was roughly the same size as Europe's northern littoral. From Nagasaki, Japan, to Shanghai, China, across the Yellow Sea is five hundred miles, about the same distance as Scandinavia to England. Korea and Japan are only one hundred miles apart, roughly comparable to the twenty-five miles that separate England and France across the Channel. Over the centuries, just as the Scandinavians invaded England and the English used their ships to invade the French, so too did Chinese, Korean, and Japanese dynasties invade each other's territory, trade with each other, sponsor piracy of each other's shipping, ally in attacks on each other, call in each other to put down indigenous rebels, and constitute places of refuge for defeated or aspiring rulers.

Dynasties of Korea, Japan, and China sometimes chose to close their maritime borders, forbidding traders from entering and citizens from leaving. These legal prohibitions typically were not effective. Traders and travelers found ways to circumvent them.[27] As also happened in Europe, local or regional powers in the China Sea region founded new ports beyond the reach of the central government. One of the most famous of such ports was Hainan Island off the southern coast of China, which served smugglers at the time of the Kublai Khan expedition and for several subsequent centuries.

Since the history of China is usually written as the history of dynasties, we might assume that the royal court of China was always the dominant power on land and at sea, but this is simply not the case. Periods of warring states were as frequent as periods of stable, large dynasties. The south of China was always difficult for a northern-based dynasty to integrate. Declining dynasties sometimes looked across the seas for a Japanese or Korean alliance.

## Monsoons and Mongols

Let us recall that for the second invasion of Japan Kublai Khan ordered a large invasion fleet from the shipyards of South China. They produced over a thousand ships in about two years (1279–1281), suggesting a substantial shipbuilding capacity. The southern provinces of China were deeply involved in maritime trade with Southeast Asia and India, much of it in Chinese vessels.

The yearly rhythm of this trade had been established for at least five centuries. May through October was the time to take the prevailing onshore winds from the islands of Southeast Asia to China. January to March was the time to return on the prevailing offshore winds. Regional traders knew the pattern. Arabs, for example, quickly earned this trading rhythm and wrote about it as early as the ninth century.

With the conquest of the Southern Song dynasty's territory in 1279, the Mongols under Kublai Khan acquired the most "developed" area of the world at the time, characterized by dense agricultural population, much investment in canals and other infrastructure, government bureaucracy, an advanced industrial base, some of the world's largest cities, and quite possibly its busiest port. The region produced both products for internal use and export and the food to support both the tens of thousands of workers in the export industries and the millions who lived in cities.

The southern region of China had developed slowly, over many centuries. It began as a tribal area with minimal agriculture and no significant cities, peripheral to the dynasties of north China. During the Tang dynasty (618–907 CE), which was centered far away to the north, sedentary agriculturalists moved into the Jin River watershed. The first agricultural settlements were on the upland boundary of the marshy and malarial coastal plain and the lower reaches of the wooded hills, which could, without too huge an investment of labor, be converted into terraced rice paddies. Perhaps a century after the first agricultural settlements, additional colonists drained some of the marshes, grew rice, and founded the port of Quanzhou at the mouth of the Jin River. Similar colonization populated the hinterland behind Guangzhou (Canton), located farther down the southern coast of China.[28]

Recall the Intan shipwreck (c. 1000) off Indonesia. Prominent in the ship's hold were a variety of Chinese manufactured goods: sophisticated cast alloy mirrors crafted for elite women of Java, silver ingots stamped by Chinese inspectors as to purity, strings of Chinese copper currency, iron pots with copper handles, and ceramics of all sorts. All these goods were produced in smaller urban centers that dotted Fujian Province of southern China.

The three centuries between the Intan shipwreck and Kublai Khan's conquest were "takeoff" years for the southern provinces of China, but especially for Quanzhou and its hinterland. The relentless pressure of the steppe armies of the Jurchen conquered northern China in the early twelfth century, and, by treaty, the emperor of the Song dynasty moved his court south to Hangzhou and conceded the north to the invaders (who subsequently ruled as the Jin dynasty). While the north was ravaged, the south prospered. Refugees boosted the population, which in any case was much larger than that of the northern provinces. Overseas trade between southern China, Southeast Asia, and India grew substantially. Several recently discovered shipwrecks of this period in Southeast Asian waters have yielded tens of thousands of Chinese export ceramics, mainly bowls and pots, the product of good-size industries employing thousands of workers. The court and Confucian officials provided steady demand for the desirable products of foreign lands: medicines and spices, such as camphor, rhinoceros horn, opium, garu wood, cardamom, cloves, nutmeg, birds' nests, liquid amber, dragon's blood (a red resin), aloe, and pepper. Also prominently imported were aromatics used in religious ceremonies, such as benzoin, sandalwood, and various tree gums. Yet another category of imports was animal and plant products used in high-end crafts, such as feathers, ivory, tortoiseshell, mother of pearl, animal horns and skins, sandalwood, and blackwood. The mineral products included copper, gold, tin, and lead.[29]

The southern ports of China served as transshipping points for goods from Southeast Asia, India, and the Middle East that were bound for Japan and Korea. A steady stream of Chinese traders migrated from the southern provinces of China to ports of Southeast Asia to sell Chinese manufactures and gather export items. These traders generally settled in Southeast

Asia and married local women, though they generally continued to consign goods to relatives in the ports of south China.

What difference did it make that this booming region fell to Mongol forces in 1279? In the short run, the empires of mainland and island Southeast Asia became targets for Mongol imperial expansion. Kublai Khan sent armies to attack what is today Vietnam, Myanmar (Burma), and Java. Burma surrendered after a long campaign (1277–1287).[30]

The even longer war to conquer Vietnam consisted of three campaigns (1257–1258, 1284–1285, and 1287–1288).[31] Overall, the rhythm of the invasions of Vietnam and the results were identical to the invasion of Japan. The Mongols were able to capture ports, but when they ventured inland, coastal Vietnam was a Mongol commander's nightmare—a muddy malarial plain laced with rivers and irrigation channels. Cavalry were virtually useless. Even worse, the plain backed to steep mountains, which provided hideouts for both kings and armies.[32] The third Mongol invasion of Vietnam was a repeat performance of Hakata Bay, on a somewhat smaller scale. The soldiers of the Vietnamese kingdom of Champa drove iron spikes into the bottom of the Bach Dang River, downstream of the Mongol base. Champa ships then lured the Mongol ships into a downriver chase. The retreating tide pushed the Mongol ships onto the stakes. Most of the three hundred Mongol ships were sunk. The Champa forces burned the rest.

The maritime attempt to conquer Java also failed, though not as spectacularly as the defeat at Hakata Bay. Initial successes on Java did not lead to solid alliances or victory. The Javanese king counterattacked and forced the Mongol army back to its ships. With the monsoon winds soon to reverse, threatening to strand the Mongol force on a hostile island, the Mongol fleet sailed away for China.

In the longer run, however, Mongol failures to conquer Southeast Asia made little difference to the broad integration of China, Southeast Asia, India, and the Middle East into a unified maritime world. Within southern China the conquering Mongols turned to foreigners, who had actively helped them against their Song enemies, for literate administrators. The Mongols also needed to promote trade for the taxes it generated. Goods flowed, taxes were paid, and foreign traders prospered. The failures of invasions probably mattered less than the expanding population of China and an apparently limitless demand for foreign goods by both the Mongols and indigenous Chinese elites. Chinese ships and merchants were active parts of this transoceanic integration. About five decades after the battle of Hakata Bay, Ibn Battuta, the great medieval traveler, saw a fleet of thirteen Chinese trading ships at anchor in the port of Calicut on India's southwest coast:

> The large ships have anything from twelve down to three sails, which are made of bamboo rods plaited like mats. They are never lowered, but turned according to the direction of the wind; at anchor they are left floating in the wind. A ship carries a complement of a thousand men, six hundred of them sailors and four hundred men-at-arms. . . . The vessel has four decks and contains rooms, cabins, and saloons for merchants; a cabin has chambers and a lavatory, and can be locked by its occupant, who takes along with him slave girls and wives.

With the conquests of Kublai Khan, China had become part of a larger empire that stretched into the steppes of Asia and the maritime world of Southeast Asia. Chinese writers of the time and historians since have treated the Mongol period as an aberration, one that had little influence on China and of little larger importance.[33]

They could not be more wrong. With the Mongol goal of world conquest, the world of East Asia became inextricably connected to Europe, both by the overland route of Marco Polo and the maritime route from the Middle East around India and through Southeast Asia.[34] It is perhaps worth noting that Christopher Columbus set off across the Atlantic Ocean for the same reason that Vasco Da Gama set off down the west coast of Africa: to find a way to the fabulous riches of the Mongol khans and discover what could be traded for them.

# 8

# BREMEN COG

In 1380 on the banks of the Weser River, a large seagoing cargo ship, known as a cog, was nearing completion. From the flat bottom rose overlapping planks, nailed together. Heavy crossbeams tied the sides together. Compared to Viking-style longships of the time, the cog was squat and tubby, with—as a modern scholar has put it—all the grace of an oceangoing storage container. Fortunately for us, this particular cog did not survive to carry bulk goods to and from Western Europe, the Baltic, and Scandinavia. No one knows for sure how the sinking happened, but most likely a huge wave swept into Bremen harbor and up the Weser River. It pulled the half-completed ship, lacking masts and some abovedeck structure, off the bank and carried it into the harbor, where it sank. Much of the hull remained intact. Silt covered the wreck.

There the ship lay, buried and forgotten, until October 8, 1962, when the dredger *Arlésienne* uncovered the wreck during extension of the Bremen harbor. The head of the harbor construction notified the State Museum of the find, and Siegfried Fliedner, curator for medieval history and ships, visited the site. Astonishingly, he and other visitors were able to walk to the wreck, which was exposed at low tide. Fliedner recognized that the ship had the characteristics of a medieval cog—a straight keel and relatively flat bottom, a single mast, quite high sides of broad joined planks, a steeply raked, almost flat stern, and a straight, raked stem. Curators of the State Museum were art historians and were not greatly interested in the cog; they allotted no funds to save the wreck. The best Fliedner could do immediately was to install a chicken wire fence around the wreck so that small pieces would not float away with the current, and begin emergency fund-raising among Bremen's citizens. Twice a day the tide flooded the site. Working by feel in the muddy water, a diver loosened the waterlogged planks, and a floating crane brought them to the surface. There was no time or money for site drawings

The reconstruction of the Bremen cog, Ship Museum, Bremerhaven.
PHOTO COURTESY OF UWE W. FRIESE, WIKIMEDIA COMMONS

or grid photography. Four years later all the major pieces of the cog rested in vats so that they would not dry out and disintegrate.

Fliedner continued raising money while Rose Marie Pohl-Weber, a local archaeologist, undertook the painstaking search of the bottom for small fragments and other remains of the wreck. She worked for hundreds of hours in a four-by-six-foot diving bell, using her hands to examine the bottom foot by foot and searching with a metal detector. She found hundreds of wood fragments, in addition to carpenter tools, clamps used in caulking, and even a dagger. The wood fragments joined the larger pieces in water tanks. The wood beams, planks, and fragments stayed in suspension for seven years while Fliedner raised the money for a special museum to house the cog.

Reconstruction then began under the supervision of a shipwright named Werner Lahn. He tried to re-create a process of building more than six hundred years old. Lahn laid the keel, which was largely intact, then began to fit the more than two thousand pieces of the three-dimensional jigsaw puzzle together. Assistants often used an overhead crane to lift the heavy, water-soaked beams and planks. The crew worked in 97 percent humidity to ensure that the precious wood would not dry out. Dowel holes in the edges of the bottom planks matched those in the keel and revealed that the bottom of the ship was perfectly flat. The side planks overlapped in a style known as clinker-built, or lapstrake. Slowly the ship took form. The reconstruction was completed in the winter of 1979–1980, but Lahn and the others were not sure that the cog would be strong enough for public display.

The intact hull was placed into an enormous stainless steel tank. A two-stage treatment gradually replaced the water in the wood's cell structure with ethylene glycol, much like antifreeze in automobiles. It was hoped that the treatment would strengthen and stabilize the medieval wood. No one knew if it would work. The Bremen cog was by far the largest wood object on which this treatment had ever been attempted. Full replacement of the water by ethylene glycol took twenty years. It turned out that the cog was remarkably strong, and on May 17, 2000, the Bremen cog became the proud centerpiece of the Schiffahrtsmuseum in Bremerhaven.[1] Though the Bremen cog never sailed, it is by far the most complete wreck of a cog ever found and provides a marvelous window into the world in which it would have sailed.

## Design of the Cog

When the cog first appeared as an oceangoing vessel (c. 1150), the Viking-style longship still ruled the seas of Northern Europe, the Baltic, and Scandinavia. These elegant vessels carried more than a hundred warriors to battle, rowing when needed, sailing when possible. Between 800 and 1000 CE Viking armies had conquered much of England, Scotland, Ireland, and part of the north of France. In the following century, even the island of Sicily was conquered by the Normans, direct descendants of the Vikings. The shallow-draft longboats allowed Vikings to attack settlements far up rivers, from the Thames to the Volga. Overall, Viking longboats were better suited to conquest and loot than trade. The deckless construction provided no protection for cargo, and the rowing crew took up virtually all the available space. During the height of Viking conquest the longboat was, nevertheless, also used for transport. A wider version of the longboat carried thousands of settler families from Scandinavia to England and France.

Scholars have long disagreed on the origins of the cog, with competing claims for Holland, North Germany, Scandinavia, and the Baltic countries.[2] The cog does seem to come from a tradition quite different from that of the Viking longboat. The cog's flat, sturdy bottom, originally without a keel, suggests a river craft, perhaps made for grounding and refloating in tidal estuaries.[3] Recent analysis of all the archaeological finds of cog-style remains suggests that boatbuilders developed the oceangoing version of the cog in Denmark and Sweden.[4] By 1200 many cogs sailed the sea-lanes of Northern Europe. By 1350 more than a thousand cogs plied the France-England wine trade alone.[5] As might be expected, the records show cogs attacked by pirates many times in the fourteenth century. The cog was the dominant form of trade vessel for two and an half centuries on the northern littoral of Europe, from about 1200 to about 1450.

What were the cog's good points? First and foremost was its large carrying capacity relative to its size. Cogs were typically about fifty to eighty feet long and sixteen to twenty-six feet across the beam. The cog was ideally suited to large-volume, low-value bulk trade. Second, the cog was cheaper to build than a Viking longship, as it was constructed of sawn planks rather than the Viking ship's laboriously split trees.[6] Third, cogs operated with much smaller crews. A Viking ship generally had over a hundred rowers, while the single-sail cog needed a crew of only fifteen to twenty.[7]

Crucial technological change improved the cog quickly. By 1225 the rudder had moved from the side (as shown on coins of Dutch, Baltic, and Scandinavian seacoast towns) to the stern. A big sternpost rudder helped with steering the ship, though the force needed to move it required either an additional steersman or a pulley system. Clearly the designers and builders thought the stern rudder well worth the additional steersman, since the innovation spread quickly and was used in all later cogs.[8] Later versions of the cog had a small mizzen mast with a triangular sail, which could assist in steering.

And what were the drawbacks of the cog design? Present-day sailors always suspected that a cog could not sail against an unfavorable wind. Typically, in order to make headway against the wind, a ship sails at first at one oblique angle to the wind, then at the opposite oblique angle, a maneuver known as tacking. Tacking is slow and requires resetting the sail on each leg of the zigzag course. The large, heavy sail of the cog made this maneuver difficult. Replicas of the Bremen cog built in the 1990s bear this out. Cogs could run before a favorable wind but could make little headway if tacking was required. Crews of cogs often waited in port for a favorable wind, for example, to take them from England to the French coast. In a less sanguine scenario, an unfavorable wind drove the cog onto rocks. The real solution to the unfavorable wind problem was the three-masted ship, which appeared only between 1400 and 1450, at the end of the period of the cog.

Builders and owners early recognized that larger cogs were more profitable. Throughout the 1200s and the 1300s archaeological and documentary evidence shows a trend toward larger cogs, eighty feet long with a beam of forty-six feet. These big cogs never, however, drove out the smaller ones. The big ones dominated certain runs, but the smaller ones worked quite satisfactorily on short coastal runs or for specific commodities. Though the Bremen cog is quite late (1380), it is rather small, only perhaps seventy-five to eight-five tons.[9]

## Shipbuilding Materials

It is perhaps worth emphasizing that the supplies to build a cog came from a dozen specialized industries, none of them local to the shipyards. The wood was from Scandinavia and the Baltic and was shipped to the many ports where cogs were built. Tar and resins for caulking came from Russia. Caulkers were a specialty trade, not to be confused with shipwrights or sailmakers. Fibers in caulk came from the skins of animals slaughtered for urban consumption. Across a broad band of Northern Europe several towns competed in the production in specialty manufactured goods for shipbuilding. Bridgeport in Dorset, for example, was the premier cordage-making town in Britain at the time. Cordage could be purchased "white" (not tarred) or "black" (tarred).[10] Bridgeport competed with other cordage centers on the Continent. Iron ship fittings came from specialized smelting and casting towns in Sweden, the Low Countries, or Germany. The iron ore was as often imported as found locally. Brittany and southwest France were the main source of canvas sails throughout the period, especially for Baltic ships.[11] Cork buoys of the period suggest a specialized trade with Spain.

## Sailing the Northern Seas

Ships generally avoided the winter on the stormy and overcast North Sea, except when unusual financial opportunity beckoned or political necessity required. Cog owners in the France-to-England wine trade, for example, knew that the earliest wine of the season commanded the highest prices, rewarding those willing to risk sailing earlier in the spring. In the wine trade at any time of the year captains were reconciled to long waits on the south coast of England or the Channel Islands for favorable winds to make the French coast.[12]

Much of the trade of the northern seas was within sight of land. Captains used their knowledge of landmarks to establish their position and avoid hazards. Landmarks could be natural, such as a distinctive tree on a promontory. Manmade objects also identified a particular place on the land, such as a church with its steeple built on a headland or a fort with its battlements on a cliff. In the cog period, some abbeys set bonfires to identify particularly dangerous rocks or shoals. For this service the shipowners paid a fee to the abbey. Along the coast of England, for example, archaeological excavations have located about two dozen early lighthouses.[13]

Because of the curvature of the earth, the higher an observer was, the farther away he could see a landmark. Early on, therefore, cog builders added a lookout platform at the top of the mast. Modern experiments have shown that this feature added almost ten miles to the sighting of a landmark.[14] Equally important was casting of the lead, which established how deep the water was under the ship. Archaeologists have found several leads of the cog period. Most have a small cavity in the top surface, which gathered mud from the bottom. Experienced captains could read the ship's position from variations in the color or texture of the mud. Cogs probably had an early version of the compass (invented in China, but first mentioned in Northern Europe in a text dated to about 1200) but no reliable charts. Captains were, nevertheless, quite capable of open-sea sailing by the stars, knowledge of wave patterns and currents, and watching for signs of land.[15]

The environmental world of the cog also included limitations of ports. Virtually all ports were on rivers that flowed to the sea. Upriver ports had three advantages over downriver ports. First, they were close to what the surrounding region produced (wool, grain, wine, coal, hides, or building stone). Moving bulk goods by road was prohibitively expensive, about ten times the cost of river transport.[16] Second, upriver ports kept oceangoing ships safe from storms while they loaded and unloaded. Third, upriver ports were somewhat more difficult to attack by sea. The principal disadvantage of upriver ports was shallow water. Large bulk carriers could not reach them, and bulk goods had to come downriver to ships by barge.

Merchants, however, wanted larger ships with inevitably deeper draft. To accommodate the new larger ships, ports eventually moved downriver, though they were more vulnerable to storms, destructive surges, flooding, and attack.[17] At the opening of the cog era downriver ports were barely developed. Unmarked narrow ship channels flowed between rocks or shoals. Only a local pilot could negotiate the shifting conditions of the port, while knowing the time that the tide produced maximum depth of water. Once safely in port, the cog was run up on a sloping bank. Its flat bottom allowed it to remain upright during loading and unloading. If the pilot got the timing of the tides wrong or the riverbanks were occupied, the ship sat on the muddy river bottom.[18] Fortunately, the cog's flat bottom allowed it to remain upright and float off during high tide.[19]

Nearby downriver ports competed for trade and set about improving the banks of their river's estuarial mudflats. Many ports built sloping wood walls to cover the natural riverbanks, creating deeper water closer to warehouses on shore. Much of the wood used in these walls came from dismantled ships. Somewhat later vertical walls of stone encased these wood walls. Today, these buried wood walls, especially along the Thames, have become one of the richest archaeological resources for cog-era ship design.[20]

### Cog Carrying Trade

Each bulk good moved in a predictable yearly pattern, which meant that cog owners knew when they should be at which harbor, what they were picking up, what they were dropping off, and when they were expected to be in the next port. The cog re-created an interconnected, specialized, networked trading world not seen in Northern Europe since the fall of the Roman Empire.[21]

What, then, were the bulk commodities? Where did they come from, and where did they go? Rhine wines and German beer moved to Russia, Scandinavia, and the Baltic countries.[22] The Baltic region competed with and eventually replaced Norway as the main source of timber to England, paid for by return shipments of English cloth.[23] English wool also supplied Flanders, which in turn supplied high-quality cloth to all of Northern Europe, the Baltic countries, and Scandinavia.[24] Cornwall tin moved just as widely. Scandinavia paid for its imports by exporting massive amounts of salted cod, which became the staple protein for urban workers across Northern Europe. Carved limestone fonts from mines in Sweden are still found in churches across the whole Baltic region.[25] Iron was no longer worked only close to iron ore mines. Cogs moved iron ore to specialty workshops in Flanders, England, and Sweden. Recall that the cog period was the age of knights in armor, and each knight normally had four horses. Denmark raised thousands of these horses, which were shipped all over Northern Europe in cogs.[26] Russia exported furs, wax, amber for jewelry and medicine, potash for the dye industry of Flanders, and tar to caulk ships. Massive amounts of grain moved from surplus areas, such as Poland, to feed the growing cities across Northern Europe. An account book of a trader from 1350 shows that cogs moved not only bulk goods but also luxuries for the rich. The trader's ventures brought to the upper class of Denmark high-quality colored cloth from Bruges, in addition to pepper, ginger, nutmeg, almonds, and figs.[27] The grain warehouses of Lübeck, the largest of the Baltic ports, give a sense of the scale of cog trade. These stone storage facilities held enough grain to feed London for a year.[28]

Fortunately, many import registers of the cog period from British ports have survived. They show that casks and barrels held a wide variety of goods, from wine to salt fish, from wax to tar.[29] Wine barrels were carefully packed in cradles, cushioned with moss or other plant material.[30] Southern fruits, such as orange and figs, were luxury items in Northern Europe and therefore also packed very carefully. Grain moved in sacks or barrels.[31] Wool was in sacks. Hides, fur, and spices were in bales. Salt, coal, tin, and lead were often loose in the hold.

Overall, the effects of cog bulk trading resembled those of other successful bulk trading networks. With adequate supplies of grain and fish to feed their population, towns and cities grew, along with demand for specialty manufactures and crafts. Specialty producers in the countryside also expanded, with new markets for their wine, beer, and wool. These producers came to rely on imported food, since their acreage was committed to single commodities rather than food production. The expansion of commercial fishing kept pace with the rising urban populations. Specialty skills, such as metalworking or weaving, were no longer tied to the mines or flocks. Low-cost bulk transport meant that raw materials moved inexpensively, and various stages of manufacture could be far removed from the mines.

Beer brewing and a developing cog carrying trade in beer illustrate the commercial network of the Hanseatic League (or Hansa, a trading association established by Northern European towns) and its subtle responses to various markets across the seas of Northern Europe. Beer making, of course, has a history that long pre-dates the Middle Ages. In the early Middle Ages, beer was typically produced in small breweries and monasteries and drunk locally. This beer soured quickly and was drunk "young," that is, soon after brewing. Until around 1300 the seaborne trade in beer was small. The scattered available documents suggest that captains carried beer for their crews and sold off any remaining beer at the end of a voyage.

Hops provided the key to beer as an export item. In eastern Germany brewers began adding the hops flower to beer to improve flavor. Around 1300 brewers noticed that hops slowed down the souring of beer (indeed, modern chemists in the brewing industry have confirmed hops's strong antibacterial quality). Hopped beer traveled well. The towns of the Hansa soon inaugurated beer exports. Newly opened land behind the Hansa ports grew the grain and the hops. The towns, especially Bremen and Hamburg, brewed the hopped beer, and the Hansa ships set out to sell it.[32]

From the first shipments, the Hansa beer could not compete in price. Local beer was always cheaper. Hansa traders insisted on a high-quality, tasty beer from its brewers and sold it as a premium product. Other Baltic towns, such as Rostock, Danzig (Gdańsk), and Wismar, soon followed Bremen and Hamburg into the hopped beer trade. Towns negotiated a standard-volume beer barrel and employed inspectors, who tasted and approved the beer before it left the docks. Specialty Hansa importers received the beer in Amsterdam, London, and Bruges, among other port cities.

Hopped beer caught on in Flanders, Holland, England, and especially Norway, which grew little grain and therefore had no local brewing industry. It failed to find a market in France. As they did with all commodities, towns of the Hansa staked out territories. Danzig, for example, supplied Norway, but political and economic conflict with the kings of Sweden and Denmark greatly reduced beer exports by the Hansa to those counties. Hamburg supplied Amsterdam, the cities of Flanders, and the towns of the lower Rhine. The beer output of Hamburg in the later fourteenth century was twenty-four million barrels a year. The beer exports to Amsterdam alone filled more than a hundred ships, each making two runs per year. Dutch import records total roughly a million and a half gallons per year.

By the opening of the fifteenth century, skills to make hopped beer had spread widely through Northern Europe. The Hansa had lost its monopoly on the process. Its response was to use the skills of its brewers to produce an even more premium beer, brewed to carefully controlled standards and sold to the luxury market. The strategy was successful for many decades, and the standards formed the basis of today's premium German beer.

As this example suggests, fortunes were made in the world of cog trading, often based on new processes, innovative business models, and nimble responses to markets. The Hansa also specialized in economic muscle and armed might. It is to this rough-and-tumble political and military world of the cog that we now turn.

## The Political and Military World of the Cog

The rise of the cog and of the loose economic confederation of the Hansa are inseparable. With the founding of the port of Lübeck, on the Trave River (in present-day eastern Germany) and the Hansa in 1159, a new business model emerged, which within thirty years included the cities of Wismar, Rostock, Stralsund, Greifswald, Stettin, Danzig, Riga, and Elbing. The Hansa's new business model made inland producers partners in bulk trading, rather than merely sellers of commodities.[33] The Hansa sought out long-term buyers for the commodities, thereby lowering risk and providing steady profits for all members. A generation later the Hansa had trading bases in Bruges and London, Bergen in Norway, Visby in Sweden, Novgorod in Russia, and had displaced Scandinavian and Russian traders from the Baltic. By the middle of the 1200s, the Hansa was shipping more tonnage of English bulk goods, such as wool and tin, than were English ships.[34]

Scholars now recognize that the Hansa was more than a formal or legal organization. It had a distinctive and recognizable culture. Similar house and warehouse styles dot the ports in which the Hansa operated. Archaeological digs have identified preferred pottery styles and colors. Members spoke Low German, though many were probably bilingual. Trading members were generally tied together by kinship and marriage alliances.[35]

The age of the cog was an age of war. Roughly half the period of cog dominance coincides with the Hundred Years War (1337–1453). The Hansa was successful not only because of a new business model, but because it developed the cog as an armed merchantman, in fact the most effective warship of its time.

At the opening of the period the Viking longboat was the ultimate ship of war. Most battles were fought on land, centering on shield walls and hand-to-hand combat. Naval battles were merely hand-to-hand combat moved onto

Note the above-deck towers, both fore and aft, of these two cogs.
Detail of altarpiece from the Saint Ursula of Cubells church (c. 1450),
now in the National Art Museum of Catalonia.

the water. Existing weaponry did not, if fact, sink ships. Nor was sinking ships the point. Longboats were much too valuable to sink. Seizing the boat and enslaving the crew or holding them for ransom were the objectives. In a typical battle, grappling hooks brought the boats together, warriors swarmed over the low gunwales, and mayhem ensued.

Cogs entirely changed this naval dynamic. Cogs stood much higher in the water, making boarding more difficult. Ship designers quickly parlayed this height advantage to a decisive military advantage. They built wood towers in the bow and stern, from which crossbowmen could wreak havoc on the open deck of an attacking longboat. Even stones thrown down on the enemy were lethal. By 1200 both kings and pirates had ceased sending longboats against cogs.[36] Refinements in the basic military array of the cog were gradual and experimental. Later, larger cogs had a third arrow platform surrounding the mast in the middle of the ship.[37]

The Hansa itself occasionally used its cogs in naval campaigns, such as against Denmark in 1234 and 1239. More significant was the naval campaign against the king of Norway in 1284 and 1285. The king had infringed Hansa trading rights, imposing taxes that the Hansa refused to pay, and he subsequently attacked Hansa ships. In return, Hansa cogs blockaded Norwegian harbors and embargoed grain bound for Norway. Norway was so desperate for the grain that the king restored the league's trading rights following an armistice.[38]

One of the few descriptions of a cog battle comes from that most-famous medieval historian and storyteller, Jean Froissart. He was born in about 1337 in the French city of Valenciennes, close to the Ardennes forest. By age twenty he had found his true calling, telling and writing stories of political rivalries between kings and especially chivalry and bravery in battle. He sought out actual participants and soldiers from both sides. For the next fifty years he moved across Europe from court to court, from patron to patron, collecting accounts and weaving historical stories. His writings were popular in his own time, and many handwritten copies still exist.[39]

Though not himself an observer, Froissart wrote a detailed account of the sea battle between the English and French outside Sluys, the principal port of Flanders, on June 24, 1340. The fleet of Philip VI, the king of France, included many swift, maneuverable galleys from the Mediterranean, whose shallow draft made them ideal for attacking ports. Froissart tells us that the French fleet numbered more than "six score," or 120 ships, including the *Christopher*, a captured great ship of Edward III of England.[40] They arrayed before the port.

The size of the English fleet is the subject of much conjecture because the royal records have been lost. Perhaps 160 ships is a conservative guess of the fleet size.[41] Most of these ships were trading cogs, pressed into the king's service. Kings paid shipowners a standard rate per month, but royal service was a risky business. Compensation for loss was sporadic and uncertain.[42] Many cogs already had "castles" at the bow and stern, built to house archers or crossbowmen and serving as a place from which to launch rocks. It seems likely that the cogs without castles were fitted with them when they were pressed into the king's service. The English ships arrived from the west and altered their course so that they would not go into battle with the sun directly in their faces. They arrayed their fleet so that a ship of infantry was flanked at either side by one of principally archers. The French fleet attacked the English ships, but the English archers poured fire down onto the open decks of the galleys. Rocks from the castles of the cogs holed and sank galleys.[43] Grappling hooks brought opposing ships together, and the battle shifted to ferocious hand-to-hand fighting. "There were many deeds of arms done, taking and rescuing again, and at last the great *Christopher* was first won by the Englishmen, and all that were within it were taken or slain.... The battle was right fierce and terrible."

The battle lasted from early morning until noon and ended with the total destruction of the French forces. Edward spent the next few days receiving fealty from the nearby lords, great and small, had his right to the crown of France declared in the marketplace of Valenciennes, and feasted his new allies.

From a naval point of view, cogs were superior fighting vessels, but they also remained the trade vessel of choice.[44] Royal documents in England have shown that the king well understood the profits of trading.[45] Cogs commandeered by the king spent roughly twice as much time engaged in royal trade as they did in ferrying troops or taking part in battle.

## Decline of the Cog

The cog's decline was rapid. Long the dominant Northern European trading vessel, it virtually disappeared from the sea-lanes after 1400. This decline can be seen as the breakdown of the boundary between two previously largely separate maritime worlds, that of the northern seas (home of the cog) and that of the Mediterranean (the rowed galley). In the thirteenth century, Mediterranean shipbuilders certainly were familiar with northern-style cogs, which were used as pilgrim ships and, later, warships in the Crusades. But no shipyard on the Mediterranean built such a ship. The rowed galley and lateen-rigged Mediterranean ships remained, for good reason, the dominant ship designs. The winds on the Mediterranean are notoriously variable in direction and force. The lateen-rigged Mediterranean sailing ship and the rowed galley could make better progress in adverse winds than the cog, even though the cog could carry more cargo.[46]

Just as cogs were not built in the Mediterranean, galleys were not constructed in Northern Europe. Even though the English kings regularly hired

Genoese galleys and their crews as warships, they could not find shipwrights anywhere in England to repair damaged galleys. The construction of a cog was so different from a galley that the skills of English shipwrights did not extend to even repairing galleys.

War and trade, however, began to connect the two worlds after about 1350. Cogs sailed around Spain, through the Straits of Gibraltar, and successfully brought cargo to Venice. In the second half of the era of the cog, Mediterranean maritime powers such as Genoa began to build such vessels themselves. By 1375, Genoese traders were shipping, for example, alum straight from the mines of the Greek island of Chios to the cloth dyeing centers in England. The new Genoese cogs were big—six hundred tons—three times the capacity of the Hansa vessels.[47] Genoese investors found that the large cogs were expensive to build but profitable. They typically paid off their cost in six to eight voyages, about a year of service in the Mediterranean.[48]

Particularly in the Mediterranean, shipbuilders sought new hybrid ships, which had the carrying and military capacity and the small crews of a cog but the maneuverability of a galley. Pictures from the 1400s show, for example, ships with a rounded deep prow and the flat, high, raked stern of a cog. The fore and aft arrow towers evolved into integrated parts of the hull and deck.[49] The hybrids dropped the single mast of the cog in favor of two masts, which gave the ship much more maneuverability.

Many of the ship design experiments centered on how to integrate cannon into the design. Shipbuilders first placed guns on the deck, which not only cluttered the deck but also produced a ship with a center of gravity too high to sail well. Guns of small caliber could be fired from the castles at the bow and stern of cogs, but anything weightier with a recoil seriously destabilized the ship. There were experiments with a square aft profile in order to install guns and protect the vulnerable stern. The solution that won out between 1500 and 1530 was lowering the guns to a raised hold level and firing out of gun ports cut into the hull, protected by closable hatches.[50]

This process of integrating guns into the design of the ships had its failures as well as its successes. The *Mary Rose* was England's largest and most heavily armed ship when it was launched in 1510. In 1545 a sudden storm caught the ship with its gun ports open and the guns run out. Water poured through the open gun ports. The ship quickly filled with seawater, heeled over, and sank. Underwater archaeologists found the *Mary Rose* in 1971. It has been raised and restored and now rests in a stunning museum in Ports-

The *Lisa from Lübeck*, a modern three-masted cog.

mouth, England. A more spectacular failure was the *Vasa*. Launched in 1628 in Stockholm, the ship was so overloaded with ordinance that it was could not be sailed or maneuvered and sank within hours of the launch. The *Vasa* was found and raised in 1961, restored over the following decade, and now forms the centerpiece of the Vasa Museet in Stockholm.

The biggest change was in the construction of the ship. The new hybrids were not built up from a flat bottom but were planked over sturdy frames. This robust construction technique made a ship strong enough to carry and fire cannon. By 1500 the new designs had become common enough to be described as new types of ships—the caravel and the galleon—the vessels of the exploration of the New World (see chapter 10).

## The Cog Today

The three replicas of the Bremen cog have shown that they were incapable of sailing against an unfavorable wind and prone to rough short-interval pitching, which makes even an experienced crew seasick.[51] A poem by a pilgrim who sailed in a cog from England to Santiago de Compostela in western Spain suggests as much. At the first sign of a storm the pilgrims could no longer eat meat and ale, but were so sick that they could only eat salted toast. The hold had to be pumped constantly, and the stench was enough to make a man "as good to be dede."[52]

The cog, nevertheless, introduced into the Northern European seas living quarters for passengers, the stern rudder, and a profile that made trading bulk goods profitable. It was vital in the developing, interconnected world of Scandinavia, the Baltic, the Low Countries, northern France, and England, with its concomitant specialization of crafts and production. It moved the necessary food to cities. It swept the Viking longboat from military dominance. The cog was central to the breaking down of the boundary between the maritime worlds of the Northern European seas and the Mediterranean. It was the precursor to the three-masted fully rigged ship, the greatest naval invention of the late Middle Ages. Its storied past is now embodied in the dark, sixty-foot hull of the Bremen cog.

# 9

# BARBARY WAR GALLEY

In April 1587, a fleet of rowed galleys from Christian Genoa chased a smaller fleet of war galleys from Muslim Algiers through the western Mediterranean. It is likely that the Algerian ships were trying to outrun the Genoese back to their home port. It was not to be. A storm blew the Algerian fleet onto the Balearic Islands off Spain's eastern coast. One of the ships foundered on the rocks of Formentera, the southern island of the two that form Ibiza. Of the crew of 250, all but 15 drowned. A dozen of the Muslim crew and three slaves who managed to break the chains to their rowing benches floated ashore on timbers and hunks of wood from the ship. This wreck was, however, destined to be more than a sad statistic of the centuries-long Muslim-Christian Mediterranean warfare.

Aboard the wrecked galley was an Englishman named Richard Hasleton, a chained Christian rower, who not only survived the wreck but also a series of adventures and colorful escapes. This intrepid sailor's dictated memoir provides a detailed description of Mediterranean slavery and the galleys, which were at the center of that world.[1]

## Galleys of the Mediterranean

What sort of ship did Hasleton and his fellow slaves row? Galleys of this period were rarely over one hundred feet long and usually about twenty feet wide.[2] Hasleton's claim that there were 250 men on board seems plausible. The Muslim crew might have consisted of fifty sailors, a majority of whom were required to hoist and set the large lateen sail amidships. (The ships often also had a smaller lateen sail aft.) A Barbary galley typically had from one to three cannons in the prow and sometimes a small gun on each side. All of these would have required a gunner and loader. Additional crew would have included cooks and helpers, plus, of course, the captain and the various overseers of the slaves. The rowing crew might have consisted of 180 slaves, thirty oars to a side and three men per oar, chained to their respective benches.[3] Barbary galleys were purely warships, built for speed. They had no holds and open decks. Food was stored in lockers under the rowing benches. The captain had the only cabin, placed aft of the rowers. A typical Barbary galley, though smaller than the one on which Hasleton served, appears in a mid-seventeenth-century Dutch painting by Lieve Pietersz Vershuier.[4]

Hasleton's memoir explains how he ended up on a Barbary slave galley: "In the year 1582, departing the English coast towards the end of May, in a ship of London called the Mary Marten . . . being laden and bound for Petrach [Petras, on the Greek coast, at that time in the Ottoman Empire] . . . we safely arrived." On the return voyage the *Mary Marten* lay virtually becalmed off Spain's southern coast, about 150 miles east of Gibraltar. Two Barbary galleys attacked the ship, boarded it, and took the crew and passengers prisoner. Hasleton and the others were beaten, their valuables taken, and they were locked in the hold of their ship. Eventually, the captured ship returned to Algiers, "where immediately after my landing I was sold for 66 doubles"—Spanish doubloons—which would be about $1,000 at today's prices. Within a month Hasleton was chained to a bench with two other rowers. He served a Barbary galley in search of other vulnerable ships on the Mediterranean. By any standard it was hard, brutal, dangerous work. He would row for four raiding seasons before the wreck of his galley on Formentera Island.

During the summer raiding season Barbary galleys captured prizes far into the North and South Atlantic. Coastal raids included Italy, France, and Spain and reached as far north as the coasts of the Netherlands, England, Ireland, and even Iceland. The vast majority of slaves taken, however, were from the coasts and waters of the Mediterranean Sea and the Atlantic Ocean immediately west of the Straits of Gibraltar. Between about 1500 and 1700, galley slavery based on the Barbary Coast of the Mediterranean was a vast and profitable enterprise.

It is worth noting that the term "Barbary" itself reflects the long-term complexities of who was considered civilized and who was not in the Mediterranean world. The term is derived most directly from "Berber," which now refers to peoples who share the Berber language group and are spread across a broad swath of western Africa that includes Morocco, southern Al-

The slave market in Algiers, from Jan Luyken,
*Historie Van Barbaryen, En des zelfs Zee-Roovers* (1684).

geria, Mali, and Niger. Berber, however, is not an indigenous term for these language-related peoples. It was given to some northern branches of this language group by Romans who fought them in the first centuries CE. Their use of the term Berber (barbarian) had the same meaning throughout the Roman Empire: a people who did not speak Latin. The term is, however, even older. The Romans borrowed it from the Greek *barbaros*, meaning a non-Greek.

## Mediterranean Slavery

Several features of this Mediterranean-based phenomenon confound common ideas of slavery. First, Mediterranean slavery turns on its head the idea that all slaves were African blacks. Mediterranean slaves were largely whites from Western Europe, which comprised some of the most advanced and powerful nations on earth at the time. The slavers were darker-skinned North Africans and Middle Easterners. Second, religion rather than race underlay the politics and economics of Mediterranean slave taking. Slave capture had a long historical association with the Crusades and was built on the ongoing hostility between Christian cities and kingdoms to the north of the Mediterranean and Muslim kingdoms to the south and east of the Mediterranean. The Christian states on the north shore of the Mediterranean captured and enslaved Muslims, just as Muslim states on the south shore enslaved Christians from the north shore. Third, unlike slaves brought to the Americas, captured Europeans were not cut off from their families. They were, in fact, encouraged to write home and tell their families of their plight, because slaveholders hoped to extract ransom. Mediterranean slavers were perfectly willing, and indeed expected, to exchange upper-class and some lower-class slaves for ransom. Fourth, in contrast to the hopeless plight of African slaves in the New World, some European kingdoms, especially Spain and France, tried to locate and free their enslaved subjects. Along with the Catholic Church, they established consuls and legations in the capitals of the slaving kingdoms and tried to keep track of slaves.

No modern scholar has yet attempted an overall census of slaves around the Mediterranean in the period of Barbary slavery. Nevertheless, piecemeal studies of particular kingdoms and periods suggest that the scale of slavery was enormous. On the Barbary Coast, Algiers had the largest number of warships, at least sixty and possibly ninety at its peak strength. Tripoli had perhaps twenty-five; Tunis, fifteen to twenty; and Salee (along the Atlantic coast of Morocco), twenty-five to thirty.[5] A conservative estimate of the number of galley slaves needed by the combined Barbary states at any one time would be between twenty-five thousand and thirty-five thousand rowers. The actual number of galley slaves in the Mediterranean was much higher. To the east, eighty thousand men were necessary merely to row the galleys of the Ottoman ruler. Throughout the sixteenth century, the numbers of galley slaves of the Christian opponents of the Ottoman Empire were similar, though the number declined in the seventeenth century as the European powers developed more sophisticated sailing vessels to replace galleys.[6]

One scholar has estimated that through the sixteenth and seventeenth centuries there were twenty-five thousand European slaves at all times in Algiers alone and another ten thousand in other cities along the North African coast.[7] The male slaves were not permitted to marry local women and thus produced no children. Therefore, every slave who died or became too weak to work had to be replaced. Perhaps a third of the galley slaves died within a year or two of capture, succumbing to overwork or endemic bubonic plague and other deadly diseases on the North African coast. The available population of rowers also decreased each year because significant numbers of

Christian slaves converted to Islam and thereby escaped the galleys. Muslims were forbidden by Sharia law to enslave other Muslims. Some slaves were freed by their masters or ransomed. A few slaves escaped. Overall, on the Barbary Coast, perhaps one in five slaves had to be replaced every year. These figures suggest that at least a million and perhaps a million and a half European men passed through the slave prisons of North Africa alone between 1530 and 1780.[8]

Perhaps the most surprising comparison is with the smaller scale of the West African slave trade across the Atlantic to the Americas. From 1500 to 1700, Barbary slavery of white Europeans was—without adding the more numerous slaves of the Eastern Mediterranean—numerically larger than slaves captured and shipped from West Africa to the Atlantic world. In fact, a single slaver from Tripoli or Algiers often seized more slaves in a single raiding season than the average of thirty-two hundred slaves transported from West Africa to the Americas in a typical year.[9]

## Ancient Mediterranean Galleys

Hasleton's galley came near the end of the incredibly long service of such craft in the Mediterranean. Scholars argue about the galley's earliest appearance because the evidence consists of only a few ship models, which lack crucial detail. By 2500 BCE, however, the evidence from Egypt is clear. As we have seen in chapter 2, early Nile boats were rowed, as depicted on tomb and temple walls. In these early Egyptian vessels a sail was at the ready to exploit favorable winds. Egyptian construction techniques were unique, found nowhere else in the Mediterranean, and therefore may have had little influence on later ship design in the Hellenic world.

The literary evidence about ancient Greek galleys is disappointing. The *Iliad*, which describes events of about 1300 BCE, contains an extensive list of the ships of the fleet bound for Troy but no description of the vessels. Perhaps the clearest literary evidence is from several passages in the *Iliad* that describe actual journeys (as opposed to journeys in which the gods magically propelled the vessel). These ships typically required twenty to twenty-five rowers, which suggests an open vessel about fifty to sixty feet long and about ten feet wide.[10]

Homer's *Odyssey* is quite useful, however, in his clear distinction between galleys of war and galleys of trade. Odysseus compares the cudgel of the

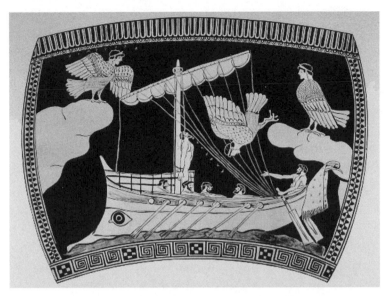

Odysseus tied to the mast of a rowed galley, scene
on a Greek stamnos, c. 480–470 BCE (British Museum).
Drawing by Adolf Furtwänger (d. 1907).

giant named Cyclops to "the mast of a broad-beamed, black-hulled merchantman that sails the seas." Merchantmen were wider than war vessels,
carried a bigger sail (hence the need for a stronger mast), and carried only
half the rowers of a war galley. (Recall that the Uluburun wreck of chapter
3 with its sturdy timbers is exactly contemporary to the period Homer describes.) For a merchantmen, speed was less important than carrying capacity. In the Mediterranean these distinctions between war galleys and trade
galleys persisted for more than two thousand years, right down to the time of
Hasleton's enslavement in the sixteenth century. There is no doubt that he
was on a war galley, built for speed, not for trade.

Images of war galleys on eighth-century BCE Greek pottery show two
banks of rowing benches, the upper one often not manned. A stone relief, in
addition to various coins and images on pottery, documents the appearance
of the three-tiered rowed galley, known as a trireme, around the mid-sixth
century BCE. This type of galley gradually became the dominant warship of
the ancient Hellenic world.[11] By the mid-fourth century BCE, the standard
complement of a trireme war galley included 170 rowers, 14 soldiers, and 21
officers and crew.[12]

Two well-documented voyages from 428 BCE show that conditions for free galley rowers in ancient Greece were considerably better than on Hasleton's slave ship. Hellenic rowers were, of course, not chained to their benches. They went ashore for a midday meal and a rest. Ships did not travel at night and were beached for rest and sleep.[13]

War galleys grew larger than the Greek trireme in the period of Rome's conquest of the Mediterranean. These galleys were termed a "four," a "five," or a "six"—that is, four, five, or six men to a rowing station, achieved by double-manning of one or more of the three tiers of oars.[14] The Roman Empire, however, generally built and fought in "fours" and "fives," using "sixes," "sevens," and huge "eights" and "nines" only for flagships. Each had its uses. The bigger ships were relatively slow but had tremendous power of attack using their ram. They sat high in the water, allowing spears and projectiles to be launched down on the opposing deck. They also carried many soldiers for an assault on an enemy ship. "Fours" and "fives" were smaller, faster, and could pursue an enemy into shallow bays or ports. In general, after the victory of Octavian over Mark Antony (30 BCE), the number of Roman warships rapidly declined. Some burned; some were stationed in provincial Gaul (France). Until the civil wars of the later third century, the Roman Empire essentially controlled the entire Mediterranean coast and had little use for a fleet of large war galleys, certainly not the monster "fives," "sixes," or larger vessels.[15] The Mediterranean naval fleet consisted of triremes and smaller galleys, particularly suited to chasing pirates and transporting members of Rome's aristocracy to posts abroad. The trade fleet was a combination of slow-sailing merchantmen and faster merchant galleys, which specialized in expensive perishable goods, such as fruit and live animals for the Roman games.[16]

In maritime terms the fall of Rome was rapid. The last naval battle to feature triremes and other sophisticated naval vessels was in 324 CE. Constantine defeated his rival and established the Eastern Roman (Byzantine) Empire, which would last for a thousand years. After 324 CE triremes were neither built nor mentioned in records or literature. In the fifth century, for example, Zosimius wrote that the secrets of trireme construction had been lost.

To date, only one shipwreck of a rowed galley has been located. Originally found in 1900 by sponge divers off the rocky island of Antikythera, the wreck yielded extraordinary treasures, including sculpture, jewelry, and a unique scientific device. At 180 feet the dives were extremely dangerous.

One diver died, and two more were paralyzed from the bends. Except for a brief exploration by Jacques Cousteau in a submersible in the 1960s, the wreck remained as the sponge divers had left it. Recent scientific analysis of various original finds has conclusively dated the wreck to the first century BCE.[17] In 2012, after years of negotiation, the Greek government agreed to a full marine archaeological expedition by the Woods Hole Institution. It is hoped that this expedition's findings will answer many questions about design, construction, and operation that remain unanswered.

## Galleys after Rome

The end of the trireme era in no way meant the end of the galley. The rationale for galleys remained the same as ever. Rowed ships were simply more efficient in the light and variable winds of the Mediterranean summer sailing season.

Galleys were still the warship of choice a thousand years after the fall of Rome, built by the Byzantine Empire, its rivals the Muslims, and for a brief period Frankish tribes. Descriptions of these latter vessels are very rare, and images nonexistent, so that our knowledge of them is sketchy, at best. Large galleys, known as dromons, had two tiers of rowers and a deck; smaller galleys featured only a single tier of oars and were not decked. Some evidence suggests that the larger ships were a bit over one hundred feet long, about the size of Hasleton's galley. Larger decked galleys also had a raised platform amidships, from which soldiers launched arrows or used a small catapult. The major shift in construction was from plank-built galleys (built up by joining planks edge to edge with strong mortise-and-tenon joints) to frame-built galleys (adding planks to a pre-built frame). Frame-built galleys were, on the whole, less expensive, required fewer shipwright skills, and were stronger.[18]

There were two significant developments in weaponry. First, the underwater ram disappeared from galleys, replaced by a large spike situated above the waterline, intended to make the attacking galley ride up and over the enemy's gunwale. Second, around 680 CE, the Byzantine fleet acquired a fearsome weapon, known as Greek fire. This napalm-like material required a special pump and siphon at the bow and a specialist to man it. Nevertheless, the results were devastating. Greek fire clung to men and ships and burned with a hot, intense flame that water could not extinguish. Fleets equipped with Greek fire rarely lost a battle. Within a few decades of the invention of

Greek fire in the Byzantine Empire, the expanding Muslim kingdom developed its own versions of Greek fire. It should be noted, however, that Greek fire was not some sort of ultimate, unstoppable weapon. Its range was short; it worked well only in calm seas; it was fired only from the bow; and ships carried a limited supply of the material. Strangely, Greek fire disappeared from naval engagements after about 900 CE. Modern scholars speculate that either the Byzantine Empire lost control of provinces that produced natural petroleum, which was the key ingredient in Greek fire, or that the secret of its formulation was lost.[19] The composition of Greek fire remains a subject of much speculation. It seems likely that naptha was the main ingredient, perhaps supplemented with tar, sulfur, or quicklime. The Chinese invented their own version of Greek fire, whose exact formula is also unknown.

Unfortunately, scholars have discovered few useful texts or accurate pictures of Muslim galleys of the Mediterranean. In Muslim documents, ship terminology consists of both Greek and Latin loan words and Arabic terms to which no particular ship design can be assigned. References by Crusader chroniclers to ships of their opponents suggest that Islamic forces continued to build large two-tier galleys. Inventories and illustrations of Christian vessels of the thirteenth and fourteenth century clearly show and describe galleys with two tiers of oars.[20]

In a final twist before the time of Hasleton, Christian states north of the Mediterranean about 1290 returned to a trireme configuration. Rearranging the benches and building slightly bigger ships allowed Venice and Genoa to increase the number of oars in the water from the standard 108 of the two-tier configuration to 150 oars in a three-tier configuration. The claim at the time was that these larger galleys were faster and more effective in battle.[21] Just as the war galley increased in size and number of rowers, so Venice and Genoa turned to building "great galleys" — big, armed merchantmen with three tiers of oars and an enormous lateen sail. They carried high-value cargo, such as silks and spices, and pilgrims, and were expected to sail without war galley escort. Some of the rowers would wield weapons if pirates or enemies attacked.

## Hasleton's Troubles in a Divided Christian World

One might imagine that after he struggled ashore from the wreck of his Muslim galley into a Christian country Richard Hasleton's problems would have been over. As soon as the three survivors arrived in the nearest village, one of his fellow slaves told the authorities that Hasleton was an Englishman and a Protestant. He was, therefore, not only a heretic but—in the politics of the day—an enemy of Spain. His troubles had just begun:

> Then I was presently carried aboard a galley of Genoa, and put in chains.
>
> And, on the morrow, was I sent over into the Isle of Iviza [now Ibiza], being within the jurisdiction of Majorca; which are all in the dominion of Spain. There I was imprisoned in the High Tower of the Town Castle with a pair of iron bolts upon my heels and a clasp of iron about my neck, there hanging a chain at the clasp; where I remained nine days, fed with a little bread and water.

From Ibiza Hasleton was consigned to a Genoese galley, chained to his bench, and rowed until the ship put in at Majorca, where he was turned over to the Inquisition. Hasleton writes that he refused to become a Catholic and was therefore thrown into a dungeon for slightly more than a year.

At this point it is perhaps worth discussing the overall truthfulness of the Hasleton memoir. He was writing for an audience who already expected a certain predictable flow of events in these Barbary slave narratives. First came the details of the ship from which the writer was captured and the abuse of the passengers and crew at the hands of their Muslim captors. Next came the sale of the passengers and the brutal details of rowing the galleys. The writer had to demonstrate his steadfast refusal to convert to Islam to better his lot and his equally steadfast faith in Christianity. English writers needed to show an equally steadfast refusal to convert to Catholicism. Typically, the narrative dwelled on the slave's daring escape. In light of these genre expectations, it is reasonable to doubt some portions of Hasleton's memoir. Particularly unlikely seems the verbatim dialogue of his discussions with the inquisitor detailing important theological differences between Lutherans and Catholics. The sections of his capture, sale, life aboard the galley, and his escapes have a sense of veracity about them. Who could have made up a story of a Christian galley slave escaping to a Christian country only to be enslaved on a Christian galley?

This series of misadventures could only have happened in a world in which England and the Netherlands fought Spain not only over the usual spoils of territory and dominance but also over men's souls. Enemies were also heretics.

Hasleton escaped from the castle dungeon of the town of Majorca by climbing the rope used to lower food to him. At night he ventured out to find an escape route.

> And, searching to and fro, in the end I came where three great horses stood tied by the head and feet. Then did I unloose the halters from their heads, and the ropes from their legs; and went [with the ropes] to the castle wall. When I had tied them end to end, I made it [the rope] fast to the body of a vine which grew upon the wall; and by it did I strike myself over the wall into the town ditch; where I was constrained to swim about forty paces, before I could get forth of the ditch.[22]

Hasleton managed to swim out of a watergate in the town wall and fled into the surrounding woods. Ten days later soldiers captured him before he could reach the port of Palma. In punishment for his escape attempt and his refusal to convert to the Roman Catholic Church, agents of the Inquisition ordered him tortured on the rack. The memoir contains the gruesome details of this experience.

> Then, the Tormentor bound my hands over my breast crosswise; and my legs clasped up together, were fast tied the one foot to the other knee. Then he fastened to either arm a cord, about the brawn of the arm; and likewise to either thigh another; which were all made fast under the rack to the bars; and with another cord he bound down my head: and put a hollow cane in my mouth. Then he put four cudgels into the ropes which were fastened to my arms and thighs.[23]

Twisting the ropes produced intense pain, increased by pouring water down the hollow cane in Hasleton's mouth.

He survived this torture and after five days in confinement managed a second escape: once again over the wall, through the watergate, and into the woods. This time he eluded capture. After three days of walking toward the coast, he found a small skiff and a hatchet in an olive grove. Hasleton cut small branches as rollers and moved the craft down to the water. He rigged his clothes as a sail and headed south for Algiers. Better the slavery of Barbary than the torture of the Inquisition.[24]

Two days later poor Hasleton landed not in the territory of the Algiers king, but in a country he termed Cabyles, or the king of Cookooe's Land. He was soon captured and taken to the capital, which seems to have been located at Bejaia, on the coast about eighty miles east of Algiers. Though Hasleton refused to convert to Islam and was initially imprisoned, he soon proved useful to the king, building gun carriages and a wood-framed house, and gained some freedom of movement.[25] He fled northwest over the first range of mountains toward Algiers but was captured by the king's soldiers and returned to Bejaia.

In a few months his luck turned and he became a paid water-carrier for the king's household. He used his wages to purchase equipment for his escape and clothes by which he could blend in with other travelers. He escaped the town one rainy night, stayed off the roads, crossed a river into Algerian territory, and soon reached Algiers.

The British consul had neither the money nor the power to protect Hasleton. After he refused to serve his old master, Hasleton was imprisoned by the king and sent back to the galleys. Three years later he finally left Algiers, probably ransomed, but the memoir leaves the circumstances unclear. Hasleton's description of the events that ended seven years of Barbary slavery concludes thusly: "by the help of an honest merchant [Richard Stapar] of this city of London, and having a very fit opportunity by means of certain [of] our English ships which were ready to set sail, bound homeward, upon Christmas Even, being the 24th of December, 1592, I came aboard the Cherubim of London; which, when weighing anchor, and having a happy gale, arrived in England towards the end of February following."[26]

## The End of the Galleys

The last large galley engagement was the battle of Lepanto (near Petras on the north coast of the Peloponnesus) a decade before Hasleton's capture. The ships of the Christian coalition left Sicily on October 6, 1571, and arrived at Lepanto a day later. The fleet included a total of 206 galleys from Venice, Naples, Spain, the Holy See, Genoa, Tuscany, Savoy, and Malta. In addition there were six galleasses, three-masted armed merchantmen with cannon firing from portholes. On board the Christian ships were approximately forty thousand sailors and slave oarsmen and twenty-five thousand soldiers. The Ottoman fleet that opposed them consisted of 205 galleys and 45 galliots (a smaller two-masted galley with provision for guns on deck), totaling perhaps fifty thousand oarsmen and sailors and thirty thousand soldiers. The fleets opposed each other in a right, center, left, and reserve array along a long north-south line. When the battle opened, the Ottoman left extended beyond the Christian fleet's right, and the Ottoman commander ordered a sweep to trap it. The Christian right moved south to counter and left a gaping hole in the line, which the Ottoman center attacked. The Ottoman right attempted a similar move but with less success, as that end was close to land. The center and both flanks tried to ram enemy galleys, and the battle soon devolved into close hand-to-hand combat. With the help of the reserve the Christian line largely held, in spite of heavy losses. In the end the Christians captured and beheaded the Ottoman commander and displayed his head on a pole. The remaining Ottoman forces broke off and fled. The Ottoman fleet lost at least two hundred ships and perhaps fifteen thousand men, in addition to thirty-five hundred captured. The Christian allies lost about eighty ships and seventy-five hundred men.

The battle of Lepanto had three important consequences. First, the Ottoman commanders observed how effective the galliots had been, and many of these type of ships were commissioned as the Ottoman Empire rebuilt its navy. Second, the battle stopped the Ottoman advance into the eastern Mediterranean. Third, the Ottoman defeat freed the kingdoms of Algiers and Tunis from Ottoman control and allowed them to become uncontrolled slaving states.

For the victors at Lepanto, the period of the sixteenth and seventeenth centuries was one of intense galley experimentation among maritime powers, such as Venice and Genoa. Those responsible for the naval fleet discussed the optimum number of tiers of oars and the advantages and disadvantages of three men rowing the same oar. They discussed the details of bench configuration and whether the motions of free rowers were more powerful and efficient than chained slave rowers.[27] These discussions were neither idle nor frivolous, but bore directly on the effectiveness of galleys in battle, and thus the raw power of these states. The Barbary states settled on a configuration of three men rowing the same sweep, which required a less trained crew and was therefore suitable for galley slaves. This configuration Hasleton knew all too well.

Unstoppable change was, however, coming from outside the bounded maritime world of the Mediterranean galley. In Spain, France, Holland, and the Baltic states, government-sponsored experiments in ship design and weapons produced sailing ships that were faster, more maneuverable, and far more lethal than earlier configurations. Three masts with independently rigged sails produced large ships not only more maneuverable than earlier sailing ships but also capable of sailing much closer to an adverse wind, lessening a galley's tactical advantage. Government-sponsored experiments also produced relatively reliable cannon of standard bore with rolling carriages suitable for use at sea. Further experiments had solved the problems of absorbing recoil from firing the cannon by use of a breech rope. Perhaps most important, these new ships were designed around the use of cannon as their principal weapon, and crews were trained to operate them relatively efficiently. By the middle of the seventeenth century, a galley could no longer hope to defeat any carrack or galleon in a pitched naval battle.

Barbary states survived by preying on relatively defenseless smaller trading ships and raiding coastal villages. The shifting political alignments of larger states often made Barbary kingdoms useful allies, much in the manner that England commissioned privateers. Barbary slavery continued well into the 1700s, but was on the decline from mid-century onward. Repeated bouts of plague had decimated the population of the North African ports. Both England and France launched repeated campaigns against Barbary galleys and especially Barbary ports, eventually extracting enforceable treaties that effectively ended Barbary attacks on their shipping.[28]

The United States also had its sailors seized by Barbary slavers, who had captured ships and sailors based in the American colonies as early as 1625. Throughout the next 150 years small numbers of American ships are recorded to have fought Barbary ships. Some escaped, but others were taken and their crews enslaved. In general, however, the treaties of Britain with the Barbary kingdoms protected the shipping of the American colonies and there were decades when American colonial shipping was not harassed.

After the American Revolution, British treaties with the Barbary kingdoms no longer covered the newly independent nation. Consequently, Barbary slavers seized the small schooner the *Maria* with its crew of six off the Portuguese coast in 1785. Later in the same year the *Dauphin* was also captured. This new country, founded on the idea of freedom and liberty, watched twenty-one of its sailors enslaved. American newspapers covered the events and expressed outrage, but little was done. The U.S. government had neither the resources to pay ransom nor the navy to either patrol the Atlantic or attack the well-fortified ports of Tripoli and Tunis. The American sailors languished and died rowing galleys or dragging boulders for Tripoli's seawall.

Assault on Algiers by the American fleet, 1805.

Then, for almost a decade, a treaty involving Britain, Portugal, and the Barbary states protected American shipping. When this treaty expired in 1793, Barbary slavers once again seized American ships. Within a year of the expiration of the treaty Barbary states had captured eleven ships and 105 American sailors, which provoked enormous publicity and a political crisis in the United States. More than a year of diplomatic negotiation between the United States and the Barbary states led to a peace treaty, which ransomed the American slaves for $1,156,000, one-sixth of the federal budget at the time.

Peace between the United States and the Barbary states lasted only until 1801, when the king of Tripoli demanded more money. The United States refused additional payment, and the Barbary states began once again seizing ships and enslaving crews. In 1803 the first U.S. military expedition against Algiers ended in disaster. The frigate *Philadelphia* foundered on shoals off

Tripoli. The ship surrendered, and its entire 307-man crew was enslaved. Over the next fifteen months much of the American navy bombarded Tripoli, and a small force of Americans, allied with a substantial number of Muslim and Christian mercenaries, captured the key port of Derna. The two actions combined to force Tripoli's pasha (leader) to seek a peace treaty. Nine U.S. marines were at the center of the invading force that captured Derna, and the Marine Corps still celebrates the victory in the second line of the Marines' Hymn—"to the shores of Tripoli." It was the French who finally ended Barbary attacks on ships and coasts when they invaded and conquered the Barbary kingdoms between 1830 and 1847.

Perhaps the most important conclusion from this exploration of galleys is the intrinsic conservatism of a bounded naval world. We have already seen such conservatism in the long tradition of Nile vessels and the slow development of superb dugout canoes in the Pacific. It was the mixing of maritime traditions, whether by war or trade, that generated new design solutions to old maritime problems.

# *LOS TRES REYES*

On August 4, 1634, the Spanish galleon *Los Tres Reyes* (The Three Kings—named for the three wise men associated with Jesus's nativity) sank either just outside or just within Cartagena harbor on the central coast of what is today Colombia. As shipwrecks go, it was not dramatic. *Los Tres Reyes* may have foundered on the notorious sandbar at the mouth of the harbor or struck a rock. Given that Spanish officials "examined" the wreck, it is likely that the ship was only partly submerged. The documents record no loss of life.[1]

Within a few days, the head of the fleet to which *Los Tres Reyes* belonged, don Antonio de Oquendo, a seasoned and competent commander, declared the ship a complete loss and hired local slaves and boats to ferry everything of value to a warehouse ashore. Colonial bureaucrats carefully logged artillery (twenty-two pieces) and cannonballs, food, medicines, household goods, intact masts, sails (four thousand square yards' worth), cables (over five tons), tackle and rigging (860 pounds). No silver is mentioned in the salvage inventory. In just over a week, slaves (whose masters were paid one to three reals per day) completed the salvage operation.

Three weeks after the wreck, Oquendo opened bidding for the stripped hulk of *Los Tres Reyes* and some salvaged materials. One Captain Agustín de Barona of Cartagena outbid others for the hull, the mainmast, the foremast, and the bowsprit. Others bought the rigging and used sails. The salvage sale brought in about 2,000 ducados, or about one-tenth the cost of the ship.[2] The topmasts and yards were redistributed within the Spanish fleet. Especially welcome would have been the cannon and shot, as galleons often carried less armament than they were in fact designed for. Though it would be months before the Spanish court knew, the once-proud galleon *Los Tres Reyes*—only six years out of the shipyard—was gone.

## The Building of a Fleet

By 1620 (six years before the building of *Los Tres Reyes*) many at the Spanish court realized that the treasure fleet coming from the Indies was dangerously under-defended. The Dutch, rebels from Spanish Hapsburg rule and its implacable enemy, had successfully attacked Spanish ports and were—year after year—looking for and hoping to capture a treasure fleet.

Between the signing of the contract for *Los Tres Reyes* and its five companion galleons in 1625 and their launch in 1628 the Dutch pulled off perhaps the most audacious and damaging attack in Spanish colonial history. Under an admiral named Piet Heyn, the Dutch fleet sighted the Spanish treasure ships near Cuba as they lumbered east toward the Atlantic. The holds of the Spanish ships were, against Spanish naval regulations, so full of the goods of passengers and the captain that crews could not deploy the guns. The Spanish commander, Juan di Benavides y Bazán, made a run for Matanzas Bay (fifty miles east of Havana) in hopes of unloading the treasure. Heyn caught the Spanish in Matanzas Bay and in September 1628 captured the entire fleet before any treasure could be moved. The booty consisted of ninety tons of silver and gold, worth more than 3 million pesos. The Dutch West India Company, private sponsors of Heyn's fleet, paid a 50 percent dividend to its stockholders, and the Spanish government went bankrupt.[3]

## Galleon Design

What sort of a ship was *Los Tres Reyes*?[4] It embodied both a long heritage of ship development and the military imperatives of a century of warfare. Builders and their owners had been searching since the fifteenth century for a ship with the strength and carrying capacity of the broad, virtually flat-bottomed Northern European medieval cog, but with more maneuverability and speed. Builders and owners recognized the need for raised platforms both fore and aft for defense against attack. Cannon were essential, but their successful placement and the solution to the problem of recoil required several decades of experimentation with different sorts of gun carriages. Most successful new ship designs used both the cog's large, centrally placed square sail and a triangular Mediterranean lateen sail on a second mast aft of the mainsail. Correctly set, the lateen sail moved the ship laterally and made it far more maneuverable. A sternpost rudder proved more effective than side rudders.

Ship model of a sixteenth-century Spanish galleon,
Museo Storico Navale di Venezia.

Overall, a century of experimentation and change (roughly 1500–1600) meant that terms used to describe ships (such as hulk, caravel, carrack, nao, and galleon) described different ships in different countries and also shifted from decade to decade. All owners wanted cargo space, speed, maneuverability, and armament, but the primacy of one or another of these factors varied from country to country. The Netherlands, Venice, and Spain, for example, required relatively shallow-draft ships to navigate their shallow harbors at home and attack the shallow harbors of their opponents. These countries realized that they could not get what they needed with a single ship design and moved toward two ship types: cargo ships with capacious hulls and few guns, and warships with narrower, longer profiles for speed, which sacrificed carrying capacity to more guns and reduced hold space.[5] This dilemma, along with this sort of solution, was, as we have seen, independently faced and arrived at by different maritime cultures, such as the various configurations of the Viking longboat; trading galleys versus war galleys in the ancient Mediterranean; and dugouts of war versus dugouts of colonization in the Pacific islands.

These sixteenth-century experiments and the ships they produced were perhaps most critical for Spain. The crown had a vast empire to defend from active attack by the French, Dutch, and English, and valuable trade and tribute to move. By the last decades of the sixteenth century, Spain had arrived at a distinctive galleon ship design, which would carry cargo and wage the king's wars for more than a century.[6] A typical galleon was 125–150 feet long, three and a half times as long as it was wide, with a crew of two hundred, in addition to passengers and about one hundred soldiers. Spanish galleons for the Indies run had a carrying capacity of four hundred to six hundred tons, though a few great galleons had a carrying capacity of a thousand tons or more.[7]

All galleons were, in modern terminology, "frame-built." The ships were constructed on riverbanks from the keel upward, with a framework of scaffolding erected to hold the first ribs in place as they were joined to the keel. Master shipwrights then attached narrow, properly bent members called ribbands from stem to stern, connecting the ribs and setting the shape of the hull. Thereafter, the rest of the ribs, bracing, decks, and planking could be shaped and joined to the framework. In all, *Los Tres Reyes* had thirty-seven ribs and two planked decks, plus unplanked bracing across or athwart the hull between the lower deck and the floor.[8]

These ships generally had two fully planked lower decks, which housed cannon, supplies, and cargo. The most visible and characteristic feature of the galleon was its sides, which actually tapered inward from the waterline so that the lower decks were larger than the main deck. This design was intended to increase cargo space, provide working room for the guns, and lower the center of gravity to make the ship less likely to roll. In this last feature the galleon design rather failed; because of its relatively short length and broad beam, the galleon was notorious for pitching and rolling, just like its predecessor the cog.

Above the main deck towered three aft decks, which housed artillery. The forward decks above the main deck were generally smaller and lower. Spanish galleons had a mainmast amidships and a large foremast, both of which carried square sails, and one or two smaller masts aft, which held triangular lateen sails used in steering. The bowsprit carried a trapezoidal spritsail. The stern of the ship had an almost flat profile, in contrast to the rounded, bulbous rear profile of the earlier medieval cog.[9]

The important point here is that the galleon evolved as a ship that merged Northern European and Mediterranean maritime shipbuilding traditions into the first truly worldwide design for a workhorse, all-purpose ship of trade and warfare. These were the ships commissioned by the crown and built by private individuals, not only in Spain and Portugal, but also in Central and South America and the Philippines.

## Building a Galleon

The records of *Los Tres Reyes* begin with an offer by one Martín de Arana to build a fleet of six galleons for the Spanish crown. The royal bureaucracy took depositions from twenty-four witnesses. All attested to the nobility of the Arana family, its long tradition of shipbuilding and ship ownership in the Basque port of Bilbao, and Arana's prior service to the king. As an ambitious noble of middle rank, Arana had both the wealth to finance in the short term the building of such a fleet, and the obligation to serve the crown by doing so.[10]

The Bilbao shipyard, though capable of producing big galleons, was hardly a sophisticated facility. Ships were built on temporary platforms supported by wood pilings driven into the muddy riverbank. The only permanent structures were sheds for materials. Bilbao, nevertheless, had the important resources to build galleons. Nearby were forests of oak from which the master shipbuilder personally selected trunks for the keel and ribs and oversaw their stacking and drying. The Bilbao region also produced iron for nails and other fittings. The port was also able to access crucial shipbuilding materials that Spain did not produce, such as sails from northern France and masts and caulk from the Baltic. Bilbao was, however, an agriculturally poor region and grew few provisions useful for a sea voyage. Wheat for biscuits, along with wine, olive oil, salt fish and pork, cheese, chickpeas, and rice, all had to be brought in from other regions, such as Navarre, Andalusia, and France.[11] One of the few places in Spain where one finds women in maritime-related employment at the time of *Los Tres Reyes* was in baking imported flour into hardtack for ship's provisions. Six of the sixteen professional owner/bakers of hardtack in Bilbao were women.[12]

By the time of *Los Tres Reyes*, the Spanish crown had sponsored three conferences of nautical experts to discuss design modifications, for example in the ratio of length to width in galleons, which might make the galleons faster and possibly pitch and roll less. Ship captains and shipbuilders argued for days and produced voluminous testimony on whether longer craft would "hog"—that is, droop in the bow and stern—and whether longer length would be more maneuverable because the spritsail would be farther from the rudder. It should be noted that none of these proposed modifications were in any way radical design changes. What was being discussed was a ship a foot or two longer or with half a foot of increased freeboard. Also discussed were modifications of the trading ship, which would make it more rapidly convertible to a war vessel. The results of these conferences became official policy of galleon design, codified as the Regulations of 1618, which included many required specifications, such as the ratio of length to beam, depth of hold, width of floor, curvature of ribs (which determined the capacity of the hold), and size and proportion of sails.[13]

By 1634, the crown had commissioned so many galleons that the basic size and lines were reproducible from the Regulations of 1618 merely by specifying the tonnage. The crown contract with Martín de Arana specified two ships of five hundred *toneladas* (a Spanish measure of both weight and volume, the same as the ancient French "sea ton") and about five hundred modern tons capacity, two of four hundred toneladas, and two of three hundred toneladas.[14] Arana offered to build the ships for thirty-two ducados per tonelada. The crown haggled him down to thirty ducados.[15]

Work began in May 1626. Arana's crew of one hundred to two hundred workers laid the keels of the two largest ships simultaneously. Construction of the other four galleons began soon after, all under the watchful eye of the inspector of ships for the north coast of Spain. The crown released payment for the ships slowly and fitfully, forcing Arana to spend large amounts of his own money to keep the project moving.

Six months from the start of construction all six vessels were well along. A royal inspection team arrived, which included four master carpenters who swore under oath that the work was well executed. A month later the king ordered the general surveyor of armadas to measure the ships' tonnage and determine whether they conformed to regulation. Finally, in late March an inspector arrived and declared the work of excellent quality and within the design ratios set by the Regulations of 1618. He recorded that the masts and the caulk were already in storage; the French sails were expected any day. Arana remained unpaid and unhappy. Only 23,000 ducados had been released from the crown treasury, but he had spent more than 70,000 ducados on the six vessels.

Although Arana rightly projected that the ships would be ready for fitting in June, various disputes between him and the crown representatives delayed completion. Who was responsible for furnishing the decorative bunting, paint, gold leaf, running lanterns, locks, and hatch hardware? Who was to rig the ship, and where was it to be done? Who was responsible for spare sails, topsails, and rigging?

In the winter of 1627–1628 Arana had assembled much of the outstanding ship fittings, only to have them commandeered by a Channel squadron that arrived in Bilbao in such bad shape that it barely made it to port. Arana surrendered his lines, tar, caulk, and spare wood to refit the Channel fleet and set about replacing the sails and other materials.[16] *Los Tres Reyes* and the rest of the fleet were not fitted, crewed, and ready for service until the summer of 1628.[17] They were turned over to the crown less than a month before the Dutch fleet under Piet Heyn captured the entire silver fleet at Matanzas Bay, Cuba. Arana eventually received his money from the crown for the galleons and a few years later received the lucrative royal appointment that motivated the building of the galleons.

### The Spanish in the Atlantic

Spanish shipyards built galleons like *Los Tres Reyes* primarily to navigate the shipping lanes to the New World, which were the basis of the empire. Within a few decades following Columbus's discoveries, ship captains and the crown understood the environmental imperatives of the seas they had conquered. Ships needed to avoid both the summer Caribbean hurricanes and the winter storms on the Atlantic, reducing the safe sailing season to the spring and the fall. By the time of *Los Tres Reyes*, Spanish maritime authorities had had more than a century to work out an optimum pattern, which consisted of one trade fleet sailing from Spain to the Indies in May and a different fleet returning from the New World to Spain in August. Each fleet wintered in the Indies, thus spending approximately a year in port and three to four months sailing.[18]

Experience had also taught the best route in both directions. To the New World from Cádiz the fleet first sailed southwest to the coast of Africa, then turned west to the Canary Islands. A west-by-southwest heading picked up the reliable trade winds, which carried the fleet to the Leeward Islands. From there, the fleet set a northwesterly course for Cuba and Veracruz. A typical voyage from Cádiz to Veracruz was about forty-eight hundred miles and took about eight weeks.

The return voyage out of Veracruz in August crossed the Caribbean via Cuba, then passed through the Bahama Channel, full of hidden rocks and narrow passages and the most dangerous portion of the voyage in both directions. Clear of the Bahama Channel the fleet turned northeast, picking up strong north winds. The fleet took advantage of the reliable eastward-flowing trade winds to make for the Azores, then on to Cádiz.

The run in both directions was, in fact, considerably more dangerous than this predictable route suggests. Often, the silver and the trade goods had not arrived in August, and the fleet did not leave Veracruz until late fall. Nevertheless, with recurring financial crises in Spain, the crown desperately needed the yearly influx of silver, forcing ships to sail outside the favorable season. Late sailing dates avoided the hurricane season but put the fleet in the path of storms in the Bahama Channel and, even worse, storms in the North Atlantic.

We might imagine that the fleet was easy prey to pirates. After all, the route—year after year—was exactly the same. Since it was known where the fleet assembled, it was only a matter of time before it loaded and showed up along the route. Then, the pirates might get lucky and weather might disperse the fleet for easy pickings.

In fact, this romantic picture of a single pirate ship attacking and boarding a Spanish treasure ship simply never happened after 1600. In part this was because military ships like *Los Tres Reyes*, which carried treasure, operated in substantial fleets and outgunned any single pirate ship. They also operated on a tighter schedule than trading fleets and were likely to be in the Caribbean and the Atlantic at the most favorable times for crossing and less likely to be dispersed by storms.[19]

Besides Piet Heyn's capture of the fleet in 1628, only one other capture of a silver-bearing Spanish vessel occurred in the seventeenth century. In 1657 a British squadron captured two silver ships as they approached Cádiz. The squadron then destroyed the rest of the fleet in the Canaries, where they had taken shelter.[20] Overall, many more treasure galleons were lost to storms and wrecks than were ever lost to pirates.[21]

## Silver and the Spanish Trading World

*Los Tres Reyes* was part of a fleet guarding the silver coming from the New World to Spain. Why, then, was there a "silver fleet" at all? Following the Spanish conquest of central Mexico (1521) and Peru (1536), soldiers and priests fanned out to explore the land that they had conquered. In 1545 a native discovered silver on the surface of a remote mountain in Peru known as Potosi. The find was, by far, the richest silver strike in the world at the time. As the Spanish forced local labor to drive shafts into the mountain, they discovered that some veins contained 50 percent pure silver. The Spanish were doubly fortunate that only seven hundred miles away they discovered mercury, which was essential to extract the silver from the ore.[22] Production reached 2 million pesos within four decades of the original strike. At the foot of the mountain the boom town of Potosi reached a population of 120,000, the largest Spanish-speaking city in the world at the time.[23]

Only a year after the Potosi strike, natives showed soldiers and priests silver ore in a remote location three hundred miles northwest of Mexico City. The mines were developed along the same lines as Potosi. The silver was, however, more dispersed than the single mine in Peru, and over the years the Mexican mines produced a smaller quantity of silver than Potosi.

Under Spanish law, the crown owned mineral rights to its colonized lands but did not finance or operate the mines. Private individuals and combines developed the mines and paid the crown one-fifth of the silver in taxes. Overall, thousands of tons of silver entered Spain from the New World in the century following the Potosi and the Mexican silver strikes.[24]

The New World silver hugely augmented a quite limited Spanish export economy of the sixteenth century. Spain's hot, dry climate affected its agricultural productivity and limited its exports to wool and wool cloth, wine, olive oil, and some iron. Without an industrial base, Spain imported textiles, linens, lead, tin, wax, cheese, and dried fish from England, hardware and paper from England and Holland, masts and naval stores from the Baltic countries and Scandinavia, grain from France, and sugar from Portugal's possessions in Brazil. Spain always ran a trade deficit, which was covered by the gold and silver shipments from Mexico and Peru.[25]

## A World of Maritime War

The silver and gold from the New World helped create the most far-flung and richest empire in the world. Most of this wealth was spent in war with Spain's rivals, which started in the mid-1500s and continued on and off for a century. Spain had had some signal successes in the half century before 1600, such as the pivotal naval victory over the Ottoman navy at the Lepanto (1571), the joining of the thrones of Spain and Portugal into a globalized empire (1581), the creation of port defenses and a strong Spanish fleet resulting in suppression of serious piracy in the Caribbean, and the forging of a broad military alliance, which included the Hapsburg possessions in southern Holland and Italy, the Catholic kingdoms along the Rhine, and more loosely Hapsburg Austria and Catholic Poland. There had also been significant failures: the defeat of the vast Spanish armada constructed for the invasion of England (1588), and Spain's failure to suppress the rebellion in the Low Countries, resulting in the successful breakaway of the Republic of the Seven United Netherlands (the Dutch republic, 1581).

The Spanish government's entire focus was on how to pay for war with its enemies, the anti-Catholic and anti-Hapsburg kingdoms of England and Sweden, and rebellious Holland. It is almost unimaginable how much Spain spent on its wars on sea and land. To crew and supply a naval ship like *Los Tres Reyes* cost each year approximately three times the amount to build the ship.[26] Spain maintained dozens of such ships in fleets in Europe and Asia, as well as the Indies. Military deployment was hard on these galleons, which had an expected service life of only ten years, with cleaning and refitting every year. On land the war with Holland cost Spain about 3.5 million ducats a year (perhaps $125 million, in today's dollars).[27] Even the income from the silver fleet could not sustain this level of crown expenses. The king and his advisers generated scheme after scheme of creative financing, such as hypothecating loans against future agricultural taxes, debasing the currency, raising existing taxes, and levying new taxes.[28]

The focus on war exacerbated serious structural problems in the Spanish economy. Faced with a crushing tax burden, peasants fled to the cities, and agricultural production steadily declined through the 1600s. Unlike the cities of Northern Europe, Spanish cites were merely administrative and courtly centers, largely without innovation or manufacture. The courtier class invested in estates and colonial ventures, not industry.[29] Peasants thus found few opportunities in Spanish cities, and many emigrated to the New World. Spain's population—decimated by starvation, plague, and emigration—steadily declined in the 1600s. By the 1640s, onerous taxation and economic stagnation produced revolt in Catalonia and the successful secession of Portugal.

The overwhelming concern with war against Spain's enemies also produced policies with negative consequences. The crown, for example, promulgated many decrees prohibiting trade with Spain's enemies, which made traders into smugglers and imports into contraband. Spain could not survive without grain from France, ship's masts from the Baltic, dried fish from Scandinavia, and manufactured goods from Holland and England. The bribery required to import these necessities corrupted the entire Spanish government and, in effect, made these items substantially more expensive.[30]

These prohibitions also widened the theater of war. The Dutch, prohibited from buying spices in the wholesale markets of Seville, challenged the Portuguese for control of spices at their source in Southeast Asia. In 1595 the first Dutch fleet arrived in Southeast Asia, consisting of four ships totaling about one thousand tons. Only 80 of the total 249 men of the crews survived, and one of the ships was lost, but the venture was a financial success and initiated repeated Dutch incursions into the spice-growing islands of Southeast Asia.[31]

A young trader from Bruges named Jacques de Coutre, who had gone to the East Indies to make his fortune, witnessed a naval battle in Manila Bay between the Dutch and the Spanish (under a common crown with the Portuguese at that point). De Coutre, whose sympathies lay with the Spanish, wrote the following account (in Spanish):

> While I was there, it so happened that a Dutch carrack [*nao* in the text] and patache sailed up to the anchorage. They stayed there for some 20 days impeding the entry of the baxeles [indigenous craft]. While this was taking place, the governor, Don Francisco Tello [de Guzmán], ordered a carrack [the *San Antonio*], a frigate [a *galizabra* in the Spanish text] and a patache to be prepared aboard which 500 Spaniards sailed, most of them were hidalgos and leading figures. They were

commanded by Doctor Antonio de Morga, who knew more about letters than arms.

[De Coutre's journal recounts that the Dutch engaged the Spanish in Manila harbor with the wind at their backs. The Spanish carrack chased the Dutch carrack to the lee of an island and boarded it. When the Spanish frigate arrived, the Dutch carrack apparently surrendered, though the Dutch patache fled. When the Spanish commander left for his own ship to pursue the Dutch patache, the Dutch retook their vessel and fired into the *San Antonio*, to which it was moored.]

When the Dutch general saw that Captain Alcega, our admiral, had left, he once again began to fire his cannons, even though our men were aboard his vessel, to such an extent that he managed to create gaping holes in the carrack of our general, Doctor Antonio de Morga. Since the latter was not a military man, as soon as he saw that his carrack was taking on water he gave orders to cut the ropes with which the two ships were tied together. When the ropes were cut, the carrack sank and everyone on board drowned; only Doctor Antonio de Morga and six men escaped on a coir mattress, which does not absorb water. The loss was deeply felt since leading figures of Manila had been killed in this incident. As soon as the Dutch general found his ship had been cut loose and our commander's vessel was sinking, he even stopped to kill those who were swimming to stay afloat; then they raised their sails and went away. Captain Alcega captured the patache [the *Eendracht*] and brought [it in] with 18 Dutchmen, 13 of whom were garrotted.[32]

Even more interesting than De Coutre's description of the battle in Manila harbor are four memorials he wrote to the Spanish monarch around 1625. He was all too aware that, following a humiliating defeat and armistice with Holland in 1609, the Spanish crown recognized that it could no longer simultaneously defend both the Americas and the Portuguese monopoly in the East Indies. Spain had suffered one defeat after another, such as the losses of Malacca and Aceh, the important port on the northwest tip of Sumatra. His first memorial begins as follows:

If Your Majesty were to dispatch 40 galleons to India with Castilians and Portuguese, like the armada that Your Majesty sent to Brazil, well equipped with men and artillery and good gunners and munitions and sufficient supplies, and if in the next year 20 galleons were sent in the same way, the aforementioned Estado [the Portuguese colonial monopoly in the East Indies] can be remedied in the following manner, because the rebels are firmly entrenched there and have many ships and very strong fortresses.

De Coutre proposed nothing less than all-out war, to be waged in the Southeast Asian islands, including conquest of indigenous mainland states and the retaking of Malacca. His strategic vision was indeed far larger than Southeast Asia, as his memorial indicates. He proposed naval attacks on Dutch fortified positions on both the east and west coasts of India and carrying the war to the Persian Gulf and the mouth of the Red Sea. His cognitive geography, which strategically united the Spanish interests in Southeast Asia, India, and the Persian Gulf, is a stunning display of the integration of three maritime worlds: the Indian Ocean, the Bay of Bengal, and the Java Sea, which may have long been joined by trade but not by political, military, or strategic thinking.[33] This vision was, of course, never to be realized by a Spain that had huge military commitments at home and declining colonial income.

Spain's prohibitions on trading with the enemy also profoundly affected the distribution of trade among the ports of Spain and Portugal. Seville desperately clung to its trading monopoly with the Indies, but crown agents were everywhere, searching for contraband. Coastal ports, such as Cádiz, were located far from crown control and were quite ready to import contraband manufactures and reexport them to the Indies in foreign ships.[34]

Overall, the Spanish crown failed to recognize that its colonies had shifted from exclusively a mining economy to agriculture and commodity production. They no longer needed the olive oil and wool that Spain produced for export, but instead required iron implements for an expanding agricultural economy and fabrics to clothe their immigrants, neither of which Spain produced. Since Spain legally and militarily forbid other countries from trading with Spanish colonies, manufacturing countries such as the Netherlands and Britain colluded with smaller, less policed ports of Portugal to circumvent these Spanish regulations. British and Dutch manufactured goods were unloaded as imports to Portugal and then reexported in Portuguese ships to the Spanish colonies. The officials of the port received taxes and bribes, the Portuguese captains had cargo to ship, and the British and Dutch had a ready market for their cargoes. It is estimated that the reexport trade of the smaller ports of Portugal cut Spain's trade with New Spain by half.[35]

Portugal, though formally part of the Spanish monarchy, had its own government and controlled its ports. Dutch manufactures, particularly cloth, formed much of Portugal's exports to Brazil. Dutch ships also took over much of Portugal's imports from Brazil, carrying sugar and dyestuffs back to the home country.[36]

Economically, the center of the Spanish Empire had shifted from the home country to the colonies. Nowhere was this clearer than in the decrease of shipments of silver back to Spain. As the colonies became more agricultural, their administrations necessarily became more complex and more expensive. The "surplus" of silver above the costs of administration available to send back to Spain steadily shrank through the 1600s, from 31.5 million pesos in 1595, with a couple of good years in between, to 3.3 million in 1656.[37]

### The Galleon in the World

In the larger picture, galleons like *Los Tres Reyes* embodied four important shifts in world history, all signaling the development of a much more integrated maritime world.

First, galleons formed the first uniformly built armed trade fleet that operated across the entire world. Galleons of Spain/Portugal made yearly scheduled runs between the Caribbean and the home country, up and down the west coast of South and Central America and through the brutal storms off Cape Horn, back and forth across the Pacific to the Philippines and China, and to and from Southeast Asia around and the Cape of Good Hope to Portugal. In spite of losses to storms, shoals, and rocks, the galleons carried the richest cargos ever assembled with a quite remarkable degree of predictability. The ships thus allowed an astonishing reach for the Spanish crown, in spite of the home country having little to export and lagging seriously in manufacturing.

Second, galleons participated in the first truly global maritime conflict. Portuguese galleons fought the Dutch for control of Southeast Asia and the China trade. Simultaneously Spanish galleons fought the English privateers in the Caribbean and off the eastern coast of South America. Spanish fleets fought English, French, and Dutch fleets off the coasts of Europe.

Third, galleons were the workhorse trade ships that made possible one of the largest rapid migrations in human history. Between 1540 and 1600 more than 250,000 Spanish and Portuguese migrated to make their fortune in Peru and Mexico, seeking out the remote silver mines. Galleons carried everything that made the mining possible, as well as the clothes, furniture, and women of the roaring boomtown of Potosi.

Fourth, the hundreds of tons of silver and gold that the galleons transported had short-term and long-term economic effects. In Europe the influx of precious metals set off a price inflation that lasted more than a century, with winners and losers, as is the case with all price inflations. The steady supply of silver and gold stimulated banking institutions, which were always ready to provide profitable loans to the chronically overspending Spanish crown. Thus, much of the silver and gold merely passed through Spain, paying for the troops and supplies for the wars with Holland and England and buying imported manufactured goods that Spain did not produce. Following the silver leads to unexpected destinations. The British, who produced nothing that India wanted to buy, used Spanish silver to pay for spices and cloth that it brought to Europe. In similar fashion, large quantities of Spanish silver ended up in China to pay for porcelains and silks. The galleons of the silver fleet, thus, centrally served the emerging world economic system.

# 11

# HMS *VICTORY*

On October 3, 1744, a strong British fleet sailed north across the English Channel, returning from breaking a French blockade of Gibraltar. The fleet had seized several enemy merchantmen and escorted valuable supplies to the British fleet in the Mediterranean. The *Victory* was the flagship of the fleet and was the largest and most heavily gunned ship in service at the time. (It is important to note that several Royal Navy ships carried the name *Victory*. This chapter's ship was not the much more famous *Victory* that served as Nelson's flagship at Trafalgar. That *Victory*—the last to carry the name—survived far longer than the *Victory* of this chapter.)

Sir John Balchan, the admiral, was a respected, experienced captain, then seventy-six years old. During the day and into the night a huge North Sea storm dispersed the fleet. Many ships lost masts, sustained damage, and were driven far off course. The ships limped into Plymouth harbor during the next week. The *Victory* was last seen on October 4 but never reached the shelter of Plymouth harbor. It went down with more than one thousand men on board.

Two weeks later British newspapers reported that some oars painted with the word "Victory" and a trunk belonging to one of the marines aboard the ship had washed up on one of the Channel Islands just off the coast of France.[1] In the months following the loss of the *Victory* a review board took depositions from a number of inhabitants of the island, as well as the light-house keeper of the infamous rocks known as the Casquets (or Caskets), of the island's west coast. Several local people reported that they had heard big guns firing in the night, signaling a naval ship in distress, but that the seas were so rough they could not launch rescue boats. No bodies of the crew ever washed up. The review board concluded that the ship had been driven onto the Casquets and broken up. There was some suggestion that the ship was improperly designed and could not survive such a storm. Neither the

*The loss of the HMS* Victory, *1744*, painting by Peter Monamy
(1681–1749), National Maritime Museum, Greenwich.

admiral nor the captain was censured, and the review board sadly concluded that the storm had simply overwhelmed the ship.[2]

The fate of the *Victory* remained one of the sea's many mysteries until 2008. That summer a commercial treasure-seeking ship belonging to Odyssey Marine (based in Florida) surveyed portions of the western English Channel with side-scanning radar and a magnetometer. Preliminary imaging located a wooden wreck with anchors and cannon one hundred meters below the surface, far too deep for divers to explore. The crew of the *Odyssey Explorer* sent down a remotely operated vehicle (ROV) to examine the site. Five dives in May and June established the presence of many cannon, though trawler nets had badly disturbed the wreck above the seafloor.

Some 2,574 square meters of the wreck site have been surveyed, revealing substantial archaeological deposits. The most highly conspicuous manifestations are the forty-one bronze cannon, which include bores ranging between four and seven inches in diameter, corresponding to six- and forty-two-pounder guns. The latter were functionally restricted to the Royal Navy's largest warships, first-rates. Elaborate royal arms of King George I and George II, as well as the foundry dates of 1726 visible on the forty-two-pounder cannon and 1734 on the twelve-pounders, place the wreck site precisely within the time frame of HMS *Victory*'s construction and operation.

What appears to be the lower end of the rudder is either protected by or repaired with a square casing of lead. The condition of the wood is extremely poor, with surfaces eroded to the extent that the rudder resembles delaminated plywood. Human bones have been recorded on the seafloor.[3]

Eighteen dives of the ROV in the fall established that important portions of the ship were still buried. The ROV cleared small amounts of sediment from the wreck, locating a copper cauldron, bricks from the cookstove, large anchors, the much-deteriorated keel, planking, and rarely found stone wheels for grinding irregularities off shot and sharpening sabers. Excavations were halted in any areas containing human remains, and the bones were reburied. The team photographed the forty-one cannon on the seafloor, and raised two of them. Cast of bronze rather than iron, the cannon lying loose on the seafloor constitute the largest collection of bronze naval ordnance in the world. As the dive report states, "With their elegant dolphins and intricate cast design and royal arms, all are exquisite expressions of bronze craftsmanship." The ROV technician Olaf Diekhoff designed and fabricated a custom tool to measure precisely the bore of the cannon, which proved a crucial piece of evidence in identifying the ship.[4]

After the fall dive season of 2008, the hunt for the ship's identity shifted from the English Channel to British naval archives. The researchers discovered in gunnery tables of the period that the seven-inch bore of the cannon on the seabed matched a forty-two-pound cannon exactly. The dates found on the guns and the royal crests narrowed the search. Only the *Victory* had bronze cannon of this caliber at this time. The wreck located by the *Odyssey Explorer* was confirmed to be the *Victory*, but it was found in the open sea more than one hundred kilometers (62 miles) west of the Casquet rocks. It suddenly made sense that no bodies had ever washed shore. The ship sank in deep water, leaving no survivors and virtually no floating wreckage.

## Ships of the Line

What was a ship of the line? In the tradition of Spanish galleons (such as *Los Tres Reyes* of chapter 10), these war vessels concentrated all their firepower in the sidewalls of the ship. They had virtually no capacity to fire forward from the bow, and severely limited capacity to fire aft from the stern. The key tactic that evolved for such ships consisted of assembling them in a long bow-to-stern line, their guns facing a similarly arrayed enemy. The two lines might use the wind to close on one another or remain at a distance and fire at each other. The goal was to outmaneuver the enemy so as to bring as many as possible of one's own guns to bear and minimize the enemy fire. As long as the lines remained intact, naval engagements rarely yielded a decisive victory.

It is perhaps worth noting that the strategy that underlay ships in a line was quite parallel to developing infantry tactics on land. Armies faced each other in lines. The man at the front of a column or rank fired his weapon, turned, and moved to the back of his column or rank to reload as the next man in line stepped up to shoot. Lethality depended on rate of fire, not accuracy. As infantry training and technology developed, the time required to reload steadily dropped. Consequently lines that formerly had required six or even eight men to complete reloading by the time a man reached the front of his column subsequently required only three men to complete loading. Lines of infantry thus became shallower, two or three men deep, and stretched out into long, long opposing lines. As in naval warfare, outflanking an enemy provided an advantage in the amount of firepower that could be brought to bear.

For more than two centuries, from about 1650 to 1850, these core ideas of naval engagement and sea power yielded similar ships across Europe. All ships of the line had three masts. Their guns fired out of gun ports. The ships all had a heavy stern rudder attached to an upright sternpost canted ten to fifteen degrees from the vertical, a design that proved superior to any other arrangement. The stern of these ships was designed to get water to the

Model of the HMS *Victory*, constructed when the ship
was in service. It was likely used in the training of young officers.
National Maritime Museum, Greenwich.

rudder quickly and efficiently. In the second decade of the eighteenth century the steering wheel rapidly replaced the tiller on larger ships. How high
a man could reach and how low he could pull set the diameter of steering
wheels at about five feet.[5]

The competing European countries—France, England, Denmark, Holland, Spain, and Portugal—all rated naval ships by the total number of
their guns (such as 24, 32, 44, 64, 74, 80, 84, 90, 100) and the weight of the
ball they shot, from eight-pound light cannons up to forty-two-pound very
heavy naval ordnance. None of the powers rated their ships for speed or
maneuverability.

A flagship of a fleet typically housed one hundred guns on three full
decks. Early ships of the line such as *Los Tres Reyes* had towers both fore
and aft armed with smaller-caliber guns. Over the century between *Los Tres*

*Reyes* and the *Victory* these towers shrank and eventually disappeared as the central space between them was filled in to become a third gun deck. Nineties (ships with ninety guns) were slightly scaled down version of hundreds, with less luxurious space for officers. Eighties were 'twixt and 'tween, with two full decks of guns and some combination of guns on the main deck and in the poop. Seventies and sixties had two decks of guns, were relatively lightly armed, and intended for some speed.[6]

## Strategy of Naval Warfare

The maritime wars of 1650–1700 were mainly between the English and the Dutch and were largely confined to the northern seas of Europe. Standard strategy placed a naval blockade outside enemy ports and attempted to punish the enemy by cutting off food and other crucial supplies. Again, this sort of strategy had its parallel on land. Armies surrounded and laid siege to cities in hopes of either taking them or starving them. Naval blockades were generally limited. Nobody wanted to be on the North Sea in the fogs and storms of winter.[7] The situation was similar on land. Generals were well aware of how difficult it was to maintain an army in temporary siege quarters outside a besieged city.

These two aspects of war—land and sea—were in constant interaction. Two of the main functions of ships of the line were to escort supply ships in support of land armies and either to maintain or break blockades. An attempt by one of the combatants to break out of a blockade triggered many naval battles of the period.

## Ships of the Line in Peace and War

The two centuries of designing and building ships of the line had a distinct rhythm. Preparation for war and actual war generally triggered sharply increased ship production, refitting and rebuilding, experiments in design, and improved technology. Periods of peace saw decommissioning of ships, little maintenance, and ossified design. It is worth noting that a ship of the line cost almost as much to supply and crew per year as the ship cost to build.

After 1714, France largely withdrew from naval competition with Britain for control of the seas. During the ensuing period of peace the British Admiralty promulgated unchanging formal design rules for various classes of naval vessels. (The reader might recall that sixty years earlier, in the period of *Los Tres Reyes*, the Spanish crown similarly generated unchanging formal design rules for galleons; a ship was ordered merely by tonnage.) From 1699 to 1739, the design, construction, and rebuilding of the navy in Britain was institutionally controlled in a way that largely precluded any experimentation in ship design. Older ships were "rebuilt" along much the same lines, with no new experiments.

These fixed rules for ship design and construction made estimating easy for shipbuilders and budgeting simple for the relevant government bureaucrats. Captains and officers generally welcomed fixed rules, since they included generous cabin space and accommodations for officers and made training of the crew easier.

Britain codified a stubby 3:1 ratio of length to breadth for its ships of the line. Both in the two-deck smaller version and in the relatively few three-deck flagships, the Admiralty knew it was getting maximum firepower from the high, squat design while keeping costs down through standardization and competitive bidding. Parliament wanted to minimize naval expenditure, as the largest single item of the national budget.[8]

Standardization and competitive bidding, however, had their own problems. Nowhere in the bureaucracy, from the Admiralty down through the Naval Board, was there adequate expert oversight of the materials used in the actual construction. The Admiralty and the Naval Board were political appointments; loyalty and service to the king were more important than technical naval expertise.[9] With competitive bidding, shipbuilders had every incentive to cut corners. Only years after launch would the results of poor-quality timber or low-grade caulk show up.[10]

Overall, the number of the larger ships of the line remained about the same, as did the tonnage. Crew increased substantially in all the larger ships of the line — for example, from 780 to 850 men in the largest of the ships of the line, though the numbers could and did go higher with the addition of marine troops for shore assaults. The life of a ship of the line even in peacetime was only about ten to fifteen years. After that it needed a full rebuilding, including stripping the planking and replacement of many timbers. Such routine rebuilding consumed much of the naval budget in the 1714–1745 period.[11]

The mandated design of British ships of the line had problems. The short, wide, stubby design made these ships poor sailors, even in good weather. They handled particularly badly in stormy conditions. And they were slow, though the large ones were about as fast as any enemy's comparable ship. Change did come, though slowly. The Admiralty withdrew the forty-two-pound heavy cannon from its ships. The ball was just too heavy for a man to handle and muzzle-load.[12] Another consistent problem was "over-gunning"—that is, installing more guns and heavier guns than the ship was designed for. The result was a top-heavy and dangerously unstable ship. Equally serious was the problem of "hogging," caused by reduced buoyancy in the bow and stern. In such a large ship, the result could mean a ship drooped by as much as two feet at either end. Heavy seas were far more likely to break over the deck, and the ship was less likely to rise out of such seas.[13] (It was not until the end of the eighteenth century that internal diagonal bracing solved the problem of hogging.)

Any navy of this period operated with many more small ships than ships-of-the-line. These included frigates for long-distance cruising (often chasing pirates), ketches, sloops, brigantines, and corvettes. Some of these smaller ships were used for shore patrol. Others were crucial components of fleets, such as message carriers. Bomb- or fire-ships were used to finish off badly damaged opposing ships of the line that could not make sail.[14]

Though the fixed designs of 1700–1750 (including the *Victory*) did not solve the problems of poor sailing and hogging in ships of the line, the period was not entirely stagnant. There were improvements to gun carriages and systems for absorbing recoil. These decades also saw the invention of a new quadrant, an improved instrument for calculating how far above or below the equator the ship was located.[15] Also of assistance to navigation was the construction and manning of numerous lighthouses around the coast of Britain and on the northern coast of Europe.

In 1745 the Admiralty generated yet another round of "establishment" rules for the building of each class of naval vessel. The new rules specified length, breadth, draft, gun placement, gun size, overhead height of decks, magazine placement, and much more. Once again this conservative approach hamstrung all experimentation, as all ships had to conform to class rules. Not until 1755, when the last of the aged members of the Admiralty board finally retired, was it possible to experiment with new ship designs.[16]

### The First Multi-ocean War

Through the 1730s and '40s Britain's absolute dominance of the seas weakened. France began building a ship that was not within the parameters of the

British naval codified rules. It carried eighty-four guns and was anything but short and stubby. The French ships were longer and larger than the British seventies and turned out to sail better in fair winds as well as storms. They were faster and more maneuverable than British ships of the line.[17]

Through 1754 England and France drifted toward a war that was already in progress away from Europe. One theater of conflict was the east coast of India. The French had much success, attacking far inland from coastal ports and allying with native kings. The Admiralty sent a fleet of six ships to Madras to reinforce the tenuous British position there.

A year later Britain and France were at war. Naval fleets from Britain and France maneuvered around each other on the east coast of Canada. The British captured two French ships of the line, but the others arrived safely at Quebec. Other French ships ran a British blockade and returned safely to France. Fleets from both sides returned to Canada in the following spring. Later in the war British naval forces built small ships in upstate New York and attacked Quebec across the St. Lawrence River.

Even before the war with France was formally declared, British ships had brought war to the west coast of India. Six British ships of the line destroyed the naval forces and forts of one Tulaji Angria, whose father had been the commander of the fleet of the Marathas, a strong regional power. His son had gone freelance, and the Marathas wanted him defeated as much as did the British, who traded along the coast.

In 1757, British ships and their troops moved north from Madras to Calcutta. The marines from the ships formed an important component of the British forces that defeated the Nawab of Bengal. In the same campaign British naval forces expelled the French from their trading station in Bengal. In 1758 the British fleet fought two major engagements with French ships of the line off the southeast coast of India. They also raised a French blockade of Madras.

In the Caribbean the war began early with the French planning an attack on Jamaica, but a British ship stationed there thwarted it. The British harried French merchant shipping. By 1758 the British stationed a fleet at the Leeward Islands, which included fourteen ships of the line and carried more than a thousand guns. The fleet eventually took the ports and the island of Martinique and prevented further French attacks in the Caribbean.

The British even sent a small fleet against French slaving ports on the west coast of Africa in 1758, followed by a much larger fleet the next year.

The important point here is that this mid-century war between Britain and France was fought in the North and South Atlantic, the Indian Ocean, the Caribbean, the Mediterranean, and the Bay of Bengal. Early in the war, twenty-seven of the twenty-eight large ships of the line patrolled the English Channel and the Bay of Biscay. A small fleet of eight ships patrolled the Mediterranean. Within a few years the colonial adventures, which had begun with smaller ships, escalated into full campaigns that drew large ships of the line and their ancillary smaller ships away from patrolling Europe. Some of the major battles in European waters were fought over blockaded money and materials intended to pursue the war in the colonies.

Half a world away from the *Victory*'s sinking, naval battles between France and England on the east coast of India played out exactly as the training and experience of the opposing commanders dictated. In the fall of 1759, for example, the French fleet had completed loading of necessary supplies and materials at Mauritius and Bourbon (Réunion) and embarked for the east coast of India. A British scout ship sighted the French fleet not far from Madras, and the British fleet set off in pursuit. The winds dropped, and the British ships lost sight of the French fleet. The British commander chose to sail north to the French port of Pondicherry and engaged the French fleet there the following day. As the naval historian W. L. Clowes put it, "The tactics of the day present no features of special interest"; the twenty-two ships of the two fleets formed up in opposing lines and blasted away at each other with a total of more than twelve hundred guns. It is a statement of the inadequacy of aiming and ranging at the time that in spite of six hours of cannonades, the French commander, late in the day, was able to break off the battle and sail back to Pondicherry with his entire fleet. The British ships were too damaged to pursue.

Though the battle seems to have had a textbook dynamic, with neither side decisively winning, this was actually not the case. The French fleet had taken almost fifteen hundred casualties and had could not readily replace them. The British settled into a blockade outside Pondicherry and challenged the French to leave the harbor. The French stayed in port, aware that four more British ships of the line were en route to reinforce the India fleet. When the British lifted the blockade of Pondicherry to restock supplies at Madras, the French fleet—anticipating no reinforcements—sailed away. This campaign ensured that England, not France, would be the dominant European power in India.

Much more than warships had become standardized and globalized in the middle decades of the eighteenth century. Commanders of fleets preferred certain kinds of offshore locations for engagements, such as a headland to protect one flank of the line, and even better if the headland contained a fort with cannon to rake the opposing fleet. A predictable offshore wind gave an attack advantage to the inshore fleet. Predictable morning fog might give a tactical advantage to a fleet already in position. The duties and responsibilities of the officers and crew had become so standardized that they could be discussed equally easily in Calcutta, Halifax, or London. Failure of a commander to fight according to accepted tenets was, in fact, quite rare, but failure to engage was cause for court-martial and, in one case during these wars, execution.

It is hard to imagine just how many men served during the worldwide naval campaigns between France and England in the middle decades of the eighteenth century. Modern scholars have looked at the crew lists and estimate that upward of two hundred thousand men served on British warships alone between 1750 and 1765.[18] In spite of large increases in the population of Britain between 1700 and 1750, with its concomitant increase in men available to serve, the navy always had trouble crewing its ships. They regularly sent out recruiters and paid a fee to a man signing up. The infamous press gangs rounded up young men in port towns and surrounding areas. They also stopped ships of the American colonies and impressed sailors into service in the Royal Navy. During wartime the navy was, of course, in competition with the armies for manpower.

### Free Ships, Free Goods

The wars of the mid-eighteenth century also created more complex maritime legal problems. While Britain fought France and Spain, Holland and the Scandinavian countries remained neutral and asserted a "free ships, free goods" policy, by which any neutral power could carry any material to any buyer. England, of course, resisted this interpretation of neutrality both in diplomatic correspondence and by blockading French and Spanish ports. The British blockading fleet regularly seized Dutch and Scandinavian merchantmen attempting to run the blockade. British diplomats dismissed all protests.

When it suited their interests, the British turned to legal niceties of earlier maritime treaties, such as various agreements that limited to a home country's ships any trade from a colony to the home country. The Dutch argued that because the Spanish had suspended such treaties, they had a right to sail to Spanish possessions in the Americas without interference. The British government took the position that no country could unilaterally abrogate colony–home country exclusivity. More diplomatic talk ensued, along with more captures by British warships.[19]

The argument expanded to neutrals carrying goods of one or another combatant. The Dutch position was that any goods carried in a neutral ship were neutral goods and should be allowed to proceed to any designated port. The British asserted that, to the contrary, all enemy goods anywhere were contraband, regardless of in what nation's ship they were loaded. The Dutch asserted their right to, for example, carry wood freely from Baltic ports to Spain and France. England countered that Baltic wood might be used for masts and therefore empowered the enemy. It therefore would impound and take to the nearest British port any Dutch ship found carrying Baltic wood.

This assertion of the "openness" of seaborne trade by the Dutch implied a new, more global conceptualization of the sea, which defined the Caribbean and, by extension, the Philippines as no longer Spanish, but part of a multi-ocean connected trading system that—in theory—welcomed all comers. The British counter-assertion that the seas remained realms of exclusive carrying trade by the home country was, of course, one of the central issues of the American Revolution two decades later. A league of neutrals (Russia, Holland, the Scandinavian countries, and the Baltic states) forced Britain to allow neutrals to trade anywhere, only agreeing not to carry goods specifically designated as contraband.

Neither in the wars of the mid-eighteenth century nor in the wars from the American Revolutionary era through the Napoleonic Wars were these issues of neutrality and openness of the oceans settled. In 1807 a British fleet waited immediately outside New York harbor and examined every departing American ship's goods and where they were bound.[20] The questions of whose ocean, whose ships, whose goods, and what was contraband, as we shall see, figure prominently both in chapter 13 (the *Flying Cloud*) and chapter 14 (the *Lusitania*). The issues remain unresolved in spite of the thorough development of international maritime law and regulation in the twentieth century. Israel, for example, created a huge international incident in 2013 by boarding and seizing in international waters a Turkish ship with supplies bound for the Palestinian Territories.

## Maritime Globalization:
## The Second Half of the Eighteenth Century

One indication of the development of a single maritime world was the emergence of Lloyd's of London as the premier ship underwriting market. No one knows when the first merchant ship was underwritten at Lloyd's coffeehouse. Toward the middle of the eighteenth century (the time of the *Victory*), Lloyd's emerged as the place to read the best shipping news and to hear the best political gossip that might affect shipping. To be up to date with ship comings and goings and be involved with the financing of shipping, one needed the network of men who read the news and made the deals at Lloyd's. Lloyd's slowly evolved from a coffeehouse with typical long tables to a roomful of small tables, divided by partitions, at which brokers sat and investors and shipowners bargained.[21]

A second feature of the globalizing maritime world in the second half of the eighteenth century was several countries' experiments with frigates. Holland, France, and England all realized that, to keep in contact with their possessions, they needed relatively fast but thoroughly armed vessels, capable of shelling ports if necessary and standing against the smaller ships of the line. Frigates could thwart those attempting to capture merchant ships of the home country and could themselves capture enemy merchantmen. The French invented the first of this new sort of ship in the 1730s. It carried seventy-four guns but was relatively larger, lighter, faster, and nimbler than a seventy- or eighty-gun ship of the line.[22] Frigates mounted a single caliber of gun on two decks, so that ammunition could be used anywhere on the ship and the crew needed training on loading and firing only one gun. Such frigates were to be the main ships of the United States after the Revolution.

A third global trend in the second half of the eighteenth century was for all countries to increase the crews of all naval ships. In mid-century a thirty-two-pound gun, for example, normally had a crew of ten. By the end of the century it had a crew of fourteen.[23] Large naval ships had crews about ten times the size of comparable merchantmen. Cramming supplies, the galley, storage of ammunition, and a place for the enlarged crew to sleep was no mean feat. Note that this sort of thinking—more men, more firepower from the same guns—also pervaded land army strategy, yielding the enormous armies of the Napoleonic era.

By the end of the eighteenth century, Britain dominated the seas. In spite of losing about two hundred ships of the line, large and small, in the mid-century wars, England had rebuilt older ships and built new ships, yielding a navy of more than seven hundred vessels.[24] Its merchant tonnage was double that of France, four times that of Holland, and ten times that of Spain.[25] Both its navy and its merchantmen operated between Britain's worldwide colonies and across the maritime world with a degree of integration never conceptualized or realized before in man's history.

## The HMS *Victory* Today

After the initial find of the wreck of the HMS *Victory* in 2008, Odyssey Marine Exploration asserted claims to ownership and salvage rights. After three years of hearings and judgments by the UK Ministry of Defense and the UK Ministry of Culture, Media and Sport (which oversees historic sites), the British government took control of the *Victory*. Management of the site was assigned to the Maritime Heritage Foundation, a nonprofit established to locate and excavate shipwrecks to high standards.

Since locating the wreck in 2008, Odyssey Marine Explorations has monitored the site, documenting year-by-year deterioration. Deep-sea trawling nets, which have heavy pointed prongs to pierce the seafloor, have broken the muzzles of two canons, deeply grooved some guns, and dragged others to new locations. One cannon is missing, illegally raised by a Dutch company. The site cannot be termed "stable," and if left in place the wreck is in danger of rapid deterioration.[26]

In 2012 Odyssey reached agreement with the Maritime Heritage Foundation on the excavation of the wreck and developed a project plan. Naval artifacts are to go to the foundation. Eighty percent of the value of trade items, such as specie, personal effects, and items of daily use on board will go to Odyssey.[27] As a commercial treasure-recovery company, Odyssey has been understandably tight-lipped about its salvage operations.

# 12

## LUCY WALKER

The mechanical problems of the *Lucy Walker*, a side-wheel steamboat, began around midday Tuesday, October 22, 1844, in Louisville, Kentucky, on the Ohio River. A main pump that provided water to the boilers was operating only sporadically. The captain and owner, anxious to depart for New Orleans, decided that repairs would be made while the boat was under way. The approximately 120 passengers included a group of evangelical ministers returning from a southern synod meeting, who had hailed the *Lucy Walker* as it passed New Albany, a couple of miles below Louisville on the Indiana side of the river. They had been waiting two days for passage downriver and counted themselves lucky as they came aboard from a small sailboat.

A short distance below New Albany in the late afternoon the captain ordered the engines stopped to make repairs, and the boat drifted downstream with the current. It is possible that the water level in the boilers had dropped to dangerous levels and they overheated. The ministers had barely put their luggage in their cabins and returned to the deck when both boilers exploded with unimaginable force.

Several eyewitnesses recounted the horrible scene. The explosion blew the central section of the boat dozens of feet into the air. One body went straight up and came down with such force that it went through the deck. Pieces of the deck, roof, furniture, and body parts were found on both sides of the Ohio River. One passenger who survived was reclining in a heavy armchair in the social hall. He and his chair were slammed into the ceiling. The explosion blew away the one man sitting next to him. Another died from head wounds. The man in the armchair suffered a thigh wound and a broken arm. Within minutes of the explosion the boat began to burn. The armchair survivor, along with other men, women, and children, jumped from the burning boat and clung to wreckage. Many drowned. A father saw his

*Explosion of the* Lucy Walker, from James T. Lloyd's
*Steamboat Directory, and Disasters on the Western Waters*
(Cincinnati: J. T. Lloyd & Co., 1856).

young son struggling in the water. The boy was able to climb aboard a floating mattress.

Fortunately, a government boat that removed submerged trees from the
river was only about two hundred yards from the *Lucy Walker* at the time of
the explosion. Captain Dunham maneuvered his boat as close to the burning wreck as he could, and his crew threw ropes to those in the water. He ordered that all bedding on board be used to keep the survivors warm.

No one at the time or since knows exactly how many passengers died, because the explosion and fire destroyed all the boat's records. The *Louisville
Courier* initially reported sixty to eighty dead, with thirty surviving. The injured received medical attention. Families in New Albany opened their homes
to the survivors. Local churches gathered clothes and other necessities.

A few days later the *New Albany Gazette* reported forty-three passengers
and crew, including the captain, known dead, or missing and presumed dead.
Sixteen were badly injured. Of the evangelical ministers, one was killed immediately, one died the next day, two had serious burns, and one was barely
injured. The boat itself broke up and sank, though pieces of it floated downstream for several days.

## The *Lucy Walker* in the News

Even before telegraph or a connected rail system, news of the *Lucy Walker* traveled fast. Initial coverage was in the *Louisville Courier* the day after the disaster, October 23. Six days later a paper in Baltimore and one in Washington, D.C., carried the *Courier* piece. The next day it appeared in two New York papers and another in Washington, D.C. November 1, nine days after the initial *Courier* story, the disaster was featured in newspapers in Boston, Charleston, Richmond, and Albany, New York. In the following weeks, the story spread to many smaller local papers on the East Coast and inland: Hartford and New London in Connecticut; Newport, Rhode Island; Newark, New Jersey; Auburn, New York; Worcester and Pittsfield in Massachusetts, Keene, Concord, and Amherst in New Hampshire; Sudbury, Pennsylvania; and Columbus, Ohio.[1]

The news spread equally quickly downriver from Louisville. The *New Orleans Daily Picayune* ran the initial *Louisville Courier* story on November 3, only eleven days after it appeared. We can assume that southbound riverboats spread the news to St. Louis, Memphis, and Natchez. The *Lucy Walker* herself had been part of this upriver and downriver flow of information. On January 22, 1843, more than a year and a half before the disaster, the *Times Picayune* had thanked the *Lucy Walker* in print for a "bundle of river papers" the steamboat had brought from upriver towns to New Orleans.

A second wave of coverage followed the *New Albany Gazette*'s publication of a more complete list of the dead, missing, wounded, and those who escaped injury. The timing of reprinting the story in other newspapers was virtually identical to the first wave of coverage.

The final wave of coverage consisted of reprints of a letter sent to the *Philadelphia Enquirer* by a survivor of the explosion. His account appeared in the New York papers the following day and spread to smaller weekly newspapers during the remainder of November.

In six days the news of the *Lucy Walker* disaster crossed six hundred miles of forest and the Appalachian Mountains to reach Washington, D.C. How was this possible in 1844? In the half-century between the landmark Post Office bill of 1792 and the *Lucy Walker* disaster, the United States Post Office had become the densest and most democratic postal system in the world. Its form and function were revolutionary at the time. In the United States, far more post offices, routes, and carriers per square mile served even the thinly settled state of Michigan than, for example, a densely populated region of northern France. The government surveyed, built, and maintained post roads and chains of post riders. In 1844 more than three-quarters of all employees of the federal government worked for the post office.[2]

Equally revolutionary was the relationship of the post to the press. Newspapers moved for a small fee from any printer in the United States to any printer in another city. The fee was no higher for a subscriber to a newspaper from a distant city. The postal system was the tissue that held the far-flung country together, providing rapid, inexpensive commercial information, contact for families, and news of elections and politics. At a deeper level, even the frontier states shared a common world of information and a trust in the ability of the federal government to provide services. The federally organized and funded post office was not some "natural" outgrowth of the spread of the United States west from the Eastern Seaboard. It was rather the outcome of some of the most contentious political battles of the early Republic, pitting the champions of a minimalist central government against those who saw the post as essential for holding the country together. We now turn to the effect of a national post and newspapers on the discussion of steamboat safety.

### The National Discussion of Riverboat Safety

Boiler explosions had become more frequent in the early 1820s when competitors substituted the more powerful and efficient high-pressure steam system for the low-pressure system used by Robert Fulton, the inventor who developed the first commercially practical steamboat. The explosions morbidly fascinated the public, which perceived the obvious benefits of steamboats but was repelled by their equally obvious danger. In the first decade of the run from New York to Albany, the steamboats *Fidelity*, *Seahorse*, and *Paragon* had all exploded.

The spectacular explosion of the *Aetna* within sight of New York City in 1824 highlighted the lack of scientific tests of boiler strength and pressure release valves. Congress took up the problem of steamboat safety, viewing it as an issue of national concern, not reasonably left to individual states. A Senate committee held hearings, but expert opinion lacked any consensus on how to make steamboats safer. Legislation drafted after the hearings failed to pass the Senate. Newspapers suggested that steamboat owners were installing more dangerous iron boilers rather than the safer copper boilers used in England. In an open letter to Congress, a steam boiler engineer descried how much public opinion was affecting the design and materials of boilers:

> The explosion of this high-pressure boat [the *Aetna*], so recently introduced upon our waters, occasioned the greatest excitement: and the opportunity was seized upon to prejudice and exasperate the public mind against the owners of managers of all steamboats which were furnished with iron boilers—those then used in the Fulton boats being of copper; . . . An active and intelligent gentleman, then acting as for one of the finest boats at that time building for our waters, . . . said "we cannot resist public opinion: the people have been instructed that iron is an unsafe material for boilers and that it is recklessly used because it is the cheapest. It is beyond our power to disabuse them in this matter; and they threaten us, moreover, that, if we will not give them a copper boiler, they procure such a one and run it against us. We have concluded, therefore, to give them a copper boiler, the strongest of its class, and have made up our minds they have a perfect right to be scalded by copper boilers if they insist on it."[3]

Several steamboat explosions occurred every subsequent year. In 1832 a congressional report estimated that since the beginning of steamboat service, fifty-two explosions had killed 256 people and seriously wounded 104.[4] Andrew Jackson mentioned the issue in his State of the Union message in December 1833. The House of Representatives, however, merely tabled draft legislation on steamboat safety.

In 1838 near Cincinnati, all four boilers of the *Moselle* exploded, blowing the boat entirely apart. It sank after drifting less than one hundred yards downriver. Of the approximately 290 passengers, 160 were killed.[5] Once again Congress held hearings, this time producing legislation on steamboat safety, including, for example, a standardized protocol for periodically examining boilers to ensure that steam safety valves were operating. Sadly, the well-intentioned legislation failed to stop disasters. More explosions followed the legislation than preceded it.

After the *Lucy Walker* disaster Congress once again turned to steamboat safety. Representatives placed into the *Congressional Record* a petition of the "Steamboat engineers of the city of Cincinnati" discussing the mechanical processes of steam engines and their safety, but no legislation cleared Con-

Explosions of riverboats continued throughout the nineteenth century.
*The Explosion and Sinking of the* Brilliant *in Bayou Goula, 1851*, lithograph
by Lewis Henry, published in *Das Illustrirte Mississippithal* (1851).

gress.[6] The spectacular explosion and much loss of life aboard the *Empire State* in 1856 generated a coroner's hearing, in which witnesses described a scene much like the *Lucy Walker*:

> I should think that the accident took place a little before ten o'clock. At the time, I was sitting in the saloon above, reading, and heard the rush of steam: and I went to the state-room, and secured my life-preservers. I saw great confusion. I noticed that it was steam, instead of smoke, that came into the saloon, and told the ladies that I thought we were safe. As soon as I deemed it safe to do so, I came down below, and saw a good deal of water on deck. I then busied myself trying to help the injured.[7]

## The Mississippi River System

The brief flurries of public concern following major steamboat explosions concealed what were in fact more serious safety problems for steamboats.

The Mississippi River system was itself profoundly dangerous. The main river and its tributaries changed course every year, which uprooted masses of trees. The trees floated downstream and often were trapped underwater and formed snags, which could rip open the bottom of a boat. Eddies and rapids flung boats onto rocks that lurked just below the surface. The lower river snaked back and forth in sinuous curves, which carved new islands and channels every season. Sandbars appeared and disappeared in days. None of these sandbars or channels were marked. The upper river froze solid in the winter, crushing any boat that had not escaped to the open water of the southern river. Low water in the summer exposed more rocks and narrowed channels.

The first vessels on the Mississippi River were canoes, followed by simple rafts, which carried furs, corn, cotton, salt, sugar, wheat, preserved pork, lead, and timber downriver to New Orleans. Around 1800 boatyards along the river developed two specialized craft to ride the Mississippi downstream: the flatboat and the keelboat. Low water in the summer on the Mississippi dictated no more than a four-foot draft. The boats had to be narrow enough to pass between rocks and long enough to carry forty to sixty tons of cargo. A ballad of the 1830s captures that era:

> Sweet Mississippi, pride of the west,
> How often I sail in the stream I love best.
> The wealth of the world now floats on thy tide
> And gladly I sing as onward I ride.
> The song of the boatman falls on my ears
> And our pilot steers unconscious of fears.
> Sweet Mississippi, sweet Mississippi,
> Pride of the west.[8]

Returning a boat upstream was a backbreaking business. Where they could, the crew pushed long poles into the muddy river bottom and, yard by yard, pushed the boat forward. Sometimes they stayed close to the shore, grabbed overhanging branches, and pulled the boat along. In stronger currents, the crew tied a stout rope to an upriver tree and pulled the boat. The captain frequently guided the boat across the river to avoid powerful currents and find calmer waters.[9] As a consequence, all rafts and most boats were simply broken up in New Orleans and sold for the wood. The crew rode a horse or walked north on the famous Natchez Trace, an ancient trail between Natchez, Mississippi, and Nashville, Tennessee.[10]

Steamboats, when introduced to the Mississippi and other rivers in the 1830s, brought rapid and remarkable changes. They dramatically cut upriver travel time. Keelboats took ninety to a hundred days for the journey from New Orleans to St. Louis. Steamboats did it in twelve days. The price of upriver freight dropped by three-quarters. The volume of downriver freight sharply increased as the price dropped.

A decade before the construction of the *Lucy Walker* in 1842, boatbuilders had arrived at an optimum shape and size of steamboat: large enough to carry freight and passengers profitably, narrow enough to maneuver through channels, shallow enough to clear shifting sandbars. Riverboats generally had three decks. The lowest deck carried freight and the boilers. Above that was a deck with cabins, an outside promenade, and a dining room. Most steamboats had a deck above the passenger deck for crew quarters, though the *Lucy Walker* did not. At the top was the pilothouse.

Nevertheless, some compromises in riverboat construction were dangerous. For speed, steamboats were built as light as possible, just strong enough to hold together and carry the freight. Single-walled hulls were incapable of remaining watertight if damaged. The boats were constructed of highly flammable wood, but boiler fireboxes routinely sent burning embers out the smokestacks. Riverboats did not carry lifeboats.[11]

Dangers of the river, careless steamboat construction, and the means of propulsion meant that steamboats did not last long. They were built to recover the initial investment in less than five years. Few lasted more than ten years. Virtually none of them were ever "retired." They sank, hit a snag, burned, or exploded. When it was possible, owners salvaged the steam engines and left the rest to rot.

The *New Orleans Daily Picayune* was, however, properly proud of the new *Lucy Walker* when it departed on its first run in January 1843.

The Lucy Walker is the name of another beautiful craft in the steamer line that arrived at our Warf on Saturday last. The Walker was built in Cincinnati the past summer expressly for the Arkansas River; she is 140 feet long, 26 feet beam, and 6 feet hold—has two fire engines, one of which is attached to the steam engine—has a sheet metal roof, and is in every way protected against fire. She is commanded by Capt. P. F. Eckert, an old and experienced commander, and we have no doubt that every person that patronizes her will be well satisfied. She will run as a regular packet in the Arkansas River, and will leave on her first trip this evening at 4 o'clock.

The *Arkansas Gazette* was equally proud of the new boat when it departed to return to New Orleans two weeks later, stating that "for elegance and comfort [the *Lucy Walker*] will compare favorably with any of her rivals, and is said to surpass them in speed."[12]

In January 1843, the *Picayune* advertised the boat's departure.

REGULAR ARKANSAS PACKET

The fast running steamer Lucy Walker, John Cochran master, will leave for Fort Gibson, Fort Smith, Van Buren, Little Rock, and all landings on the Arkansas River, on Tuesday the 27th instant, nt. 4 o'clock P.M., positively. For freight or passage apply on board, foot of Girod street or to WALTON, SANFORD & CO, 54 New Levee.

Note the emphasis on speed in both these quotes. Passengers and freight shippers paid a premium for a speedy boat, and captains raced steamboats from the early years of steamboats on the river. Even on ordinary runs captains sometimes ordered stokers to fill the bunkers and push the steam pressure beyond safe limits to beat a rival to port. Companies sponsored time trials known as "record" runs, on which the boat carried virtually no freight other than a few passengers. The captain pushed the boat beyond its limits to establish a new record from, for example, New Orleans to St. Louis. The bragging rights were immediate and visible; the fastest boat mounted the largest set of antlers the captain could find on the wheelhouse. Equally storied were actual races between boats, avidly followed in the press throughout the Mississippi basin. This ethos of speed encouraged captains to push boilers into dangerous pressures and was a contributing factor in explosions.

The upriver cargo was probably cloth and clothing, advertised as "newly arrived on the Lucy Walker" in a Little Rock newspaper. On February 10, the *Lucy Walker* arrived back in New Orleans with 611 bales of cotton.[13] On March 15, 1843, the *Arkansas State Gazette* noted, "There has been a slight rise in the river, and the Steamers Arkansas and Lucy Walker, have passed up, the later having on board upwards of two hundred Seminole Indians, on their way to the west. . . . We have seldom looked upon men of finer mould or more muscular power than these sons of the forest seem to display."[14]

Unloading goods along the Tennessee River
from the steamboat *City of Savannah*, 1910.

Steamboats on these rivers were the lifeblood of small farms. Boats like the *Lucy Walker* carried supplies in and produce out. Captains and pilots knew farm families all along their route. For pickup of a passenger or freight, someone stood on the bank and either hailed the boat or waved a handkerchief. The boat would blow its whistle to alert a farm of delivery. The boat then nosed in, and the deck crew dropped the landing stage.

The physical survival of the steamboat depended on the training and skill of the captain and pilot. Only their knowledge prevented the boat from grounding on a sandbar or crashing into a rock. The apprenticeship of a riverboat pilot was formal, lengthy, and rigorous. To steer the correct course, pilots scrupulously memorized landmarks on shore and the necessary course adjustments.[15] As Mark Twain observed from his experience in the early 1860s, when pilots got together they discussed particularly tricky sections of the river:

"Jim, how did you run Plum Point, coming up?"

"It was in the night, there, and I ran it the way one of the boys on the 'Diana' told me; started out about fifty yards above the wood pile on the false point, and held on the cabin under Plum Point till I raised the reef—quarter less twain—then straightened up for the middle bar till I got well abreast the old one-limbed cotton-wood in the bend, then got my stem on the cotton-wood and head on the low place above the point, and came through a-booming—nine and a half."[16]

For the most current information on the ever-changing rivers, pilots nailed boxes to trees near particularly dangerous portions of the river. Up-bound pilots left notes for down-bound pilots of what they had just seen, and vice versa.

By the 1850s all pilots, new as well as experienced, were periodically tested and licensed for sections of the rivers they navigated. The exams consisted of "singing" a portion of the river before a group of experienced pilots and captains—that is, visualizing and describing appropriate course changes to the river's twists and turns, sandbars, currents, obstructions, islands, bridges, and tributaries.

### Steamboats in the World

The problem of upstream river navigation was common across the world. In China, for example, boats were rowed upstream on the coastal plain but required hundreds of men and oxen to drag them through canyons in steeper sections. The Ganges had favorable winds for upstream travel only three months of the year. Much of the Nile had only a very gentle rise, so that boats used oars. Predictable southerly winds made sailing upriver possible for only a few months of the year. It was never possible to sail, for example, up the Amazon; variable and inconsistent winds made tacking through the sinuous curves of the lower river difficult, and making headway against a two-to-four-knot current was virtually impossible. Sailing up the lower Rhine was possible, but the rocky upper portions were too dangerous for sailing vessels.

The steamboat revolution of the middle decades of the nineteenth century was a worldwide phenomenon. The engines were perhaps the most sophisticated technology of the time and were exported from England, France, and Germany to China, India, Egypt, and South America. Scientists and engineers discussed technological possibilities and problems of boilers across national boundaries. Steamboat engineers from Cincinnati, for example, who filed their petition on the causes of steamboat explosions to Congress in 1845 cited research and discussion from France and England.[17]

Countries attempted to make the rivers safe in common ways. Just as on the Mississippi, navigation of the Rhine, for example, was professionalized in the 1850s and 1860s, with formal apprenticeship and exams. A commission with representatives from countries bordering the river began testing and licensing pilots and captains. The commission installed beacons and markers, blasted dangerous rocks, and dredged channels.[18]

Across the world, steamboats made travel to the heartland easy, comfortable, and relatively swift. By the time of the *Lucy Walker* in 1844, the gloomy towers and medieval towns of the Rhine hosted hordes of tourists, arriving by steamboat. Inns were equipped for large numbers. Illustrated guidebooks to the Rhine were printed in French, German, and English.[19] Woodcuts and etchings of sites along the river were sold as souvenirs. Shopkeepers casually quoted prices in kreutzers, Prussian dollars, or French francs. In the last half of the nineteenth century a steamboat tour of the Nile to see Egyptian ruins was an essential part of the grand tour of Europe. Whether their travel was on the Mississippi, the Rhine, or the Nile, tourists wrote and published memoirs of their experiences.

In a less sanguine role, steamboats also played a part in worldwide disease transmission. On the Nile, for example, steamboats hastened the spread of deadly rift fever when the river was in full flood. On the Mississippi River, poor sanitation and polluted water spread cholera, and rapid upriver travel of steamboats spread epidemics more quickly. By 1830, for example, there had been several serious cholera epidemics that moved up from New Orleans to St. Louis. Some had even reached Minnesota.[20] Yellow fever recurred throughout the lower river. In 1867 an epidemic in New Orleans killed thirty-two hundred of a population of forty-one thousand. In spite of quarantines of riverboat traffic from New Orleans, the epidemic spread upriver. In Memphis, six thousand people died out of a population twenty thousand.[21]

Inexpensive upriver and downriver steamboat transportation offered similar opportunities to river cities across the world. Along the Mississippi and its tributaries cities such as St. Louis, Cincinnati, Kansas City, Pittsburgh, and Minneapolis shifted to manufacturing, rather than merely exporting raw materials and importing manufactured goods. The waterfalls at

Minneapolis/St. Paul proved ideal for the milling of grain from the western prairies. General Mills, Pillsbury, and Robin Hood Flour became national brands. Cincinnati and Kansas City became meat-processing centers. St. Louis developed from a city that supplied settlers heading west into a major manufacturing city.

Mississippi River cities were generally competitive because their factories were new compared to those in the cities of Europe or the Eastern United States, and used sophisticated machines that employed cheaper labor than older, craft-based manufacturing methods. They were also closer to markets as settlers moved into the land beyond the Mississippi. In much of the newly settled land, farming was profitable and the market for windows, side tables, shoes, and store-bought clothes developed apace. The river towns and cities generally had a "go-ahead" image.

Smaller cities along the river also shifted to manufacturing in the later decades of the nineteenth century. Cape Girardeau, Missouri, for example, located about fifty miles north of the confluence of the Ohio and the Mississippi, had originally only supplied settlers headed west, its manufactures limited to barrels for flour and meat. By the later decades of the nineteenth century, the town had several brick kilns utilizing clay from the surrounding region, a foundry making agricultural implements, a woolen factory, a factory fabricating doors and windows, several large flour mills, and a shoe factory.[22]

Steamboats were equally important to the development of the Rhine River and its tributaries. In addition to the traditional downriver transport of grain, wine, and stone, steamboats moved machinery, farm equipment, rails, and tools out from the manufacturing towns of the Ruhr valley. They also moved specialty manufactured goods and dyes from a dozen river towns downriver to the sea for export.

The other use of steamboats worldwide was military. Throughout history infantry moved upstream at a marching pace, rarely covering more than ten miles in a day. Steamboats provided the first rapid transport upstream for armies. Tactics and strategy were forever changed. The Union army, for example, commandeered riverboats and in only a few days moved far up the Tennessee River, splitting the Confederacy and forcing the battle of Shiloh. The Union won largely because steamboats brought reinforcements during the night after the first ferocious day of battle. In a similar fashion steamboats rapidly ferried the khedive's troops from Cairo up the Nile in the 1860s to put down a rebellion.

## The Disappearance of the Steamboat World

Across the world the core, unsolvable problems of steamboats were similar. The river went only exactly where it went and, because of low water or freezing, was navigable only part of the year. The Mississippi ran north to south, but the country's main supply lines needed to go east to west. Entrepreneurs well understood these problems and built short rail lines well before the Civil War. These short lines only needed to be linked up and standardized for railroads to provide direct connections between mines and fields and processing centers. Railroads took finished products directly to wholesale distribution locations. They ran in the winter while the riverboats sat idle in St. Louis. By the 1870s thirteen rail bridges crossed the Mississippi. Railroads replaced riverboats for travel and general merchandise throughout Europe and elsewhere, including in Egypt, Russia, India, and China.

What had been a revolutionary technology in the 1830s was obsolete by 1900. Steamboats were practically gone in the United States by the 1920s. Popular music reflected this change with songs of nostalgia for the romantic days of the steamboat.

> Don't you hear those whistles blowing,
> There's going to be a jubilee down where the
> Mississippi's flowing.
> They searched the country until they found
> All those old time steamboat racers of great renown.
> Grand old boats with all their beauty,
> Gray-haired captains still on duty.[23]

Today the Mississippi, the Rhine, the Yellow River, and most navigable waterways worldwide handle mainly heavy goods in flotillas of barges pushed by tugs. On the Mississippi, standard barges are 120 to 200 feet long and 30 to 40 feet wide. The river carries more than three hundred million tons of cargo each year, such as grain, coal, petrochemicals, sand and gravel, and chemicals.[24] Tourist boats on a variety of the world's rivers hark back to the heritage of the steamboats like the *Lucy Walker*, but none are steam driven. Better technology, dams, lights, channel markers, and government dredging have made rivers immeasurably safer than the nineteenth-century world of the *Lucy Walker*.

# *13*
# *FLYING CLOUD*

On June 17, 1874, that most famous of clipper ships the *Flying Cloud* lay at anchor in the port of Saint John, in the Bay of Fundy in the province of New Brunswick on the east coast of Canada. The glory days of the gold rush, racing, and Chinese silks and tea long behind her, the ship waited to load wood. During the night a late spring gale drove the *Flying Cloud* ashore, breaking crucial structural members. There it lay for a year, until the insurance underwriters declared the ship a total loss and hired a team of local men to douse it with kerosene. They burned the *Flying Cloud* on the beach in the Bay of Fundy in order to recover several tons of copper and iron. The maritime world had so profoundly changed in two decades that the event went completely unnoticed in the American and world press.[1]

## Colonial Shipbuilding

Shipbuilding came early to the American colonies. Wood was plentiful, and some colonists came with woodworking skills. The demand for ships was obvious. The thirteen colonies were strung out along the Eastern Seaboard of North America. Long before the Revolution the northern, central, and southern colonies had developed specialized exports: fish, turpentine, and wood from the North, grains from the central colonies, and tobacco from the South. Exports were essential for the colonists to purchase what they did not have, such as iron tools, cloth, fashionable clothing, and tea.

Britain never regulated or restricted colonial shipbuilding, which thrived in the Boston area, Maine (then part of Massachusetts), on the coasts of Connecticut and Rhode Island, and in the cities of New York, Philadelphia, Baltimore, and Charleston. Britain, however, banned colonial ships from carrying the most lucrative global commodities, such as Indian cotton and spices, Chinese tea, porcelains, and silks, and British manufactured goods. Many of the colonial ships were small, suitable for fishing or coastal trade. Others were larger and undertook voyages to the Caribbean, trading fish, meat, and grain for sugar and bills of exchange, used to buy British imports.

## A Tradition of Speed

During the Revolution the thorough British blockade of American shipping put a premium on speedy colonial ships that could outrun British naval vessels. The continuing war between England and France at the opening of the nineteenth century saw blockades of the American coast by both countries. American ships in most instances could not compete militarily with British naval vessels, so all they could do was run, fostering a focus on speed.[2] The War of 1812 was fought in part over the practice of British ships stopping American vessels and "impressing" their seamen to serve on British ships.

The earliest American long-distance trading ships were substantially faster than the lumbering European merchantmen to India, China, or Southeast Asia. The American ships were much smaller, averaging around four hundred tons.

No scholar has yet proved that the new, faster American ships of smaller carrying capacity were substantially more profitable than the older-style, slower European vessels. Still, there was logic to the American pursuit of speed. The English East India Company and the Dutch East India Company had monopolies on their trade to their respective home countries and could set high prices even if their ships were slow. The Americans had no such monopolies and could only sell what their markets would pay. If an American shipowner could manage one additional trading voyage in a year, it might well mean the difference between profit and loss.

Up and down the Atlantic Seaboard the dynamic of profit through speed generated competitive experiments with new ship designs, new ways to add sail and increase cargo capacity. By the 1830s these new, larger trading ships, dubbed "clippers" (from "clipping right along"), were "sharper," that is, longer relative to beam. By the middle of the 1840s the design had fully arrived. Clipper ships had become literally "sharper" in forward profile; their prow was built to cut through waves rather than batter over them, as did older merchantmen. The shape of the ship, if one looked down at the deck from high on the mast, was quite different from traditional merchantmen, tracing out a long oval with its widest point well ahead of the midpoint of the ship. A fully rigged clipper ship hoisted an enormous amount of canvas, consisting of more than twenty individual sails. Two masts carried five sets of squared sails, from mainsails below to skysails (also known as moonrakers) at the top. The mizzenmast aft carried four square sails and supported a spanker. Between the bowsprit and the foremast were a triangular staysail, jib, and a flying jib, in addition to staysails between the three masts. Even more sail, known as studding sail, could be added for a fair following wind. Most clippers sailed fastest with a wind off the rear quarter of either side of the ship, allowing all sails to fill; however, the ship's deep draft made it also able to sail closer to the wind.[3]

Designers, owners, and captains continued to discuss the placement of the mainsail mast, whether it should be exactly amidships or placed slightly fore or aft. They also argued about how the ship should ride, with the deck relatively parallel to a calm sea surface or somewhat canted upward from the back to the front of the ship. Experiment after experiment faced the ultimate test, the sea itself, from the light winds around the equator to the gales of Cape Horn. No one designer, nor owner, nor port got all the pieces exactly right, but each owner watched the performance of the ships of others and learned. Progress was steady and incremental. One milestone was the realization that flatter bottoms did not, as expected, diminish the speed or sailing qualities of these long, narrow ships. Flatter bottoms did, however, yield much larger spaces for valuable cargo. A second milestone was the realization that a crew of fifty to seventy-five (larger than ships of similar size but with less sail) could handle banks of sails on extremely tall masts. Clipper ship masts were far taller and wider at their base than a single tree and also needed to be stronger than any single tree could possibly be. Shipbuilders developed a technology for banding with iron three or more trunks into a single lower mast. Rising above the composite lower mast was a single-trunk mast and yet another lighter, single-trunk mast above that. (It is perhaps worth recalling that a similar process of experimentation and refinement in the same period among competing boatyards produced the efficient and speedy design for Mississippi riverboats.)

### A New World of Navigation

Navigation to distant ports had much improved in the 1840s, based on the efforts of a single mapmaker named Matthew Maury. In his youth he sailed in the United States Navy and noticed the lack of good charts of winds and currents both in the Atlantic and the Pacific. Back in the United States in 1834 he produced his first book on navigation.[4] In 1835 he was assigned to the navy's cartography department and later took over the navy's Depot of Charts and Instruments. There he studied thousands of ship's logs and developed a uniform method of tabulating the mass of data on winds and currents. He first published charts for the navy showing the best routes across the Atlantic, collating data from hundreds of ship's logs. He next expanded this study to the entire world and produced for the navy comprehensive charts of winds and currents, again based on ship's logs. His tabular method of recording wind and current data spread through the naval fleet and was quickly adopted by merchant captains. Maury actively collected this data and incorporated it into later charts. By the 1850s smart captains and navigators owned and used Maury's superior wind and current charts, thereby shaving days, and often weeks, off a run.

In Maury's conception the world's oceans had become a single maritime environment. The winds and currents of Antarctica were just as essential to the whaling ships of Massachusetts as was the Gulf Stream off the Carolinas. The Humboldt Current was as important off Alaska as it was off Mexico.

The second breakthrough for navigation and particularly for speedy passages was the chronometer. The problem of longitude had plagued ocean sailing for millennia. Simple instruments could, from the height of the sun above the horizon at noon, calculate latitude—a ship's position above or below the equator.[5] Figuring out how far the ship was east or west of home port proved devilishly difficult. Over the centuries, astronomers, mathematicians, and philosophers proposed any number of incorrect or impractical methods. In 1714 the government of Great Britain offered the Longitude Prize for the development of a practical method of determining a ship's position. It would go unclaimed for fifty years.

By the later decades of the eighteenth century, many understood that a navigator already could easily calculate how fast the ship traveled but did not know for how long the ship had sailed. The problem was to fabricate a very accurate clock, which could keep time in the pitching, rolling, and wet environs of a ship. In 1765 a clockmaker named John Harrison, after more than thirty years of research and testing prototypes, proved that his clock was accurate within five seconds across the Atlantic. Though essential for calculating the ship's actual position, accurate ship's chronometers remained very expensive and entered wide use only in the middle decades of the nineteenth century, the era of clipper ship building.[6]

## Coasting and Whaling

The new clippers must be placed in the larger context of American ship-building of the time. American shipyards produced other important types of transoceanic ships in the first half of the nineteenth century, for example whaling ships. Captains and owners made fortunes in hunting whales for their oil, used in lamps. This chantey, like most, takes the point of view of the seamen:

> 'Tis advertised in Boston, New York and Buffalo,
> A hundred hearty sailors a whalin' for to go, singing
>
> Blow ye winds a mornin' and blow ye winds hi ho,
> Clear away your runnin' gear and blow, boys, blow.
>
> They tell you of the clipper-ships a-going in and out,
> And say you'll take five hundred sperm before you're six month out.
>
> It's now we're out to sea, my boys, the wind comes on to blow;
> One half the watch is sick on deck, the other half below.
>
> Now comes that damned old compass, it will grieve your heart
>     full sore.
> For theirs is two-and-thirty points and we have forty-four.
>
> Next comes the running rigging, which you're all supposed to know;
> 'Tis "Lay aloft, you son-of-a-gun, or overboard you go."
>
> The Skipper's on the quarter-deck a-squinting at the sails,
> When up aloft the lookout sights a school of whales.
>
> "Now clear away the boats, my boys, and after him we'll travel,
> But if you get too near his fluke, he'll kick you to the devil!"
>
> But now that our old ship is full and we don't give a damn,
> We'll bend on all our stu'nsails and sail for Yankee land.
>
> When we get home, our ship made fast, and we get through our
>     sailing,
> A winding glass around we'll pass and damn this blubber whaling![7]

Whaling ships stayed at sea for months and away from their home ports for years. Their captains pushed farther and farther in pursuit of whales: down the east coast of South America, up the west coast of South America, north to the cold Alaskan waters, across the Pacific to Japan, eventually into the Antarctic.

In 1828 the congressional Committee on Naval Affairs recommended that a navy ship be dispatched to the Pacific to chart islands and locate dangerous rocks. The bill failed in Congress. When hearings were again held in 1836, a Mr. Southward of the committee summarized the importance of whaling to New England ports:

> No part of the commerce of this country is more important than that which is carried on in the Pacific ocean. It is large in amount. Not less than $12,000,000 of capital are invested in and actively employed by one branch of the whale fishery alone; and in the whole trade there is, directly and indirectly, involved not less than fifty to seventy millions of property. In like manner, from 110,000 to 900,000 tons of our shipping, and from 9,000 to 12,000 of our seamen are employed, amounting to about one-tenth of the whole navigation of the Union. Its results are profitable. It is, to a great extent, not a mere exchange of commodities, but the creation of wealth, by labor, from the ocean. The fisheries alone produce, at this time, an annual income of from five to six millions of dollars; and it is not possible to look at Nantucket, New Bedford, New London, Sag Harbor, and a large number of other districts upon our northern coasts, without the deep conviction that it is alike beneficial to the moral, political and commercial interests of our fellow-citizens.[8]

The number of whaling ships produced by American shipyards was far larger than the number of clippers. By the middle of the nineteenth century, the American whaling fleet numbered more than five hundred.[9]

Clippers were always a small proportion of ships built in American yards, far outnumbered by sloops, brigs, and schooners, the vast majority being fishing boats, coastal carriers, and vessels for basic commodities (such as grain, or timber for building).[10] Even in the middle of the nineteenth century, at the height of clipper ship building in America and England, clippers were globally only a small percent of ships undertaking transoceanic crossings, especially if we include, for example, indigenous Asian ships, which carried manufactured goods from China to Southeast Asia.[11] Indian cloth and spices, Dutch plantation crops, and most immigrants to America, Australia, and South Africa traveled by slower, if less spectacular, ships. American shipyards built clippers only when specific economic opportunities made them profitable. To those we now turn.

### The North Atlantic and All the Tea in China

The first opportunity for speed translating to profit was on the transatlantic run. In the 1820s a few American shipowners figured out that passengers would pay a premium for fewer days on the rough, cold Atlantic. They would also pay a premium for a predictable schedule of departure, rather than waiting around Liverpool or New York until a ship filled with cargo and departed. These new scheduled shipping "lines," most based in New York, built and operated mainly small vessels of four hundred tons and under.[12] Speedy runs were, however, lauded in the press and built a line's reputation. Potential passengers noticed.

The second opportunity for American ships to enter a market where speed made money was the China-to-England tea trade. England and America's taste for tea produced steadily increasing demand, but the East India Company held a monopoly on the tea trade to England. Tea traveled on the company's large, slow trading ships (literally a "slow boat to China"), often arriving a year from embarkation in Canton (Guangzhou). American ships loaded tea for New York and Boston and made good profits.

In 1834, however, Parliament ended the East India Company's monopoly on the tea trade to England. Wealthier tea-drinkers in both Britain and America knew that fresher tea was more flavorful. Tea importers knew that the freshest tea of the year's crop commanded a huge premium over later shipments. Speed thus meant profit. The fastest ships commanded the highest freight rates for carrying each year's tea from China around the Cape of Good Hope to an awaiting England.

When American ships first entered the tea trade in the mid-1830s, the Chinese court permitted Europeans to operate only in the port of Canton. Long-established ties between the British traders and local officials made American access to tea difficult. With the end of the East India Company's monopoly, however, new British traders demanded more open Chinese ports. When the Chinese court refused these demands, the British navy shelled Chinese ports and initiated the Opium Wars between England and

China in the later 1830s. By 1840 British gunboats had forced the Chinese court to open four additional ports to foreign traders. The race was on to bring the freshest tea to England. American ships produced faster and faster runs, gradually displacing British ships and producing vast profits for clipper ship owners. The best of the American clippers could make the voyage from China to New York in less than ninety days. Nevertheless, even after mid-century the numbers of clipper ships in the China trade was small; never more than two dozen entered the yearly race.[13]

## California Gold

The discovery of gold in California in 1849 proved a perfect match for American clipper ships. Suddenly there existed a huge demand for passengers and goods to reach California. Men sold all they had to take a chance on a gold strike. Any ship that might survive the gales of Cape Horn immediately found passengers, but every gold-rusher wanted to arrive in California as quickly as he could afford. A folk ballad of 1851 catches the spirit of the times:

> Came from Salem city
> with a washbowl on my knee,
> I'm going to California,
> the gold dust for to see!
> It rained all night the day I left,
> the weather it was dry.
> The sun's so hot I froze to death,
> oh brothers don't you cry!
>
> *Chorus:*
> Oh California!
> That's the land for me!
> I'm off to San Francisco
> With a washbowl on my knee!
>
> I jumped on board the Lisa ship
> and traveled o'er the sea,
> And every time I thought of home
> I wished it wasn't me!
> The vessel reared like any horse
> that had of oats a wealth,

I found it wouldn't throw me,
so I thought I'd throw myself!

I thought of all the pleasant times
we've had together here,
I thought I ought to cry a bit
but couldn't shed a tear.
The pilot's bread was in my mouth,
the gold dust in my eye,
Although I'm going far away,
dear brothers don't you cry!

And when I get to Frisco boys,
it's then I'll look around,
And when I see the gold lumps there,
I'll pick them off the ground.
We'll scrape the mountains clean, me boys,
we'll drain the rivers dry!
A pocket full of rocks bring home,
Oh brothers don't you cry!

Even more important than passengers for the profitability of clipper ships
was the freight they carried, supplies for surviving in the goldfields, such as
barrels of meat, picks, clothing, tents, and wagons. Cargo worth $100 in New
York could be sold for $1,000 in San Francisco. Even with lay-ups for refit-
ting, a fast ship had the potential for two or even three trips from the East
Coast to San Francisco in a year.

Getting to the goldfields quickly became a national obsession. The mys-
tique of the clipper ships went hand in hand with newspaper coverage. With
so many ships heading to San Francisco and China, the development of racing was probably inevitable. There was youthfulness, recklessness, and a
passion for speed in the ethos of the country at the time. Recall that this was
the same period as the famous steamboat races on the Mississippi. An 1851
sea chantey captures the sailor's point of view:

It's a bully ship and a bully crew
    With a ho down, ho down.
And we're the boys to put her through
    With a ho down, ho down hey.

*Chorus:*
So blow boys blow
    For Californio.
There's plenty of gold so I've been told,
    On the banks of the Sacramento.

It's round that capstan we must go
    With a ho down, ho down,
To hoist the anchor from below
    With a ho down, ho down hey.

And when we wallop around Cape Horn . . .
You'll wish to God you'd never been born . . .

When we get 'round to Frisco town . . .
My dear stay clear of Shanghai Brown . . .

I thought I heard our captain say . . .
Those Frisco girls will steal your pay . . .

She would not steer, she would not stay . . .
She sailed high seas both night and day . . .

I thought I heard our bosun say . . .
Just one more turn and then belay . . .

Steamboats could return their cost of construction with four trips. A clipper could do even better. Some repaid their investors in two trips, and a few paid off in a single trip from New York to California, then to China to load tea, next around the Cape of Good Hope to England to sell the tea, and finally back to New York loaded with passengers and manufactured goods.[14]

## Building and Provisioning a Clipper

The *Flying Cloud* made its name on the New York to California run during the height of the California gold rush mania. The ship came out of the well-respected Boston shipyard of Donald McKay. Constructed of more than a million board feet of white oak, maple, and pine from the first-growth forests of New England, and tons of copper, both for sheathing and as the main component of brass fittings, the *Flying Cloud* was, at 1,782 tons and 235 feet

*The American Clipper Ship* Flying Cloud *at Sea
under Full Sail,* painting by Antonio Jacobsen (1913).
PHOTO COURTESY OF BOTAURUS, WIKIMEDIA COMMONS

long, one of the largest ships completed in 1851 as the gold rush peaked.[15] The company that originally contracted the ship received numerous bids while it was still under construction and promptly sold it, almost doubling their $50,000 investment. It is difficult to compare the dollar then and the dollar now. Strictly based on inflation, the second buyer paid about $2 million in today's money for the *Flying Cloud*. In actual buying power, however, the cost was much higher, perhaps as much as $5 million. In any case, the *Flying Cloud* was a good investment, its cost recouped within a few years.

On its maiden run the *Flying Cloud* carried only six passengers. Freight made the voyage profitable. Stevedores loaded the holds with cargo sure to garner a high profit in San Francisco, such as crockery, whiskey, bales of cloth, barrels of flour, tools, books, shovels, boots, twine, apples in casks, cheese, and candles.[16]

The sixty necessary crewmen were recruited. Local labor pumped forty-eight hundred gallons of water into a tank and seventeen hundred more into barrels, the quantity set by recent federal regulations. Vast amounts of provisions arrived: salted beef, pork and fish in barrels, crackers, oysters, lard, flour, butter, oats, and livestock. Hundreds of chickens cackled in cages on deck.

The provisions and cargo of the *Flying Cloud* suggest how the United States had expanded since the opening of the nineteenth century. The apples likely came from upstate New York or far inland Massachusetts. The salted beef and pork in barrels likely came from Ohio. The crockery and tools, which would have earlier come from England, might have been manufactured in New England or the relatively new cities of Syracuse or Buffalo. Cleveland might have produced the iron from Lake Superior ore. All these commodities moved to the East Coast on the Erie Canal from Buffalo to Albany, an engineering marvel that had opened in 1825.

### Sail and Steam to California

The stirring story of the *Flying Cloud*'s record-setting run to San Francisco has been told many times, from a variety of viewpoints: the design of the ship by the McKay firm, the determination of the captain to keep sail aloft even in dangerous gale conditions, the courage of the crew in cutting away broken masts in horrendous seas, and—most recently—the crucial role of the captain's wife, a trained and skilled navigator who used Maury's charts to plot the optimum course. The *Flying Cloud* crossed the equatorial doldrums, sped through the "roaring forties" (strong winds typical of the latitude forty degrees south), survived the monster waves and gales of Cape Horn, and arrived in San Francisco in eighty-nine days and nine hours, a record that stood for more than a hundred years.

Even in 1851, however, there were hints of a coming revolution in transportation. Forty-Niners, in fact, went to California mainly by steam power. One route began with a steamship from the Eastern Seaboard to the Isthmus of Panama (where the Panama Canal would be built half a century later) and a weeklong canoe and mule trek across the isthmus. Passengers then boarded another ship, either steam or sail, to San Francisco. This route was typically shorter in time than a clipper voyage but twice as expensive.

A third route to the California goldfields crossed the entire United States by land. From the East Coast a Forty-Niner could reach St. Louis by train in only two weeks and book passage on a steamboat up the Missouri to Kansas City. From there, however, the going was rough, fifteen hundred brutal miles over the Rocky Mountains by wagon train, a trip that could easily take three months, depending on season. Overall, perhaps half the Forty-Niners went by sea and half by land, but many more went by steam power than by clipper.

## Racing Down Under

Only two years after the California gold rush came the discovery of gold in Australia in 1851. The gold finds were enormous and close to the surface. One Australian gold strike produced 2.4 million pounds of gold in a single year, as registered in the assay offices of surrounding towns and cities. In 1852 three ships arrived in London together carrying more than eight tons of gold. The madness of the California gold strike was duplicated.[17] People willingly paid high fares for passage, the swifter the better. In the 1850s almost three hundred thousand people migrated from England to Australia, as did almost twenty thousand Americans.

While many men mined for gold, some women mined for gold of their own, as this ballad from 1853 shows:

> She arrived in November eighteen fifty-two,
> And a chap come aboard for a wife;
> He offered her marriage, and also to do
> His best to support her through life.
> That he was a government clerk she'd no doubt,
> And although she admired his figure,
> She frowned, and said quite plump out,
> "You don't look like a lucky gold digger."[18]

The Australian gold rush was ideal for sailing ships.[19] The continent was beyond the range of the coal a steamship could carry. Though coaling stations existed in India, they had not yet been built along the remainder of the route to Australia. Just as in the California gold rush, great profits were made in transporting equipment, supplies, and passengers.

## The End of an Era

The end of the clipper ship era came hard and fast.[20] It was a typical boom-and-bust cycle. The East Coast shipyards overbuilt as capital rushed in to make a killing in speedy transport to China, California, and Australia.

Within a few years overcapacity cut freight rates. When a more general recession began in 1857, owners sold off many clipper ships to European buyers. The new owners shortened masts and reduced sail, requiring fewer crew and producing less overall strain on the ship. These reconfigured clippers passed into humdrum freight service, carrying grain, wood, cotton, and guano for fertilizer.

In the larger picture there was a shift in the contours of American entrepreneurial activity. In the early decades of the nineteenth century the United States was a coastal country, facing the Atlantic Ocean. Entrepreneurial men thought of ships and shipping. By the 1830s this was no longer true. Opportunities in farms, mines, and lumber beckoned, as did founding banks in new towns, building steamboats, and digging canals. The future was in westward expansion.

And then there were the steamships. Design steadily developed in the 1840s and 1850s. The ships made scheduled runs that easily bettered the times of the great clipper ships. By the 1860s, composite steam-and-sail ships displaced sailing ships on all time-dependent runs, especially the transatlantic mail and passenger runs.[21] The idea of predictability and a regular schedule was immensely attractive. In the late 1850s the only routes remaining profitable for fast sailing vessels were the very long-distance runs to China and Australia, for which steamers could not carry enough coal. That all changed with the opening of the Suez Canal in 1869. While the rocks and shallows and light winds of the Red Sea made the canal of no use to sailing ships, the canal shortened the run for steamships by four thousand miles and put both China and Australia well within range.

But even before the Suez Canal opened, a fatal blow to clippers had been dealt by the Civil War. The attacks by the Confederacy on Northern shipping were very effective. More than fifteen hundred ships were attacked and burned during the course of the war, many of them clipper ships. By the end of the Civil War, few clipper ships remained. They had been burned, reconfigured for regular freight service, lost at sea, or simply worn out. With a life expectancy of only sixteen years (as calculated by the London maritime insurance industry of the time) and few yards building new clipper ships, it is no surprise that they largely disappeared within a decade after the Civil War.[22] The last production of large, multi-masted sailing vessels with massive amounts of sail was around 1900, built for the specialized grain trade to Australia.[23]

Of the thousands of clippers built between 1835 and 1860, only the *Cutty Sark* remains today. Built as a tea clipper in 1869, it made only a few runs and then was converted to a wood carrier to Australia. Later it had Portuguese owners and served as a training ship. In the 1950s the *Cutty Sark* was transferred to permanent drydock at Greenwich, England.

The era of clipper ships, though brief, illustrates important mergers of the maritime world. Until clipper ships, it was mainly governments or government-sanctioned monopolies that sent their vessels on long, world-girdling voyages, such as the East India Company's to India and China or the Dutch East India Company's voyages to Southeast Asia. The clipper ships (and whaling ships) also made these globe-circling voyages, but they were privately owned. With new navigational guides and tools, the clippers sought out any run that would yield profit for speed. Along with the whaling ships of the same period, they demonstrated that the seas were truly one world, and profits from it were for the bold.

# 14

## LUSITANIA

On the afternoon of May 15, 1915, in the midst of World War I, a grand liner of the British Cunard fleet approached the Irish coast. The *Lusitania* was the fastest passenger ship afloat at the time, but it slowed to eighteen knots for the last stage of the voyage, which was along the southern coast of Ireland. The liner, commissioned in 1907, was on its two hundred-and-second scheduled transatlantic run. On eastbound voyages the ship usually crossed the Irish Channel at night and docked at Liverpool in the morning. It was not to be. A German submarine waited off a rocky peninsula known as the Old Head of Kinsale, twenty miles south of Cork. Three months earlier, German U-boats were instructed to attack "transport ships, merchant ships, and warships." Two U-boats had been dispatched around Northern Scotland to a station off the Irish coast. The German command believed that large troopships would be crossing the Irish Channel in the ensuing weeks.[1]

The *Lusitania* was a perfect, textbook target, steaming relatively slowly on a straight course, presenting a full side view of the ship. The liner had no warship escort. The captain of the submarine, following his standing order, moved to the ideal position and torpedoed the *Lusitania*. A second large explosion quickly followed the torpedo's initial blast. The huge ship quickly listed so seriously that the crew managed to lower only a few of the lifeboats. Many survivors told stories similar to that of Mrs. Jane Lewis, a second-class passenger traveling with her husband:

> When the awful noise came people came pouring through the dining room from other parts of the ship. People fell down, people walked over them, you couldn't do anything because the boat was going sideways. We got out, luckily, because we were near the door, otherwise we never would have got out. Then we went down the stairs, instead of going up they went down [because of the heavy list], and I fell down

them. We got out onto the deck and then we stayed there, we were standing by a lifeboat, there was nobody about where we were, but there was plenty in the water. . . . We got away eventually, I was thrown into the boat, because we had to be so quick. We were rowed away from the ship, and there were people in the water everywhere.[2]

Eighteen minutes after the torpedo struck the *Lusitania*'s hull the bow went under, the stern rose high in the air, and the ship slid into the sea. Nearby fishing boasts rescued many, but hypothermia took the rest. In the following days hundreds of bodies washed up on the Irish coast. Only when the authorities compared the living with the passenger list did they understand the scope of the loss. Of the 1,959 passengers and crew aboard the *Lusitania*, 1,198 died. At the historical distance of a century it is hard to imagine how important the liners were and how complex and connected were the mental and physical worlds they occupied.

## The Marvel of the *Lusitania*

What sort of a ship was the *Lusitania*? It was—by the standards of the day—enormous: 790 feet long, 87 feet wide, and 31,500 gross tons. If the ship could have been set upright on the pavement in New York, it would have towered 150 feet taller than the Singer building, then the tallest skyscraper in the world. As it was built, the press across the world hailed the *Lusitania* as a miracle of the modern age, man's most sophisticated engineering achievement. At its launch, the chairman of the Cunard Line characterized the ship as "by far the largest vessel that had ever been put into the water. In length, breadth, and capacity she exceeded any other vessel that had been designed, whilst her engine power would be such as to send her across the Atlantic at a speed never accomplished, except by a torpedo boat destroyer."[3] Its four huge funnels made the *Lusitania* look powerful and fast.

With completion of the cabins, suites, dining rooms, exercise room, steam room, library, lounges, and shops, the *Lusitania* was ready for 552 first-class passengers, 460 second-class passengers, and 1,186 third-class passengers. First class cost the princely sum of $400 ($9,500 in today's currency) for one-way passage. Business owners and the rich occupied magnificent cabins on the boat deck, the top of the ship. Public rooms featured rare woods, marble, and stained glass. Families crossing the Atlantic, students traveling to Europe, and salesmen often traveled second class, which consisted of the rear half of five lower decks. Its dining room could seat 260 and included white pillars, a circular raised ceiling, and a mahogany sideboard. Its lounge had rose carpets and satinwood furniture. Third class (perhaps fifty dollars per passenger) consisted of small cabins, not the large dormitories typical of ships of the time, and included a women's lounge and a men's smoking room and some protected deck space. The press hailed the ship as the most elegant and sophisticated liner afloat.

The *Lusitania* also carried cargo in the hold. The manifest of its last voyage was typical, including 200,000 pounds of sheet brass, 11,762 pounds of copper, several lots of machinery from Boston, 217,157 pounds of cheese, 342,265 pounds of beef, 43,160 pounds of lard, 185,040 pounds of bacon, and several automobiles.[4]

Twenty-five huge boilers in four separate boiler rooms powered the four bronze propellers, each sixteen feet in diameter and weighing sixteen tons. The ship normally carried seven thousand pounds of coal (a week's worth of steaming), laboriously hand-loaded from coal barges. It used eight hundred to a thousand pounds of coal per day when cruising at its normal fast speed of twenty-three knots. On its last voyage, a total of 104 trimmers, in three shifts, set out coal for 138 firemen who shoveled the coal into the fireboxes.[5]

## Passengers as the New Cargo

By the middle of the nineteenth century, the shipbuilding community was well aware of the limitations of sailing ships. They were subject to the winds and not capable of a predictable, scheduled crossing. The focus on merchant shipping was the valuable cargo in the hold. Accommodations and food for passengers might be adequate, but cabins were tiny and never elegant. The deck was crowded and busy, as large crews hoisted and lowered sails.[6]

The demonstrated need for scheduled crossings of the Atlantic between Europe and the United States triggered innovation and experiment, such the screw propeller and the iron hull. By 1850 a few iron-hulled, propeller-driven ships had demonstrated the practicality of steam-driven ocean travel. Over the next few decades steam-driven ships less and less resembled wooden sailing ships. Masts shrunk, and by the 1880s the use of sails on steamships largely disappeared. Hulls changed contour, as they no longer needed to resist the strains of sails. By the 1870s further experiments in steamship construction included the double hull, watertight compartments, and improved propellers. Efficiency was improved with the invention of the double-expansion engine, which used extremely hot steam to drive one set of pistons and vented the steam directly into another set of pistons for lower-pressure expansion. Much of the crew worked in the engine rooms and was far less visible than on sailing ships. In the 1880s Britain was the nation sponsoring these innovations and building the largest, fastest, and most luxurious ships on the transatlantic run.

Steam propulsion and iron hulls made it possible to redesign ships primarily for passengers. Ships designed for the North Atlantic run attempted, in every way possible, to keep passengers away from the cold, rough, foggy, gray world outside. The activities were all inside. The idea was an interior space that was luxurious and inviting and lulled one into a sense of safety. The gym was the preferred exercise venue, along with the steam room. These ships barely had a place to walk around the deck, even if weather were good enough to warrant it.

Interior design in transatlantic liners from the 1880s onward echoed various elegant periods and places in European history, beginning with Rome. Some liners had in prominent public places columns with Roman capitals, friezes of dancing nymphs, and relief carvings of gods and goddesses. Other liner interiors featured silk panels, white trim, and inlaid furniture typical of the eighteenth-century French court. Still others evoked the carved wood paneling of English Tudor country houses or the hunting prints and tufted leather furniture of London clubs. Even Moorish interiors showed up in baths and workout rooms.[7]

Below the elegant first-class cabins and lounges was second class, mainly occupied by business travelers and families touring Europe. These decks lacked the fine woods and marble of the first-class lounges, but had simpler versions of French or club designs. Each cabin had a tiny bath.

Below the second-class accommodations traveled the immigrants to the New World. Transatlantic liner companies actively promoted opportunities in America or Canada on posters across Europe and opened offices in distant European cities for immigrants to book steerage passage.

The term "steerage" has a long history and refers to space deep in the stern, close to the rudder, the least expensive space on a ship for passengers. At the time of the *Lusitania*, steerage passage was cheap relative to first class and second class (the average steerage passage cost about $30, ranging from

$25 to $50—that is, $596 to $1,193 in today's currency), but conditions were generally appalling, much worse than those on the *Lusitania*.[8] In 1909 the United States Immigration Commission directed several of its agents, both men and women, to pose as poor immigrants and document the steerage conditions aboard all twelve major immigrant-transporting transatlantic carriers. Their findings, in part, were as follows:

> Generally the passenger must retire almost fully dressed to keep warm. Through the entire voyage, from seven to seventeen days, the berths receive no attention from the stewards. The berth, 6 feet long and 2 feet wide and with 2½ feet of space above it, is all the space to which the steerage passenger can assert a definite right. To this 30 cubic feet of space he must, in a large measure, confine himself. No space is designated for hand baggage. As practically every traveler has some bag or bundle this must be kept in the berth. . . . The open deck available to the steerage is very limited, and regular separable dining rooms are not included in the construction. . . . When to this very limited space, and much filth and stench is added inadequate means of ventilation, the result is almost unendurable. . . . The number of wash-basins is invariably by far too few, and the room in which they are placed is so small as to admit only by crowding as many persons as there are basins. The only provision for counteracting all the dirt of this kind of travel is cold salt water, with sometimes a single faucet of warm water to an entire wash room.[9]

The women agents were particularly appalled by the crew's ogling, fondling, and attacking of immigrant women.

> To get anything from an upper berth, to deposit anything in it or to arrange it, it was necessary to stand on the framework of the one below. The women often had to stand thus, with their backs to the aisle. The crew in passing a woman in this position never failed to deal her a blow—even the head steward. If a woman were dressing they always stopped to watch her, and frequently hit and handled her. . . .
> One night, when I had retired very early with a severe cold, the chief steerage steward entered our compartment, but not noticing me approached a Polish girl who was apparently the only occupant. She spoke in Polish, saying, "My head aches please go on and let me alone."

But he merely stood on and soon was taking unwarranted liberties with her. The girl, weakened by seasickness, defended herself as best she could, but soon was, struggling to get out of the man's arms. Just then other passengers entered and he released her.[10]

The numbers of immigrants were truly staggering, providing a large, steady, and profitable human cargo for the transatlantic liners. Between 1900 and the outbreak of war in 1914, twelve and a half million immigrants fled an increasingly troubled Europe for Canada, the United States, and South America. Though liners carried other cargo, their most valuable cargo was always people.

## Subsidies and National Rivalries

The era of scheduled steam transatlantic crossings began in 1840. Yet from the very beginnings of scheduled ocean travel, liners needed government subsidies to turn a profit.

Samuel Cunard, founder of the British and North American Royal Mail Steam-Packet Company, came from a family of staunch Loyalists. His father, a master carpenter, left America ahead of the Revolution, settled in Halifax, Nova Scotia, and found work in the shipyards. Young Samuel Cunard, however, cultivated American ties, living for time in Boston as a ship broker. The family firm, A. Cunard and Sons, expanded from the Halifax docks to Chatham (Miramichi), New Brunswick, building up a large trade in fish and timber. Samuel bought ships and nurtured Canadian colonial contracts, such as the monopoly of distributing East India Company tea and carrying the mails between Halifax and Boston. The move to carrying mail by steamship was a natural one for a forward-looking maritime entrepreneur like Cunard.[11] He would personally head the line until 1878 and had a no-nonsense obsession with safety, in preference to speed or opulence.

By the 1890s, liners had become a matter of national pride and rivalry. The "liner race" began in 1889 when Germany's Kaiser Wilhelm II visited the White Star Line's *Teutonic* during a review of British naval ships. He returned from the review convinced that such ships were an important means of demonstrating to the world his nation's engineering and metallurgical expertise and industrial might. With direct government funding, eight years later a German shipping company launched the 14,300-ton *Kaiser Wilhelm der Grosse.* The ship was 655 feet long, 66 feet wide, carried 1,970 total passengers, and was formally recognized as the largest and fastest steamship afloat. Its maiden voyage attracted crowds in the thousands at Bremerhaven, Southampton, and New York.[12] Germany produced six similar liners in the next nine years, deeply threatening both Britain's transatlantic shipping business and, more important, its self-image as the world's dominant maritime power.[13]

It is worth noting that other routes and destinations did not generate the intense national attention and national pride embedded in the transatlantic run. The famous British-owned Pacific & Orient Line, for example, began much like Cunard in the middle of the nineteenth century, subsidized by the government to carry mail. The government also paid for many of the passengers, who were soldiers, missionaries, and administrators heading for jobs in the colonies of India, Singapore, and Australia. P&O ran steamships from its earliest days and also made substantial profits carrying cargo, such as the transport of opium from Bombay to China and tea from China to Britain. Nevertheless, when the British government canceled its mail contracts in 1867, the company was headed toward bankruptcy until the government reversed its policy. In the later decades of the nineteenth century, P&O built new liners incorporating all the latest technological developments, such as double hulls and multiple propellers. Its first-class cabins and public areas were luxurious.[14] The P&O liners were, however, half the size (at about six thousand tons) of the new transatlantic liners and were not in the public eye. They did not inspire German competition or German press demands for competing ships.

The British government's response to the German building program of the 1890s was to open talks with Cunard, the principal British transatlantic liner owner, about construction of larger, faster, and more luxurious liners.[15] In 1904 a deal was finalized. Cunard would build two superliners, which would be faster, larger, and more luxurious than the German competition. The government would heavily subsidize both vessels, first by loaning Cunard £2.6 million at 3 percent, half the then-current commercial interest rate, payable over twenty years. The second subsidy was £150,000 annually to keep both vessels "war-ready." Third, the government guaranteed £68,000 annually for carrying the Royal Mail.[16] In return, both the *Lusitania* and its sister ship, the *Mauritania*, were built to military standards, including slightly thicker hulls, stronger bulkheads, more powerful engines, and propulsion machinery below the waterline. The intent was rapid conversion, if necessary, to carrying troops or chasing and destroying submarines.[17] Germany, of course, knew about these military specifications, and contemporary German liners were also built for conversion to armed cruisers.

Ten years later, during World War I, it became obvious how ill-suited the big liners were for combat. The configuration of liner decks precluded large guns. The liners, therefore, carried insignificant weaponry compared to a destroyer, much less a battleship. The converted liner *Carmania* fought the converted German liner *Cap Trafalgar* off the coast of Brazil in 1914. During the battle the two ships closed to within a few hundred yards of each other and fired every gun they had for ninety minutes. Though the *Carmania* took seventy-three hits, it won the day, sinking the *Cap Trafalgar*. The *Carmania* was, however, severely damaged, losing its bridge and holed below the waterline.

The most successful of the conversions was perhaps the *Kronprinz Wilhelm*, a fast German liner. At the beginning of the war in 1914 the ship was equipped with two rapid-firing 88-millimeter guns, a machine gun, and thirty-six rifles. The ship intercepted unarmed enemy freighters off the coast of South America—as much for its own endless pursuit of coal as for seizing contraband. The big liner typically overawed freighters by its sheer size, boarded them, removed the crew and goods, and dynamited them. The *Kronprinz Wilhelm* sank thirteen freighters. In April 1915, dwindling coal supplies and pervasive malnutrition aboard finally forced the ship into Newport News, Virginia, where ship and crew were interned for the remainder of the war.

The launch of the *Lusitania* in 1907 and its sister ship *Mauritania* a year later were large public events. Thousands upon thousands of the curious toured both ships before launch. The newspapers, both at home and abroad, described every detail of their size, speed, and elegance in breathless prose, and the ships were much photographed. Throughout the *Lusitania*'s seven years of service, the press always noted important people aboard.

In the period of the British-German superliner competition, the two nations also accelerated a more expensive and more lethal battleship rivalry. In the 1880s British naval strategy focused on France and Russia, not Germany. Britain launched eight new, larger battleships, which featured thicker hulls and a central battery of twelve-inch guns. Britain intended this fleet to be stronger than any two competing powers combined. Both France and

The *Lusitania* on its maiden voyage, in New York harbor, 1907.

Russia responded with new battleships, as did the United States, Japan, and Italy. Germany, however, rapidly became England's principal competition for dominance of the seas. By 1898 Germany had commissioned thirty-eight new battleships. Launched in 1906, the same year as the *Lusitania*, the British battleship *Dreadnought* featured heavier armor and more powerful turbine engines and proved the effectiveness of large-caliber turret-mounted guns as the sole armament. The *Dreadnought* set off another furious round of battleship building by Germany and other competing nations, this time including Austria, Turkey, and even Brazil and Argentina.[18]

## War and Blockade

With the outbreak of the Great War in July 1914, Great Britain moved its formidable fleet to blockade German shipping. The traditional blockade (immediately off the coast) worked well in the Atlantic, bottling up dozens of German ships in New York harbor. A traditional blockade was rather less effective on German ports because of the complex coastline and frequent fog. Britain tightened the blockade in three ways. First, it published a long list of contraband items, such as iron and brass, eventually including basic foodstuffs, thereby justifying stopping and diverting many ships from neutral countries. Second, in early November 1914 (seven months before the torpedoing of the *Lusitania*), Britain declared the entire North Sea a war zone. It asserted its right to engage not only all German ships, both naval and civilian, but also the right to stop and board any ship of a neutral country, seizing both contraband and escorting the ship to a British port. Practically, the British fleet needed only to patrol the "choke-points" of the North Sea, namely the English Channel and the passage north of Scotland. Three months later Germany retaliated, declaring all seas around Great Britain a war zone, within which any and all British ships, naval as well as civilian, would be attacked. Neutral shipping could be searched. A month later President Wilson sternly announced that Germany would be held "strictly accountable" if American citizens were hurt or killed by German attacks in the declared war zone around Great Britain, though he did not spell out what America's response might be.

Germany's declaration would seem pointless, since its fleet was incapable of blockading the entire coast of Great Britain, much less directly competing with its navy. Germany did, however, have one weapon that it could send into the newly declared war zone: submarines.

### Conventions and the Realities of War

In the months leading up to the sinking of the *Lusitania*, both Germany and Great Britain played fast and loose with established principles of a war zone, blockade, neutral shipping, protocols for seizing and boarding an enemy vessel, rights of neutral passengers, unarmed shipping, and items of contraband. Perhaps this situation was inevitable. Many of these conventions were decades old and referred to sailing ships. Rapid advances in technology made some conventions obsolete. A three-mile blockade limit, for example, put shore cities beyond the range of mid-nineteenth-century naval cannon. By the time of the Great War, naval cannon could hit targets from fifteen miles off a coast.

Many conventions reflected the relatively slow pace of sailing ships. A naval vessel was required to announce its intention to stop a vessel by a shot across the bow, by flag, or even by hailing. If the ship attempted to escape it could be fired upon and sunk. If it hove to, then an officer and crew of the naval ship boarded and examined the ship, identifying and seizing contraband, and separating enemy nationals from citizens of neutral countries.

Enemy nationals were arrested and removed, along with contraband. A ship deemed neutral was then released to continue its voyage.[19] An enemy ship was to be sailed to a home or allied port.

Early in the war Germany, in fact, tried to follow most of these conventions. The first ship sunk by a German submarine was a British freighter, the 866-ton *Gitra* bound from Scotland to Norway. The sub surfaced, challenged the freighter, allowed time for the crew to lower and board lifeboats, and towed the lifeboats closer to the Norwegian coast before returning to the *Gitra*, opening the stopcocks, and sinking her.

The British were aware of U-boats in the North Sea, but most naval experts discounted their threat. Germany had only about thirty submarines. At any time, a third were headed to assigned positions, another third were returning to base, and only nine or ten hunted British shipping. In September 1914, however, a single German submarine sank three substantial British warships, each about twelve thousand tons, a convincing show of their lethality.[20]

By the end of February 1915, the formalities of capture seemed less and less relevant to submarine warfare. German submarines had sunk ten British ships totaling thirty-two thousand tons. In about half the attacks the submarine had surfaced and practiced the formalities of capture. From the British viewpoint, March was considerably worse. Submarines sank twenty ships, totaling over sixty thousand tons, few with prior warning. The Admiralty recruited much of the British commercial fishing fleet to search for mines and submarines off the coasts of Great Britain. These tactics had some success. April's losses dropped to eleven ships, totaling twenty-two thousand tons. The German submarines adjusted to the patrols of the trawlers. In May, German submarines sank nineteen ships of eighty-four thousand total tons, including the *Lusitania*'s thirty-one thousand tons; virtually none of the attacks included prior warning.[21] It is perhaps worth noting that Germany rapidly expanded its submarine fleet to 115 submarines.[22] By the later years of the war, submarines would sink half a million tons of Allied shipping per month, which was more than the tonnage sunk in the entire first year of hostilities.

## Liners and Submarines

Early in the war the Admiralty assumed that the fast British liners could outrun the slower submarines. Both sides knew that prior warning was particularly unlikely in a confrontation between a submarine and a liner. If a submarine surfaced to announce its presence and intentions, it was quite vulnerable to even a couple of four-inch or six-inch guns mounted on the ship.[23] And it had no way of knowing whether or not the liner was armed. Other British liners, such as the *Carmania*, had indeed been converted and armed. The only reason the *Lusitania* had not been armed as a submarine-destroying cruiser was that the Admiralty decided it used too much coal for long-distance patrolling. It was more valuable on its regular New York to London–Southampton run, bringing crucial supplies and people to England.[24] Even if it were completely unarmed, it is hard to imagine a huge liner with a crew of several hundred peaceably surrendering to boarding and capture by perhaps half the thirty-five-man crew of a submarine, much less the submarine's crew somehow sailing the liner to a German home port (which in any case was blockaded by the British fleet). Both England and Germany were well aware that a British liner, if threatened by a surfaced enemy submarine, was under Admiralty orders to ram and sink it, though there were no actual encounters in which a liner rammed a U-boat.

## Aftermath: A World of Moral Outrage

Telegraphic news coverage of the torpedoing of the *Lusitania* reached major newspapers around the world within a day. The American press generally covered the event as a barbaric attack on an innocent, unarmed vessel. Political cartoons accelerated the portrayal of Germany as barbaric Huns. Politicians, from President Wilson on down, deplored the attack and particularly the death of Americans. The torpedoing of the *Lusitania* became one of the standard arguments for America's entry into the war on the side of Britain and its allies and a regular feature of military recruitment posters in Great Britain.

The debate over the morality of the sinking of the *Lusitania* continued for decades. In the 1920s, families of Americans killed on the *Lusitania* sought reparations; Germany summarily denied their claims, citing not only their presence on a British ship in a declared war zone but also pointing out England's prior "illegal" blockade.[25] The debate has continued in law journals and in books ever since. The case for murder has been asserted repeatedly, most recently in a book by Diana Preston titled *Wilful Murder*.[26] The opposite point of view stresses that Britain knew the risks of continuing to run the

Political cartoon of Uncle Sam delivering note of warning
to the kaiser after the torpedoing of the *Lusitania*,
from the *Philadelphia Record*, 1915.

*Lusitania*, Americans knew the risk of traveling on a British vessel into a declared war zone, the Admiralty did little to protect the *Lusitania*, and Britain had violated the rules of naval warfare at least as much as the Germans.
The fullest development of this position was laid out three decades ago in
*The Lusitania Disaster: An Episode in Modern Warfare and Diplomacy*, by
Thomas Bailey and Paul Ryan. Perhaps the most balanced recent discussion
is David Ramsey's *Lusitania: Saga and Myth* (2001).[27] The authors accept
that the *Lusitania* was hardly an innocent civilian liner and that the torpedoing was hardly simple cold-blooded murder. The ship carried crucial
war matériel, such as brass, iron, and shell casings. Secondary explosions

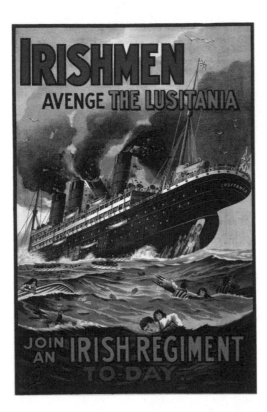

World War I recruiting poster.

suggest the ship carried ammunition. As in most long-standing historical debates about actions in wartime, one's viewpoint depends on one's selection of the "facts" of the event. Whatever the judgments of later writers and scholars, it does seem clear that the Admiralty had the option of laying up the *Lusitania* for the duration of hostilities and chose not to do so, either because the supplies it carried were essential to the war effort or its continued running provided a psychological boost in the dark days of war.

## Postwar Liners

World War I produced winners and losers in the transatlantic trade, which reflected the winners and losers of the war. Cunard lost nine liners to German torpedoes, but four returned to service. Nevertheless, the company was financially sound, benefited from government subsidies, and built thirteen new ships in the 1920s.[28] Smaller lines from Great Britain had suffered losses but built new liners. The pattern was much the same for the Allies, except for Russia, which had never had much presence on the transatlantic run. French and Italian lines and the government of the United States received German liners as war reparations. France used them and then replaced them with new vessels. The United States gave the German ships to a new American company, but the experiment failed. Novices on the route could not compete with the experienced English lines. The neutral countries, by and large, did well. German submarines had not attacked their ships, and their economies were largely intact. The two big German lines suffered. Without liners or any chance of subsidies from a German government saddled with massive war reparations, the lines struggled but survived. They bought back a few reparation ships from the United States and managed to build more in the 1920s.[29]

All lines depended on the immigrants in third class probably more than they depended on the luxurious first class. When the United States Congress passed the Johnson-Reed Act of 1924, it effectively ended the period of mass immigration from Europe to the United States. Quotas reduced immigration to a trickle, virtually stopping immigration from Italy and Eastern Europe. Many of the smaller lines, which were heavily dependent on immigrant traffic, simply failed and disappeared. Others shifted to freight service.

Even the large British and French lines scrambled to fill the lower-class cabins. They advertised on American college campuses, promoting student travel to Europe for the summer or a semester. They advertised in the national magazines, promoting the idea of a European vacation for the middle class.

Several lines experimented with winter cruises, shifting the liners to warm locales. These early cruise experiments encountered a host of problems. Liners designed for the North Atlantic run were, for the most part, inward looking. They lacked an outdoor pool and poolside seating, an outside bar. Dining rooms and lounges did not open to the outside tropical sunshine, which was the point of a cruise. Air conditioning was another problem, unnecessary on the Atlantic run but very desirable for tropical cruising.

The liners were also set up for complete physical separation of the various classes of traveler. Stairs and elevators did not go from one class to the other. Different classes ate in their own dining rooms and walked on deck out of sight of each other. In contrast, while some cabins on a cruise ship certainly cost more than others, the cruise experience was to be a shared one. Passengers were to eat together, mix around the pool, and generally enjoy the tropical climate outside together. Unlike the Atlantic run, the cruise itself was the destination. The ship and its experience had to be delightful enough to produce satisfied customers who would recommend the experience to their friends. Therefore, entertainment, shore shopping, and land trips became central concerns of the cruise line.

The world of seaborne passenger travel did not, therefore, quite yet constitute a single, global maritime world. At least through World War I, liners of different countries were built in their country's shipyards and looked somewhat different.[30] Their crews were nationals. They were built for particular runs. P&O Line ships, which mainly sailed in warm climates, were configured differently from ships of the cold North Atlantic run. Passenger ships all carried freight, but the portion of the ship given over to freight varied from ship to ship and run to run. The full separation of freight from passengers and the true emergence of a single cruising world were still decades away.

# *15*

# *EXXON VALDEZ*

On March 24, 1989, the *Seattle Times* carried the first, fragmentary story on the wreck of the *Exxon Valdez*. The information came from the Coast Guard. The 987-foot-long tanker had departed the Valdez oil terminal at the head of Prince William Sound, in Alaska, bound for Long Beach, California, when the ship encountered large chunks of floating ice and maneuvered to avoid them. Twenty-five miles southeast of the terminal, the *Exxon Valdez* was far outside the marked ship channel. At 12:20 a.m. the ship grounded hard on Bligh Reef (a known and charted hazard) and began to leak oil. As the paper reported, there was plenty of oil to leak. The *Exxon Valdez* carried "at least" 1.2 million barrels, or over 50 million gallons of Alaska crude.

Though the *Seattle Times* headline of March 24 read "Tanker in Massive Spill off Valdez," the initial information from the Coast Guard was, on the whole, optimistic. A Coast Guard oil strike team and experts from Exxon were flying to Valdez. Though oil was still leaking, it was leaking "slowly," and the estimated leak was perhaps 150,000 barrels, or 6.3 million gallons. Offshore winds would keep the spill from the coast. The plan was to deploy booms to contain the spill, pump off the surface oil, and dispose of it at the terminal. Another tanker near the *Exxon Valdez* would pump oil from the stricken ship into its empty tanks. There was concern about the "structural integrity" of the *Exxon Valdez*.[1]

Within hours, news of the wreck of the *Exxon Valdez* spread around the world. Featured stories appeared, as might be expected, in the *Washington Post*, *New York Times*, *Boston Globe*, *Toronto Star*, *Chicago Tribune*, *San Francisco Chronicle*, and *Los Angeles Times*. On March 25, coverage also appeared in newspapers in many smaller cities, such as the *Orlando Sentinel*, the *St. Petersburg Times*, the *Austin American Statesman*, the *Providence Journal*, and the *Orange County Register*. Even more compelling was the TV coverage. Small planes and helicopters flew over the ship and the spill all

High-pressure steam hoses in the cleanup of the *Exxon Valdez* spill.

day. By the time of the evening news, pictures of the spreading slick reached millions of homes.

Twenty-four hours later things looked worse—much worse. As the *Seattle Times* reported the next day, the *Exxon Valdez* had massively leaked for more than twelve hours. Spill estimates rose to 8.4 million gallons, the largest in U.S. history. An oil slick more than five miles long extended into the ice-filled waters of Prince William Sound and closed the port of Valdez. Local manpower struggled to contain the spill with booms and water sprays.[2]

It was difficult at the time for people to conceptualize the quantity of oil that had leaked into Prince Edward Sound. It still is. It was enough oil to give a gallon jug of oil to every man, woman, and child in New York City and have plenty left over. It could have filled the tank of every car and truck in San Francisco or Philadelphia. It would fill a football-field-size swimming pool to a depth of twenty-four feet.

In the next couple of days ominous rumblings of bigger problems began to appear in news stories. The *Anchorage Daily News* headlined "Valdez Spill Oil Officials React Slowly to Disaster" as the slick spread to thirty-two square miles. A reporter interviewed local fishermen who worried about the impact on their livelihood.[3] Some articles emphasized that the huge spill would soon come ashore and that containment efforts were already failing. The press the following day reported alcohol testing for the captain and crew of the *Exxon Valdez*. A long piece by Larry Prior in the *Los Angeles Times* suggested that the debate over the safety of drilling in the far north was about to be reopened.[4]

Reporters and photographers descended on Prince William Sound. The defining photos of the disaster emerged: oil-covered rocks and beaches; black, oil-covered birds; dead whales; the big eyes of dying sea otters and frantic efforts of local people to clean them. The ship, the oil, the ecological disaster, the local reaction, the moral outrage, and the legal process of assigning responsibility and restitution each define a world to which the *Exxon Valdez* belonged. The major litigation was quickly settled, but the cleanup would last for years. The debate on the environmental damage continues to this day. Let us begin with the ship.

## The World of Oil Tankers

What sort of ship was the *Exxon Valdez*? Oil transported by sea was one of man's earliest trade commodities. Recall, for example, the oil amphorae of the Uluburun shipwreck in chapter 3. Oil transport remained in casks and barrels for millennia, through the large-scale whaling operations of the middle decades of the nineteenth century.

The discovery of petroleum in Pennsylvania in 1859 produced a lamp oil much cheaper and easier to obtain than whale oil. A decade later, John D. Rockefeller's well-funded Standard Oil Company began bringing his lamp oil—in barrels—to the world.[5] Many within the developing petroleum industry realized that barrels were slow, costly, and inefficient. The first ship designed specifically for bulk oil transport was the *Zoroaster*, built by the brother of Alfred Nobel (inventor of dynamite) in 1877. It carried the oil in several tanks, divided both fore-and-aft and transversely. Both Standard Oil and Shell Oil quickly adopted this design. The next significant design innovation was the *Gluckhauf* (1886), which placed the oil in divided compartments surrounded by a double hull. By 1891, about seventy ships, largely British or American, had been custom-designed for service in the petroleum trade.[6]

By 1900 the electric lightbulb was displacing oil lamps, but two major markets for petroleum opened up. One was the use of fuel oil to replace coal in propelling ships. The second was gasoline to power automobiles. The 1920s were boom times for oil, the market almost entirely controlled by three British firms and the eight companies that emerged from the breakup of Standard Oil. It was a time of discovery of new oilfields, negotiation for foreign oil concessions, and exploration of new markets.[7]

With the approach of World War II the United States Navy was in desperate need of oil transport for its fleet and created a standard tanker vessel design, which could be built in any large shipyard. The navy specified and paid for more powerful engines for greater speed and other wartime modifications. During the war the United States built a total of 481 standardized oil tankers (523 feet long and 21,100 ton displacement) on an assembly line basis.[8] Many went into commercial service after the war. These ships proved a template for worldwide postwar tanker production.

Since World War II, oil tankers have followed a simple, functional shape, which is basically a long, flat box, rather like a box for tall boots. The bottom is essentially flat, and the top is slightly crowned for seawater runoff, with a series of hatches to fill the tanks.[9] The bow is contoured to ride through waves, and the stern features a multistory control tower, below which are the engine room and bunker oil tanks to run the engines. Loading the oil merely requires it to flow down from onshore storage into the ship's tanks. Unloading requires complex onboard piping, and pumps located just ahead of the engine compartment. To maintain stability tankers must incorporate large amounts of ballast (mainly water) distributed throughout the ship.[10]

The important point here is that oil tankers have become a worldwide, internationally regulated product.[11] There is nothing distinctive about a vessel's design that would identify it as having been constructed in Japan, Sweden, or Indonesia. Procedures at oil terminals, safety protocols, and pollution control practices are equally internationally regulated, if not always so in practice.

### The Economic World of the *Exxon Valdez*

Just as truly as the *Exxon Valdez* was grounded in Prince William Sound, so was it stuck in the economics of oil transport and the American politics of oil. Let us first look at the worldwide oil fleet. For three decades prior to the *Exxon Valdez* disaster, the total oil tanker fleet remained at about three thousand ships. The tanker fleet capacity, however, expanded from about 60 million tons to around 300 million tons as new, larger vessels came online. In the early 1960s no tanker was over 100,000 tons capacity; by 1983, 823 tankers were over 100,000 tons, and 27 were over 400,000 tons. The largest ships of the fleet now transport two million tons of crude or more. Company ships like the *Exxon Valdez* moved oil from company-owned terminals to

The *Abqaiq*, a typical large modern tanker, photographed in the Persian Gulf, 2003.

company-owned cracking plants and formed about 40 percent of the fleet. The remainder of the fleet was privately owned, many by Greek magnates.[12]

Privately owned tankers formed a complex international web of leases and charters. Registry largely depended on the country with the lowest taxes. In the 1980s about 30 percent of the private tanker fleet was registered in Liberia, another 5 percent in Panama. Ten percent were registered in Japan, reflecting that country's heavy dependence on foreign oil. Greece, Norway, the United States, Great Britain, and France each flagged between 5 percent and 8 percent of the fleet. The rest of the tanker fleet was divided among dozens of countries with a few ships.[13]

At the simplest economic level, oil transport depends on supply and demand, but both factors can be complex and fast moving. Tankers compete with long-distance pipelines for transport from the fields to the processing plants. A new pipeline can displace many tankers. Economic development of an oil-producing country may keep the oil at home. Government policy may shift energy needs to nuclear, wind, or solar power, decreasing the overall consumption of oil. Oil prices respond to political crises, which are perceived by oil brokers as potentially or actually disrupting supply. In 1969, for example, Egypt closed the Suez Canal and forced all shipping to go around Africa, producing suddenly higher transportation costs for oil. In 1973 the oil-producing countries of the Middle East formed a marketing group (OPEC) and set higher prices. The United States responded with programs to import less oil, while private citizens drove less and set their thermostats down. Demand for oil dropped, and tankers were taken out of service, anchored in any suitable location from Borneo to the Norwegian fjords.

Although worldwide crude oil production has steadily increased (topping a billion tons in 1960 and two billion tons in 1965[14]), the tanker business is characterized by boom-and-bust cycles. Fleet owners order tankers in good times, and the tankers sit idle in the next down cycle.

A tanker was expected to last about thirty years, but between 1960 and 1989 fleet owners replaced smaller tankers with larger ones at a much faster rate. In some years between 1960 and 1985 more than a hundred tankers were scrapped and about as many came into service. In lean years of low demand for oil, only a handful of tankers came out of the shipyards.

One constant in these long-term trends and short-term crises is that a tanker only made money if it moved oil. Companies and private owners established an industry standard of only seventy-two hours for turnaround time at both oil terminals and cracking plants. A tanker might lay up for twenty days a year for cleaning and refitting. Otherwise, today's oil fleet of three thousand tankers constantly plies the world's oceans. Instantly communicated deals decide where a ship will next collect oil and where it will take it. The closest land-based analogy to the oil fleet is the day-to-day or hour-to-hour dispatch of a truck fleet for pickups and deliveries.

## Tankers and the Environment

Let us begin with four truisms. First, oil is intrinsically polluting to any land or water with which it comes in contact, whether by natural seepage, at a wellhead, issuing from a broken pipeline, or simply thrown out behind a gas station. Second, no technological process is risk-free. Parts wear; humans fall asleep or make incorrect decisions. Third, the beneficiaries of a technology, whether nuclear power, electric lightbulbs, or a car, expect it to work safely and efficiently without much conscious thought or effort. Fourth, the tanker industry resists any new regulations—whether environmental, safety, pay of labor, or number of crew onboard—that slow turnaround time or raise costs.

In the decades after World War II when the oil-delivery technology apparently ran smoothly and safely, there was no "news," and people mainly ignored how gas got to their pump or heating oil to their furnace. The most powerful influence on government regulations and international policy was the oil lobby. Voices speaking against all-out drilling and for environmental preservation were generally weaker and less effective.

Nevertheless, spills had been a periodic feature of the oil business. Between, for example, 1967 and the year of the *Exxon Valdez*, 1989, there had been seven major tanker spills, ranging from four times to nine times the size of the *Exxon Valdez* disaster. Running aground caused three; two were collisions, and one was an explosion and fire.[15]

The most famous of these spills was *Torrey Canyon* (1967) off the coast of Cornwall. Estimated at thirty-five million gallons, it was the largest spill in history, at the time. Within twenty-four hours of the wreck the oil spill was twenty miles long. The British government was unable to control the slick as it spread across 150 miles of the south coast of England, the Isles of Scilly, and 150 miles of French beaches. An unusual pattern of wind kept the oil from fouling much more of the nearby coasts. The ship broke in half on the rocks, which precluded any attempt to pump out oil. Navy planes dropped ten thousand tons of chemical degreasers, dispersing some of the oil into tiny droplets, which were, unfortunately, highly toxic to fish, sea animals, and birds. Estimates of birds killed varied wildly, from 25,000 to 150,000. In the end the government directed the air force to burn the ship, which also failed. Eventually the ship sank and continued to ooze oil for years and fouled the ecosystem for decades. The most concentrated damage was on the island of Guernsey. The government pumped three thousand tons of oil that threatened its coastline into an unused quarry, where it still kills birds regularly.[16]

The debate in Parliament was surprisingly subdued. British Petroleum, which had chartered the *Torrey Canyon*, disclaimed any responsibility but eventually paid a small amount of compensation. The main political impact of the oil spill was on international regulations. Two years after the wreck many signatories passed the International Convention on Civil Liabilities for

Oil Pollution Damage, which defined who was liable in the event of a spill. A decade later, many countries signed the International Convention for the Prevention of Pollution from Ships (MARPOL), which addressed both routine marine activities and large-scale spills.[17]

Some features of the *Torrey Canyon* disaster prefigured the *Exxon Valdez* spill, such as ineffectual efforts to contain the spill and its immediate impact on birds and sea animals. Local fisherman rightly worried about their livelihood. Much, however, had changed in the two decades between the two wrecks. Those concerned about the environment were no longer a fringe and ineffectual minority. Mainstream media took the *Exxon Valdez* spill seriously and covered the tragedy relentlessly. The wreck and its consequences dominated the nightly news for weeks. Ordinary citizens could not avoid the question of how oil and its delivery technology threatened the environment. Commentators questioned what seemed like inadequate regulation. Environmental organizations became heroes, gained members, visibility, and governmental attention. Questions of how the disaster could have happened were followed by who was responsible. There was no question of Exxon disclaiming responsibility. The environmental crisis spurred debate in city councils and state legislatures. National legislatures debated how vulnerable their coastlines were to similar spills. Various international maritime bodies and the United Nations debated the adequacy of regulations.[18]

## Restitution

Unlike the *Torrey Canyon* wreck, the *Exxon Valdez* spill almost immediately triggered extensive citizen lobbying for improved regulations and planning. Congressional hearings followed. It is important to recall that the port of Valdez was the southern terminus of the Trans-Alaska Pipeline, the building of which had generated one of the most fiercely fought battles ever between environmentalists and oil interests. Throughout congressional hearings and in news interviews the oil industry assured Americans that the pipeline would be safe and would not harm the environment. Spokesmen described migrating elk passing along the pipeline and Alaska's pristine waters staying pristine. The degree of public moral outrage following the *Exxon Valdez* spill reflected citizens' feelings of having been misled.[19]

Within months, with bipartisan support, Congress passed the Oil Pollution Act of 1990, which established a basic framework for the federal government to initiate and lead the response to an oil spill disaster. The bill required and provided the budget for the Department of Commerce to consult with state and local governments to develop site-specific oil spill contingency plans. It provided funds for purchase and local storage of booms and other oil spill equipment and up to a billion dollars per incident for dealing with major oil spills. The legislation clarified the shipowner's financial and legal responsibility for an oil spill and its cleanup, based on the contingency plans. The legislation also mandated that owners of ships carrying oil, drilling-platform owners, and oil transfer facilities develop specific site-based spill contingency plans. A ship company's federal liability began with $1,000 per barrel spilled, but could go to $25,000 a day if the company did not comply with federal cleanup orders. The act emphasized that these limits did not apply to states, which had no limits on the size of damages for which they could sue.[20]

In the months after the *Exxon Valdez* disaster the federal government began litigation for damages from Exxon. The need for hard evidence of immediate effects of the spill generated a large number of scientific studies of damage to fish, birds, and marine animals. Other research focused on economic loses to fishing, recreation, public lands, and local subsistence-based Native American groups.[21] Two years later, in October 1991, in an out-of-court settlement, Exxon paid over a billion dollars for cleanup and restitution. Exxon would eventually pay another billion dollars in claims.

Evidence at congressional hearings in 1993 suggested that effects of the spill were much wider and longer lasting than Exxon predicted. A Native American elder, for example, spoke of the fouling of the shores and the disappearance of seals two hundred miles from the wreck.[22] As in no other oil spill, science was brought to bear on the effects. The need for hard evidence for the government's lawsuit generated hundreds of scientific environmental studies, on salmon, herring, trout, fish, birds, lichens, sea otters, mussels, kelp, tidal grasses, barnacles, and plankton. Specialists counted species, examined samples, and judged what had happened. This data and the resulting conclusions initially remained unknown to the public, hidden in the lawsuit's evidence. After the settlement these studies became public; more were funded by the settlement.

The results should have alerted the public to the complexity of shoreline and riparian ecologies and the equally complex long-term impacts of oil spills.[23] Not everything that ate the oil necessarily died. Certain species of microbes flourished on oil, shifting the proportions of organisms in the oil-laden areas, which in turn affected populations of small crustaceans and fish, right up the food chain.[24] Much of the research, however, was too specialized, too short term, or covered too small an area to be of much use in formulating policy.[25] Much of it was too complicated for the public to even understand.

What happened to the oil of the *Exxon Valdez* spill? The details depend on water temperature, waves, and currents, but spills display a general pattern. Crude oil is a mixture of shorter and longer carbon chains. In a spill the shorter, more volatile fraction of the oil, perhaps 20 percent of the total volume, evaporates within a couple of days. Newsmen flying over the Valdez reported the sickening stench of oil. The next heavier fraction of the oil, perhaps 14 percent of the spill, disperses into the water in tiny droplets, which may travel long distances and enter the food chain via microbes that eat the carbon. The remaining oil from a spill, perhaps 50 percent, is heavy and sticky. Perhaps half this oil comes ashore, fouling beaches, coating birds, and killing seals. Some goes to the bottom, and some forms floating balls. As much as 20 percent cannot be accounted for. Biological breakdown of heavy oil proceeds very slowly, sometimes producing toxic by-products. The heaviest fraction of the oil usually forms balls and ends up embedded in beaches. More than a quarter century after the *Exxon Valdez* spill many beaches along Prince William Sound have either a layer of oil or balls of oil a few inches below the surface.[26]

What happened to the *Exxon Valdez*? Eventually the ship was floated off Bligh Reef and towed from Alaska to the San Diego shipyard from which it had been launched three years earlier. Boulders embedded in the hull had to be removed, the entire bottom and starboard side replaced, and the tanks rebuilt.[27] The company changed the ship's name to the *SeaRiver Mediterranean*, and it returned to service in late summer of 1990. The ship carried oil without incident for more than twenty years, though barred from Alaskan waters. The ship was converted to a Chinese-owned ore carrier in 2011 and finally scrapped in 2012.[28]

## Tankers after the *Exxon Valdez* disaster

The Oil Pollution Control Act (U.S.) and the international MARPOL regulations significantly lowered maritime oil pollution. One of the most important and least noticed provisions changed discharge of ballast. Before these new laws, tankers simply discharged ballast seawater, which was fouled with oil, into the ocean. Every year a volume of oil equivalent to a major oil spill reached the ocean from this routine practice. Under the new regulations such discharges became illegal, and companies quickly developed methods that concentrated and recovered the oil before discharging the seawater ballast.[29] New practices in tank cleaning also limited oil reaching the oceans. In a radical departure from previous practices, the new regulations also allowed the U.S. Coast Guard to board and inspect tankers for an on-board disaster plan and safety equipment, and search for illegal polluting practices.

Navigation technology has also dramatically improved, principally with the introduction of satellite-based global positioning systems after 2000. Internationally agreed shipping lanes in crowded channels have decreased collisions. Bow and stern thrusters make tankers more maneuverable when docking in a harbor or at an offshore facility.

A major direct effect of the wreck of the *Exxon Valdez* was on tanker design. For decades maritime engineers and other specialists had discussed the benefits of double-hull construction. The logic of such construction seems obvious. If the ship runs aground or collides with another ship, a second interior hull might stay intact and prevent an oil spill. Tanker owners had resisted double hulls on the grounds of cost and unproven benefit in a grounding or a collision. The new legislation, however, mandated double hulls in new construction and the phasing out of single-hull tankers as they were taken out of service.

The new regulations have, by and large, worked. There has not been a major tanker spill since two in 1991: the *M/T Haven* off the coast of Italy (45 million gallons) and the *ABT Summer* in the South Atlantic seven hundred miles west of Angola (51–81 million gallons).

The two largest oil spills in history were, however, yet to come. The first was the opening of valves at the principal Kuwaiti oil terminal and aboard docked tankers by retreating Iraqi troops along the coast of the Persian Gulf in 1991. That spill has been estimated at 380–550 million gallons and produced a four-inch-thick layer of oil across three thousand square miles of the Persian Gulf. The second disaster was, of course, the underwater explosion of the *Deepwater Horizon* oil rig, which leaked 206 million gallons of oil into the Gulf of Mexico in 2010. It is still too early to access the possibly profound effects on the ecology of the Gulf.[30]

# The Unified World of Oil Tankers

Understanding oil tankers today is now possible only within a fully integrated worldwide perspective. Oil tankers share a common design whether they are built in the United States, Europe, Russia, or any of several countries in Asia. Ownership of the total fleet is fragmented and global. If a broker set out to find a ship to carry crude from a field in the Middle East to China, he or she might contract a ship from Poland or Brazil. Contracts for shipping oil are also standard across the world, specifying duration of charter, pickup and delivery locations, turnaround time, and penalties for failing to meet schedule.

Another global feature of the tanker trade consists of well-known companies, which rate the safety and reliability of both individual ships and whole fleets. Shipping underwriters, such as Lloyd's of London, likewise rate tankers across the entire world.[31]

All tankers now operate within an international regulatory world, which specifies safety features, disaster preparedness, and post-voyage cleaning procedures. Protocols for entering and leaving harbors and offshore terminals apply to every tanker, regardless of ownership. In similar fashion a captain of a tanker must have up-to-date information on shipping channels in crowded locales, whether it be the English Channel or the Strait of Malacca.

Crewing a tanker has also gone global. Owners know that a crew from the Philippines might receive only a quarter of the wages of an American or European crew. Across the globe cheaper labor has forced out more expensive labor on tankers. Global competition has steadily led to smaller crews and more automation. Today, a tanker the length of three football fields is run, day and night, by twenty to twenty-five men.

The big oil companies have been global for decades, exploring and developing fields from Southeast Asia to the Arctic. Even they have taken an environmental stance with their advertising, stressing their conservation ethic and the stewardship approach. They know all too well that a public once burned by the *Exxon Valdez* and twice burned by the *Deepwater Horizon* would extract heavy penalties if such an accident were to happen again. They want to build tankers to global standards, use the global positioning and communications systems, comply with the global environmental regulations because they must, but stay out of the global news spotlight that a spill would trigger.

# COSTA CONCORDIA

The last voyage of the *Costa Concordia* began like any other since its launch in 2006. The big, modern cruise ship departed Savona (about twenty-five miles west of Genoa) on the Italian Riviera, sailed west to Marseille and Barcelona, then returned to Rome via the Balearic Islands, Sardinia, and Sicily. The last leg of its cruise was north along the Italian coast from the port of Rome to the *Costa Concordia*'s home port of Savona.

On the night of January 13, 2012, the Italian news agency ANSA reported that the *Costa Concordia* had run aground on the small island of Giglio on the west coast of Italy. Initial details were sketchy, but at least six people were known dead, and all 4,234 of the passengers and crew had to be evacuated. The ship's severe list was, as a company spokesperson said, "making more difficult the last part of the evacuation."[1]

The following day more harrowing information came from interviews with the shaken passengers. The disaster began during dinner. The ship hit something, most likely a submerged rock. Silverware and dishes crashed to the floor.[2] The lights went out and the ship lost power, upright but drifting. Almost an hour later the ship hit the reef in two places and began to roll, the list still only fifteen degrees. The first lifeboat was launched an hour and ten minutes after the ship hit the rock. In the next hour the list increased to seventy degrees. People were thrown down the steeply canted floors. Below, passengers struggled against water, which flooded the ship. Passengers below found stairways at crazy angles. The only lights were the flashing beacons of life vests that passengers grabbed. Most of the passengers got off the boat in this critical period. The list of the *Costa Concordia* became so severe that it was impossible to lower most of the lifeboats.

Over the next six hours, Italian Coast Guard helicopters ferried the remaining fifty people on board to safety. More than sixty passengers and crew were injured. Through Saturday night and into Sunday morning divers

The *Costa Concordia* heeled over on the Italian coast.

PHOTO COURTESY OF RVONGHER, WIKIMEDIA COMMONS

searched the water-filled areas belowdecks, hampered by cold water and masses of floating furniture and mattresses in submerged hallways. The divers found a Korean couple alive and later a surviving member of the crew. The Coast Guard divers found three bodies—two French passengers and a Peruvian crewman—killed in the initial impact. Two more passengers in life jackets were drowned below. In the early hours it seemed that nine passengers and six crew were missing, though such counts were tentative at best. One diver found the ship's black box recording its last moments. Eventually the cruise company would acknowledge that thirty-two people died that night.

By dawn TV footage flashed around the world the signature image of the *Costa Concordia* disaster, a huge ship on its side impaled on jagged rocks.[3] Newspaper articles appeared in Mexico, Russia, South Africa, the Middle East, India, and China.[4] The wreck generated more than three thousand newspaper articles in multiple languages over the next month.

A day after the rescue, passengers and the Coast Guard reported that the captain had left the ship by lifeboat shortly after the accident and watched the rescue from shore, refusing to return to the ship. The shipowner guardedly reported that there "had been procedural errors." The following day the captain was arrested and jailed.

For the next year private reviews within the company, public hearings, and court cases would take testimony from the captain, the crew, and passengers. The *Costa Concordia* may have been trapped on the rocks, but it still sailed just as dangerous economic, political, and legal waters.

## Cruise Ship Design

What sort of a ship was the *Costa Concordia*? The ship's design was, paradoxically, both old and new. About a century before the launch of the *Costa Concordia*, owners of transatlantic liners clearly understood a problem. Transatlantic passenger traffic fell off in the winter months. The Atlantic was cold, the weather gray, and the seas rough. In the 1890s a handful of lines decided to divert a ship or two to sail the warm, calm waters of the Caribbean, whose storm season was in the summer. The plan attracted wealthy leisure travelers.

Traditional transatlantic liners were ill suited to tropical waters. Everything about their design directed passenger attention inward to luxurious lounges, libraries, and formal dining rooms. Deck space was relatively small and cramped. Pools were tiny. Another problem with the use of transatlantic liners for cruising was their rigid divisions of travelers by class. It is hard to imagine anyone choosing the bare-bones layout of third class for a vacation.

In 1899 the head of the Hamburg-American Line opted for a radical experiment. Over the objections of his board he ordered the *Prinzessin Victoria Luise*, a ship specifically designed for luxury cruising. Compared to transatlantic liners of the time, it was small, only four hundred feet long and fifty feet wide. The ship carried no cargo, so that cabins could be large and luxurious. There was plenty of room for reading and socializing on deck. The ship looked and felt more like a big yacht than a small liner. Rich Americans and Europeans booked cruises.

The life of the *Prinzessin Victoria Luise* was, unfortunately, short. Only five years after launch its captain confused lighthouses on the coast of Jamaica and drove the ship onto rocks outside Kingston harbor. Unable to back the ship off the rocks, the captain retired to his cabin and shot himself. The passengers and crew survived, but the ship was a total loss. It was to be seven decades before any line would again design a ship explicitly for cruising.

After World War I, transatlantic lines did what they had done before the war—move liners unneeded in winter from the Atlantic to cruise the warm climates of the Mediterranean and the Caribbean. All these ships, of course, carried cargo, and none of them were built specifically for the warm climates. Their attraction was mainly the destinations: Havana, Puerto Rico, the Bahamas, or Egypt, Tangier, Italy. It is perhaps worth noting that the Mediterranean in the winter is stormy and relatively rainy, but certainly warmer than England or northern France. (The idea of modern cruising—that is, that the ship constitutes the destination—was still decades away.)

All these cruises were ancillary to a liner's main functions: moving cargo, mail, businessmen, and government functionaries.[5] When the fleets required rebuilding after the losses of World War II, design reflected these core priorities, not tourists and cruising. Designs looked much like those of prewar liners. Lifeboats dominated the exterior profiles. Decks were mainly taken up with vents, winches, and other machinery. Many cabins had only a tiny porthole or none at all. No cabins had balconies.

The new liners of the 1950s had air conditioning, which made cruising in tropical waters more attractive. Lines based in the United States, such as the United States Line and the American Export Line, benefited from the country's unprecedented prosperity. European lines, such as Cunard and Holland America, competed for European passengers with cruises to the Caribbean, Mexico, and the north coast of South America.

Few of the lines or their ships survived the revolution initiated by jet planes in the 1960s. Within a few years, businessmen, most mail, government officials, even families relocating traveled by air. Some lines dropped passengers and specialized in cargo. Others bought dock facilities or hotels.

A few entrepreneurs bought surplus liners at a steep discount, made modifications to open up more deck space, ran economical cruises to the Caribbean, and demonstrated a continuing demand for winter-weather escapes. In the 1970s only a few investors were willing to back new ships specifically designed for the Caribbean cruising trade.

One of the first of these new cruise ships was the *Pacific Princess*, first built for a Brazilian company and launched in 1971. How, then, did a ship like the *Pacific Princess* differ from a traditional transatlantic liner? Note the name. Not the serious "Queen this" or the nationalistic "United States that," this ship was a younger "princess," quite capable of fun in a tropical setting. A cruise vacation was no longer mainly about seeing other countries or exotic cultures. The ports of call were diversions and add-ons, not the crucial experience. The vacation was mainly about the ship as a destination.

Cruise ships, even early in their development, had a characteristic shape and features: slab sides, with no main deck for walking or machinery; as many exterior cabins as possible; the entire top deck configured for a pool; an aft veranda. The aft main deck was entirely devoted to a pool, sunning chairs, and a bar. The deck above the pool had "wings" for outdoor seating that looked down on the pool area. Designers consolidated the three or four stacks of transatlantic liners into a single stack aft, which dispersed fumes behind the ship. The stack was often brightly painted, replacing the multi-stack ocean liner's image of power and speed with one of relaxed fun. Several of the new cruise ships included an interior atrium, a design feature borrowed from enclosed shopping malls and upscale hotels.

Cruise ships also functioned differently from liners. There was no cargo, mail, or immigrants. The travel was done for leisure, not business or family relocation. Purpose-built cruise ships had larger and smaller cabins, but unlike liners, cruise ships were designed as a single class; all passengers ate in the same dining room, lounged around the same pools, and used the same workout room. Elevators and stairways connected all passenger decks. With the ship as the destination, on-board amenities assumed much greater importance. What was the quality of the evening entertainment? How good was the food? Were there interesting shops? What was the size of the pool? Did the pool area have an interesting bar?

The *Pacific Princess* was featured in the popular TV series *The Love Boat* (1977–1986). All America saw a romantic, sunny alternative to dreary, cold winter. Who could resist even the opening montage, which offered love in a warm climate with blue skies, interesting locations, and a perky, friendly American crew?

Companies competing for cruise passengers quickly figured out that bigger was better. With more passengers, cruise ships could offer larger pools, a casual lunch location, a bigger movie theater, more lavish evening entertainment, gambling, and balconies. Average tonnage of a cruise ship climbed steadily in the 1980s, from about 45,000 tons to about 70,000 tons. The trend has continued, with cruise ships passing 100,000 tons in the 1990s and 150,000 tons in the 2000s. Today, cruise behemoths top 200,000 tons.

In 2014 the cruising fleet (including river cruise boats and small "adventure" ships) consisted of 410 ships. Fourteen new ships were launched in 2014, several in the smaller "adventure" category, and eight large cruise ships are on order for 2015.[6] The *Costa Concordia*, at 114,000 tons, was middling size in today's cruise fleet.

The cruise industry is still overwhelmingly U.S.-dominated. Of the nineteen million total cruise passengers (2013), over ten million were from the United States. The next-largest cruise passenger market is England, with a million and a half passengers. Americans have traditionally cruised the Caribbean on American ships, while Europeans cruised the Mediterranean on European ships. The cuisine, furnishings, entertainment, and crew all are geared to one audience or the other.[7] Even within the European market the Dutch, English, and Scandinavians tend to choose ships from their own country. In total, Europe, the Mediterranean, and the Caribbean still constitute more than three-quarters of all cruise passengers.[8]

Cruise lines have made largely successful efforts to appeal to and develop market niches. Carnival and Disney have targeted families. Their tactics include onboard classes for children and recreation geared especially for children. Waterslides have proved popular. Other lines have played to mid-career couples without children, expanding the beauty salon into a full-service spa and offering cooking and other classes. They might add a Thai restaurant with exotic, lighter cuisine than is usually found on a cruise ship. Still other lines have focused on relatively less expensive cruises for the younger set, including couples, newlyweds, and singles, both straight and gay. Understandably, discos, bars, and casual dining spots are important design features on the ships of these lines. Many lines cater to retired well-off travelers, with suitable classes and entertainment. Some explicitly market grandparent-grandchildren cruises.

In the last decade the big cruise lines have also attempted to widen the horizons of potential passengers, offering cruises, for example, to the mainland and islands of Southeast Asia, Sri Lanka, and the ports of India. More recently they have targeted Asian passengers with Asian destinations. A variety of lines now take Japanese tourists around the various ports of Japan.

The true globalization of the cruise industry has, however, not come from the big cruise lines but from a different set of companies, which build and operate smaller, more specialized ships. Known as premium travel or adventure travel, smaller vessels can go where big ones cannot. These smaller cruise ships range downward from about four hundred feet and typically have simple, informal dining, minimal evening entertainment, and often no pool, disco, or gambling. The draw is the destinations, such as the Amazon, Antarctic coves and glaciers, the inside passage along the East Coast of the United States, Alaskan glaciers, the Galapagos, small islands in the South Pacific, or the smaller ports of Indonesia. Sophisticated travelers relish talks by specialists who know the plants and animals of the region or its history and culture. Travelers enjoy frequent opportunities to meet and talk with others aboard the smaller ship. The companies often espouse an environmental ethic, seeking to experience a place without destroying it. Today, this specialized cruise fleet gains nine or ten new ships a year, while only three or four mega-ships are built. (The passenger capacity of one of these mega-ships is, however, about the same as all the smaller ships combined.)[9]

## *Costa Concordia*: The Aftermath

In the immediate aftermath of the *Costa Concordia* disaster, columnists—especially in England—worried that the whole cruise industry would be adversely affected. The photos of the stricken ship on its side on the rocks would put tourists off a cruise vacation. An industry specialist asked in a headline in the *Daily Telegraph*, "So Will This Sink the Cruise Industry?" The answer was no, for two reasons. First, the ship was Italian, with mainly Italian passengers. The fragmentation of the market put very few English aboard the ship. Of wider consequence was that, from the first, the cause of the disaster was perceived as human error, not a fault in the design of Costa's ships. The prompt arrest of the captain on manslaughter charges helped. In fact, the *Costa Concordia* disaster had no observable impact on cruise passenger numbers, with 2012 and 2013 bookings growing at at least the same rate as in previous years.[10]

The chaos in the hours following the grounding was, in part, attributed to the passengers, who, according to the *Daily Telegraph* columnist, pay little attention during lifeboat drill. The columnist mused that instructing passengers in an emergency to return to their cabins and get their life vests was a bad idea. When a ship had four thousand people aboard, this practice seemed a prescription for chaos.[11]

During the week following the *Costa Concordia* disaster, various countries announced the fate of their nationals aboard. More than a hundred Russians were safe. So were the Koreans and the Ukrainians.

Law firms initiated claims on behalf of the passengers. As might be expected, there were immediate transnational points of contention. Costa's tickets explicitly stated that any claims against the company had to be filed only in Genoa. Some lawyers proceeded to file in Italy. Other lawyers sought larger suits in the United States against Carnival Lines, the owner of Costa. One firm filed in Florida, seeking $160,000 for each uninjured passenger. Simultaneously, a Chicago firm filed a $100 million class action suit against Carnival. A week later Carnival offered $14,460 to each uninjured passenger, which both law firms treated scornfully.[12]

Within two weeks the international maritime insurance industry weighed in, anticipating heavy losses. Moody's (the rating agency) estimated that the wreck would cost Carnival and its insurers over $1 billion, possibly affecting the whole structure of marine insurance. They further worried that a loss of this size would decrease earnings of Carnival enough that banks and investors might be reluctant to invest both in the company and in the industry.[13] European estimates were much lower, ranging upward from $30 million. Moody's predictions turned out to be quite wrong. Investors continued to back both Carnival and the cruise industry, and new ships were built at a steady rate in the subsequent years.

Over the months following the disaster, a spokesperson for the international maritime unions suggested that emergency staff training was inadequate and that the sheer size of the mega-ships demanded rethinking the whole question of disaster management on such large vessels.[14] The *Costa Concordia* disaster pushed cruise owners to design emergency stations and to store lifejackets at the stations rather than in cabins. Many owners retrofitted emergency stations into existing ships and changed rules to make boat drills more serious.

## Cruise Ship Disasters

Is cruise travel, as the industry blandly asserts, "the safest travel in the world," or is it closer to the seafarer union's judgment of almost inevitable disasters? The industry calculates risk simply by dividing the number of deaths (not of natural causes) or injuries aboard the cruise fleet by the number of miles traveled. This math, indeed, yields a result that cruise ships are a safer means of travel than cars, bikes, trains, buses, or even walking. This calculation does not, however, quite catch the essence of a cruise ship disaster as a major public event, which dominates the news, even if only for a few days.

Let us consider for comparison airplane crashes. There has not been fatal crash involving a major airline in the United States in a decade (though there have been fatal crashes involving regional carriers and several near misses, such as the successful landing of an airliner on the Hudson River). Nevertheless, the serious fear of flying remains quite common. Childhood memories of round-the-clock news coverage of earlier airplane crashes are vivid enough that therapy is often necessary to get fearful passengers onto a plane. Calculable, risk-management sort of risk is not what keeps these passengers off planes. The perceived risk of death and the lack of control initiate the phobia.

Cruise industry disasters often occur in faraway places and are rarely considered as an ongoing problem. Understandably the cruise industry does not record and post these incidents, though the maritime insurance industry surely tracks them. What follows here is a scattering of cruise ship disasters culled from newspapers and other public records. The list is surely incomplete, but cruise disasters are surprisingly frequent over the last two decades.[15] In 1991, the engine room of the *Oceanos*—an old ship built in 1952, with many name changes, sailing under a variety of flags, and in 1991 chartered to Starlight Cruises of Johannesburg—caught fire off the coast of South Africa. An explosion holed the hull, and the ship began to sink. A heroic effort by South African navy and air force helicopters saved the passengers and crew. A year later the *Royal Pacific*, of Greek registry and managed by Tony Travel of Piraeus, collided with a fishing boat in the Strait of Malacca and sank. Of 570 aboard, 30 died and 70 were injured. Two years later the *Club Royale* went down in a hurricane. Fortunately, it was traveling empty. Eight of the crew of eleven died. In 2005, sixty-two cabins of the *Norwegian Dawn* (Norwegian Cruise Lines) were flooded by a seventy-foot wave. There were no casualties. In the same year the *Seabourn Spirit* (Seabourn Cruises) fought off Somali pirates. A year later a fire started on the passenger decks of the *Star Princess* (Princess Lines). One passenger died of smoke inhalation. The crew managed to save the remaining passengers and contain the fire, although it destroyed seventy-nine cabins and damaged two hundred more. Repairs took two months, after which the ship returned to service. In 2008, two hundred miles east of New Zealand, huge Pacific waves tossed the *Pacific Sun* (P&O Cruises), sending furniture flying across cabins, lounges, and kitchens, injuring seventy-seven passengers and crew. Two years later the *Louis Majesty* (Louis Cruise Lines) encountered three huge rogue waves, which crashed more than fifty feet over the foredeck and smashed the fore lounge. Two died and eighteen were injured. In 2011, an engine fire left the *Carnival Splendor* (Carnival Lines) without electricity, toilets, air conditioning, or the ability to navigate. The ship drifted in the Caribbean for days before a tug brought it to port. Two years later the *Carnival Triumph* had a similar engine fire and floated without power for six days.[16]

Medical disasters have been a regular feature of cruise ships for decades. Thousands of passengers in close proximity form the ideal breeding ground for norovirus, which causes severe diarrhea, vomiting, and weakness. The virus can be spread extraordinarily quickly by an infected person touching any surface. There is no vaccine, because the virus mutates quickly, and there is no cure. The hapless victim has to suffer and see the disease through.

The Centers for Disease Control has tracked cruise ship norovirus outbreaks since the early 1990s, but reporting has become more thorough since 2002. Every year between fifteen and twenty ships have outbreaks serious enough to report to the CDC.[17] There is no easy fix. Crews now clean the entire ship between cruises, scrubbing with bleach. As ships get larger, the probability that a passenger brings the virus aboard also rises. Once a ship is under way, only aggressive hand washing by passengers and crew can keep the disease at bay. The problem remains unsolved. In the cruise season of 2014, the *Explorer of the Seas* (Royal Caribbean) returned to its New Jersey dock two days early with almost seven hundred passengers sick. The *Caribbean Princess* also cut short a cruise, with 178 sick passengers aboard.

These medical crises on board cruise ships now affect passenger bookings directly. Cruise lines advertise across the world on the Internet, but potential passengers also do their own research. Dozens of sites review lines and their ships. The reviews, written by passengers, spare no problem, but also praise good service and amenities aboard. Norovirus outbreaks immediately appear on the cruise review sites, and lines must show diligence in keeping the ship clean or immediately lose business. Every cruise ship sails in the virtual worldwide waters of the Internet just as surely as it sails in the Caribbean or the Mediterranean.

## The Last of the *Costa Concordia*

A year after the disaster, the Costa Company commissioned a costly, complex, and risky procedure to free the severely damaged ship from the reef. The plan was to roll the ship back into vertical, resting it on a massive shelf that divers had built underwater to support the hull. Then huge flotation chambers would be attached to the sides to support the ship. By winter 2014 the ship had been righted; in the spring and summer it was floated and towed to an Italian scrap yard.

The end of the *Costa Concordia* will by no means be the end of the examination of the disaster. A Swedish maritime safety expert has questioned much of the official account of the accident. He has argued that the loss of power, list, and eventual capsizing of the ship were the results of internal flooding caused by illegal doors connecting various compartments below the waterline, probably open at the time of the ship's hitting the rock. He attributes many of the deaths to lack of crew training in disaster procedures and lack of teaching of passengers how to reach mustering stations.[18] With multiple liability lawsuits pending, these opposing narratives of "irresponsible actions by the captain" versus "company operating a non-seaworthy vessel" will play out in Italian and American courts for years.

An early gambit in this long legal battle took place only a few months after the accident. The family of a German passenger killed in the disaster filed an "admiralty and maritime claim" in the U.S. District Court in Galveston to attach the *Carnival Triumph* as the "defendant's joint and collective property." The judge ruled that the claim was valid, and the ship was in fact impounded, though passengers and cargo continued to board.[19] The company posted a $10 million bond, and the ship was allowed to proceed.[20]

## Cruise Ship Globalization and Its Limits

The cruise industry is in some respects fully global. Information about sailings, lines, and ships is readily available anywhere in the world on the Internet. So are reviews and passenger critiques. Satellite contact between the ship and its home offices is instantaneous and expected. Passengers expect and have the same continuous global contact.[21]

Cruise ships of the same size look virtually identical. Many have been built for various lines in the same shipyards. Competition between lines is global and fierce. Innovations on one line's ships are quickly copied by other lines. Water slides, for example, proliferated in just a few years.

Cruise ships are, however, not as fully standardized and globalized as are oil tankers. Moving oil to meet demand is different from moving leisure passengers, who have expectations, needs, and desires. Cruise passengers generally seek a familiar cultural environment on the ship, but they also want (1) a warm, sunny climate, (2) wonderful beaches, (3) interesting shore excursions, and (4) quality shopping. A limited number of ports large enough for the big cruise ships can provide all four factors. And these places can absorb only a limited number of cruise passengers before one or more factors deteriorate.

Does this mean that cruise ships will inevitably run into limitations? Possibly not. Lines have offered three solutions. One is to persuade passengers to go farther afield, to ports in places such as India and Southeast Asia. A second strategy is to develop alternative harbors in the Mediterranean and the Caribbean, and encouraging new businesses to provide interesting shopping and food, to meet passenger expectations. A third approach is to buy and develop an uninhabited tropical island, designed specifically to meet passenger expectations. The cruise company then brings in local workers from other islands for eight-hour shifts.

Perhaps the logical development of larger and larger cruise ships is the Atlantis resort, built on a small island. It has a warm climate, beaches, lagoons, quality shopping, and underwater experiences without getting wet. It has none of the inconveniences of boarding a ship, no disaster drills, many places to eat, and rooms substantially larger than shipboard cabins. Atlantis may be the wave of the future.[22]

# CONCLUSION

# MARITIME HISTORY AS
# WORLD HISTORY

In the strictest sense, ship design over human history has been an evolutionary process. In the beginning, human maritime habitats were small and local. Early boats evolved to function in a single small habitat. As in nature, similar but independent solutions, such as the dugout canoe, were invented in many local habitats. Environments with different resources generated different boats, such as the skin boats, birch bark canoes, or reed rafts.

As in nature, there could be long periods during which the shipping environment did not demand much change. Tried-and-true designs were reproduced (Egyptian craft on the Nile, the sewn ships of India and Southeast Asia, the design of the junk in China, dugout canoes). At other times there might be rapid changes in a ship's environment, such as new economic opportunities (the gold rushes, whaling, the tea trade, cotton on the Mississippi, immigrants to America). Rapid change could also come from a changed political or military situation (the Greek trireme arms race, the development of the armed Spanish merchantman, the pre–World War I battleship race, the production of World War I submarines). New marine technology usually came from real needs (new naval cannon and carriages, the chronometer, shipboard telegraph, watertight bulkheads, double hulls). There were also abrupt changes that threatened existing shipping (the development of steamships, the demand for a standard galleon, an upsurge of piracy in the Caribbean).

As in nature, change also came from the breakdown of boundaries between habitats. Trade, war, or migration sometimes produced new forms of ships, based on the experience of the groups doing the merging (the merger of the northern seas cog and the Mediterranean galley; steamships on the Mississippi). Competition for dominance of the seas played just as active a role as peaceful learning. Some types of ships, however, were so suited to a specific environment that they could not be transferred to new environments (the Mediterranean galley, the Egyptian barge, the birch bark canoe).

As the chapters of this book show, we can conceive of the long arc of human history as the gradual, halting process of the integration of local maritime activities into larger and larger regions. The Eastern Mediterranean, the coastal India–Southeast Asia nexus, and the China-Japan-Korea triangle seem to be important early nodes in this process. It is important to note that this process of integrating larger maritime regions was neither continuous nor inevitable. The fall of the Indus Valley civilization (1700–1600 BCE), for example, ended the Indus-Mesopotamia maritime region. Similarly, by 1000 BCE, with the fall of the Hittite kingdom and the conquest of Mesopotamia, the maritime trading world of the Eastern Mediterranean collapsed, only to reemerge centuries later.

Man's subsequent history reveals important makers of greater and greater maritime trans-regional integration: Imperial Rome's demand for luxuries, which connected the Indian Ocean and the Mediterranean; European colonization of the sixteenth century, which connected the Atlantic, the Pacific, and the Asian Seas; global maps and global piracy in the seventeenth century; the first global maritime war in the eighteenth century; whaling as the first truly global maritime resource extraction in the nineteenth century; scheduled transoceanic travel and the successful movement of huge numbers of immigrants in the second half of the nineteenth century.

In the twentieth century the maritime world became unified and global. Naval fleets moved around the globe in both war and peace. Multi-country treaties hammered out a functioning law of the sea. Global environmental laws governed ocean pollution by ships. The pursuit of scarce resources, such as oil, pushed merchant shipping into harsh climates, such as the Arctic. Navies and merchant shipping relied on universally adopted, much-improved charts, tide tables, and navigational instruments.

Ships themselves have become a standard commodity moving other standard commodities across the globe. It does not matter what is in the container — toys, table linen, machinery, furniture — the container is packed at its origin and moves to its destined port. Oil is the same. A standard ship moves it from source to cracking plant. The industry barely notices where the ship was built, its country of ownership, the nationality of its captain or its crew. Only the most efficient schedule of filling and emptying really matters. Cruise ships move people through a hopefully pleasant experience with little regard for where the ship was built. All these ships depend on a fully globalized communication and navigation system.

Thus, what has changed over the millennia is the size of that human maritime habitat, which has expanded from local needs for fishing and trade to our world of globalized commodities, instant communications, and just-in-time schedules. Today there is only one global maritime environment of trade opportunities, regulation, technology, and information, in which ships must prove their fitness.

# ACKNOWLEDGMENTS

I would like to thank the following colleagues for continuing conversations on the themes of this book: Richard Tucker, Richard Eaton, Patrick Manning, Emma Flatt, and Daud Ali. My mental discussions with historians John Richards and Robert Frost carry on, though both have passed. I wish to thank the organizers for allowing me to explore the book's ideas at several talks at colleges across the Midwest. I am grateful to the curators and staff of the following libraries: Hatcher and Clements Libraries at the University of Michigan, the Library of Congress, and the Cleveland Public Library. I would like to thank Stephen Hull, my editor, for thoughtful and productive critiques, and, as always, Roger Williams, my agent, for his support and advice.

# NOTES

## Introduction

1. This estimate is contained in a UNESCO press release from a 2004 conference, "Protecting Underwater Heritage from Treasure Hunters." See http://www.unesco.org /confgen/press_rel/291001_subaqua.shtml.

## 1. Dufuna Dugout

1. The Dufuna site is about two hundred miles west of Lake Chad, into which the water from the Komadugu Gana River empties.

2. My description of the Dufuna site and its excavation follows Peter Breunig, Katharina Neumann, and Wim Van Neer, "New Research on the Holocene Settlement and Environment of the Chad Basin in Nigeria," *African Archaeological Review* 13, no. 2 (June 1996): 116–117.

3. Personal communication from Peter Breunig.

4. Breunig, Neumann, and Van Neer, "New Research on the Holocene Settlement," 118–120. A recent find of six-thousand-year-old incised pottery on the eastern rim of ancient Lake Chad is the first material evidence of what might have been the culture of the area.

5. One large unsolved problem in the chronology of early boat construction is how the aborigines got to Australia fifty thousand years ago across one hundred miles of open water. There is no evidence of a land bridge at that time, so they must have come in some form of boat. Even more puzzling is recent archaeological work on the most ancient of the coastal aboriginal sites, which suggests that a group of over a thousand constituted the original immigrants.

6. Ancient dugout boats have also been found in Denmark, Poland, the Czech Republic, England, along the Rhine River, and in coastal South America. For a buried boat to survive requires favorable conditions, such as cold water or a highly arid climate. Future excavations in other parts of the world will undoubtedly turn up more ancient dugout boats. China seems a likely prospect. I do not find productive the discussion of what were the earliest boats, with its hidden assumption that other types of boats somehow evolved from the earliest ones. The more important question is what was locally available. The environmental range of trees that produced a bark suitable for canoes was, in fact, quite limited. Skin boats worked well in northern climates where hides were readily available but large trunks of trees were not.

7. Paul Johnstone, *The Sea-Craft of Prehistory* (Cambridge, MA: Harvard University Press, 1980), 46–48.

8. Connecting two hulls together as a solution to instability was independently invented in Poland, where it was used for carrying heavy materials.

9. The find was announced in *Science News*, August 12, 2012, www.sci-news.com.

10. Janet M. Wilmshurst, Terry L. Hunt, Carl P. Lipo, and Atholl J. Anderson, "High-Precision Radiocarbon Dating Shows Recent and Rapid Initial Human Colonization of East Polynesia," *Proceedings of the National Academy of Sciences* 108, no. 5 (November 22, 2010): 1815–1820.

11. E. Matisoo-Smith and J. H. Robins, "Origins and Dispersals of Pacific Peoples: Evidence from mtDNA Phylogenies of the Pacific Rat," *Proceedings of the National Academy of Sciences* 24, no. 101 (June 15, 2004): 9167–9172.

12. I am generally following the magisterial work on Pacific Ocean dugouts by A. C. Haddon and James Hornell. Both men traveled the region extensively in the 1920s, amassing notes, sketches, and interviews. Haddon also did archival research and corresponded with Europeans living on various islands. Many of the broader tentative conclusions of the movements of peoples are no longer valid, but the details of construction and the illustrations of the boats are invaluable. See Haddon and Hornell, *Canoes of Oceania* (Honolulu: Bernice P. Bushop Museum, Special Publication 27, 1936).

13. Ibid., 20–22.

14. Ibid., 144–145.

15. See Bronislaw Malinowski, *Argonauts of the Western Pacific: An Account of Native Enterprise and Adventure in the Archipelagoes of Melanesian New Guinea* (London: Routledge and Kegan Paul, 1922).

16. For a review of the elegant dugouts of the West Coast of native North American tribes see Jeanne E. Arnold and Julienne Bernard, "Negotiating the Coasts: Status and the Evolution of Boat Technology in California," *World Archaeology* 37, no. 1, *Archaeology in North America* (March 2005): 109–122.

17. Haddon and Hornell, *Canoes of Oceania*, 242.

## 2. Khufu Barge

1. The story of the recovery and reconstruction of the Khufu boat is found in four related books. In the 1960s the Antiquities Department of Egypt issued archaeological reports that documented the find, its removal, and the beginning of reconstruction. See Mohammad Zaki Nour, Mohammad Salah Osman, Zaky Iskander, and Ahmad Youssof Moustafa, *The Cheops Boats* (Cairo: General Organization for Government Printing Offices, 1960). In 1970 Björn Landström assembled all the available evidence and produced a book of stunning, if somewhat speculative, drawings of ancient Egyptian boats. See Björn Landström, *Ships of the Pharaohs: 4000 Years of Egyptian Shipbuilding* (Garden City, NY: Doubleday & Co., 1970). In the early 1980s Paul Lipke, himself a trained

boatbuilder, interviewed Youssof Moustafa (the lead restorer) for over one hundred hours and recorded not only the human struggle but also his thinking along the way. See Lipke, *The Royal Ship of Cheops*, BAR International Series 225 (Greenwich: National Maritime Museum, Archaeological Series no. 9, 1984). Two decades later Cheryl A. Ward put the Khufu boat in the context of other Egyptian buried boats excavated by archaeologists in the last half of the twentieth century. See Ward, *Sacred and Secular: Ancient Egyptian Ships and Boats* (Philadelphia: University Museum Publications, 2000).

2. The conservators finally settled on polyvinyl acetate in a solution of acetone and amyl acetate with an admixture of DDT to discourage insects.

3. Since the 1950s, archaeologists have known that the Khufu boat was one of several buried boats surrounding the Cheops pyramid, another on the south and four on the north side. The paired boat on the south side, though near the reconstructed one, remains unexcavated. In the late 1980s a team drilled through a limestone block and inserted a miniature still camera and a small video camera. The images showed similar stacking to the first boat, but it had deteriorated badly. Much of what was visible was decking and superstructure, identifiable from parallels to the first boat. The woodworking relied on mortise-and-tenon joints. Air samples showed high humidity, perfect conditions for rot. It is not known exactly why the first boat remained in such ideal conditions for preservation. One possibility is that the second boat was constructed mainly of local woods rather than the highly rot-resistant cedar of the first boat. No wood samples of the second boat were taken, so this remains speculation. Also intriguing is the much greater number of oars visible on the second boat. Perhaps it was, in fact, a real working boat and was actually rowed. Massive oarlocks, not found on the first boat, also suggest this possibility. The boats on the north side of the pyramid likely originally contained some wood, possibly an entire boat. What remains are boat shapes cut into the native limestone. They have the same overall hull shape, proportions, and timber details as the excavated boat. The best discussion of the full range of boats associated with the Cheops pyramid is in Ward, *Sacred and Secular*, chaps. 6 and 7.

4. For the many independent appearances of the sewn boat see Sean McGrail and Eric Kentley, eds., *Sewn Plank Boats: Archaeological and Ethnographic Papers Based on Those Presented to a Conference at Greenwich in November, 1984* (Oxford: BAR International Series 276, 1985).

5. Barbara Bell, "The Oldest Records of the Nile Floods," *Geographical Journal* 136, no. 4 (December 1970): 569–573.

6. Robert O. Collins, *The Nile* (New Haven, CT: Yale University Press, 2002), 14–15.

7. Fertile productive river deltas have been central to many kingdoms—the Yellow, Yangtze, Red (Vietnam), Mekong, Brahmaputra, and the Irrawaddy, for example. All these river deltas share the same problems of flooding. In most cases the kingdom controlling the delta did not control the headwaters or the middle reaches of the river.

8. Kenneth Kitchen divides the land west of the Red Sea into five parallel bands, running north and south: (1) the desert adjacent to the Red Sea; (2) the Nile; (3) the desert

west of the Nile; (4) the chain of oases; (5) the western desert. See Kitchen, "Ancient Polities and Interrelations along the Red Sea and Its Western and Eastern Hinterlands," in *Connected Hinterlands: Proceedings of Red Sea Project IV Held at the University of Southampton September 2008*, ed. Lucy Blue, John Cooper, Julian Whitewright, and Ross Thomas, Proceedings of the Red Sea Project IV, BAR International Series, no. 2052 (Oxford: British Archaeological Reports, 2009), 3–8.

9. The seaworthiness of boats constructed of bundles of reeds should not be underestimated. Reed boats are considerably more seaworthy than reed rafts. See Tom Vosmer, "The Magan Boat Project: A Process of Discovery, a Discovery of Process," *Proceedings of the Seminar for Arabian Studies* 33, papers from the thirty-sixth meeting of the Seminar for Arabian Studies held in London, July 18–20, 2002, 49–58.

10. The boats would have been a prominent feature of the landscape. It appears that they were originally only partially mounded, so that twelve ghostly white boat shapes might have appeared to sail across the desert. Later, blowing sand fully buried them. The sequence of burials and their overall time span are among the many unknowns of the Abydos site.

11. See David O'Connor, *Abydos: Egypt's First Pharaohs and the Cult of Osiris* (London: Thames & Hudson, 2009).

12. Preliminary survey of the site goes back to the mid-1970s, with strong suggestions of nautical focus, such as unfinished boat anchors. In the 1980s archaeologists located shrines built of inscribed anchors, which recounted voyages to a land termed "Punt." The caves were located in 2001.

13. A group of archaeologists took known data from ancient Egyptian boats and generated carrying capacity. Workboats of the type suggested by the Lisht timbers could easily carry one or even two huge obelisks. See J. V. Wehausen, A. Mansour, M. C. Ximenes, and F. Stross, "The Colossi of Memmon and Egyptian Barges," *International Journal of Nautical Archaeology* 17 (1988): 295–310.

14. See Ward, *Sacred and Secular*, chaps. 9 and 10.

15. This tomb inscription is quoted in the useful and well-illustrated introduction to ancient Egyptian beliefs and religion by Lorna Oakes and Lucia Gahlin, *Ancient Egypt: An Illustrated Guide to the Myths, Religions, Pyramids and Temples of the Land of the Pharaohs* (London: Hermes House, 2002), 137.

16. Proponents of the anti-market viewpoint have produced literally tens of thousands of studies exploring apparently pre-market worlds. Marx wrote extensively about such a golden age and the difference between "oriental despotism" and Western modern capitalism. In the twentieth century both Max Weber and Karl Polanyi championed the characterization of most cultures as nonmarket. Marshall Sahlins explored Stone Age economics as fundamentally different—with utterly different rules—from modern economics. From their fieldwork anthropologists developed ideas of gift economy, mutual obligations across generations, honorable behavior, nonmonetized work, and ritual display, all of which superseded market transactions. Emanuel Wallerstein developed

the idea of a world system in which Europe spread market-based capitalism to the rest of the world. The anti-market viewpoint is not some relic of past thinking. It is a vibrant tradition today with smart, active proponents. It is at the center of the criticism of globalization and the discussion of the corroding influence of market values on education and health care. In contrast, for the latest discoveries of markets in ancient Egypt see András Hudecz and Máté Petrik, eds., *Commerce and Economy in Ancient Egypt*, BAR International Series, 2131 (Oxford, Archaeopress, 2010).

17. Angela Murock Hussein, "Beware of the Red-Eyed Horus: The Significance of Carnelian in Egyptian Royal Jewelry," in *Perspectives on Ancient Egypt: Studies in Honor of Edwar Brovarski*, ed. Zahi Hawass, Peter Der Manuelian, and Ramadan B. Hussein (Cairo: Supreme Council of Antiquities, 2010), 185.

18. On the voyages see Joyce Tyldesley, *Myths and Legends of Ancient Egypt* (London: Allen Lane, 2010), chap. 3. Much more depth and detail on Ra are found in Stephen Quirke, *The Cult of Ra: Sun-Worship in Ancient Egypt* (New York: Thames & Hudson), 2001.

## 3. Uluburun Shipwreck

1. The discovery and initial exploration of the Uluburun wreck are well described in George F. Bass, "A Bronze Age Shipwreck at Ulu Burun (Kaş): 1984 Campaign," *American Journal of Archaeology* 90, no. 3 (July 1986): 269–296. See also C. Pulak, "The Bronze Age Shipwreck at Ulu Burun, Turkey: 1985 Campaign," *American Journal of Archaeology* 92 (1988): 1–37. For a later consideration of the three dive seasons see C. Pulak, "The Uluburun Shipwreck: An Overview," *International Journal of Nautical Archaeology* 27 (1998): 188–224.

2. See Cemal Pulak, "The Cargo of the Uluburun Ship and Evidence for Trade with the Aegean and Beyond," in *Italy and Cyprus in Antiquity: 1500–450 BC*, ed. Larissa Banfante and Vassos Karageorghis (Nicosia: Costakis and Leto Severis Foundation, 2001), 24.

3. There might even have been copybooks available to tomb painters, showing how ships or animals or gardens should be portrayed, though no actual examples of such copybooks have been excavated.

4. Several of these features are present in a simple terra-cotta ship model found at Enkomi on the east coast of Cyprus. The model was, however, found on the surface and cannot therefore be accurately dated.

5. Cheryl Ward, "Pomegranates in Eastern Mediterranean Contexts during the Late Bronze Age," *World Archaeology* 34, no. 3, Luxury Foods (February 2003): 529.

6. Thomas Cucchi, "Uluburun Shipwreck Stowaway House Mouse: Molar Shape Analysis and Indirect Clues about the Vessel's Last Journey," *Journal of Archaeological Science* 35 (2008): 2953–2959. See Also François Bonhomme, Annie Orth, Thomas Cucchi, Hassan Rajabi-Maham, Josette Catalan, Pierre Boursot, Jean-Christophe

Auffray, and Janice Britton-Davidian, "Genetic Differentiation of the House Mouse around the Mediterranean Basin: Matrilineal Footprints of Early and Late Colonization," *Proceedings: Biological Sciences* 278, no. 1708 (April 7, 2011): 1034–1043.

7. Sturt W. Manning, Bernd Kromer, Peter Ian Kuniholm, and Maryanne W. Newton, "Anatolian Tree Rings and a New Chronology for the East Mediterranean Bronze-Iron Ages," *Science*, New Series, vol. 294, no. 5551 (December 21, 2001): 2532–2535.

8. Quoted in Shelly Wachsmann, *Seagoing Sips and Seamanship in the Bronze Age Levant* (College Station: Texas A&M University Press, 1998), 39–40.

9. Ibid., 40. The importance and volume of trade in the Late Bronze Age Eastern Mediterranean are much debated in the scholarly literature. See the chapters by H. W. Catling, A. M. Snodgrass, G. F. Bass, and M. Melas in *Bronze Age Trade in the Mediterranean*, ed. N. H. Gale, Studies in Mediterranean Archaeology, vol. 90 (Paul Åströms Förlag, 1991). See also Stuart W. Manning and Linda Hunt, "Maritime Commerce and Geographies of Mobility in the Late Bronze Age of the Eastern Mediterranean: Problematizations," in *The Archaeology of the Mediterranean Prehistory*, ed. Emma Blake and A. Bernard Knapp (Oxford: Blackwell, 2005), 270–303.

10. Andreas Hauptmann, Robert Maddin, and Michael Prange, "On the Structure and Composition of Copper and Tin Ingots Excavated from the Shipwreck of Uluburun," *Bulletin of the American Schools of Oriental Research*, no. 328 (November 2002): 2.

11. See Nöel H. Gale, "Copper Oxhide Ingots: Their Origin and Their Place in the Bronze Age Metals Trade in the Mediterranean," in Gale, *Bronze Age Trade in the Mediterranean*, 200. Good answers to questions about the method and its results are found in Sophie Stos-Gale, "Trade in Metals in the Bronze Age Mediterranean: An Overview of Lead Isotope Data for Provenance Studies," in *Metals Make the World Go Round: The Supply and Circulation of Metals in Bronze Age Europe*, ed. C. F. E. Pare (Oxford: Oxbow Books, 2000), 56–69.

12. I recommend to the reader the marvelous article by Paul T. Craddock on early copper smelting in the region, "From Hearth to Furnace: Evidences for the Earliest Smelting Techniques in the Eastern Mediterranean," *Paléorient* 26, no. 2 (2000): 151–165.

13. Microanalysis of core samples of the Uluburun copper ingots found a consistent and distinctive structure of voids and boundaries of grains and large slag inclusions throughout the sampled ingots. The microstructure of the relatively low-grade Uluburun ingots contrasts sharply with the much more highly refined bun ingots of the period from Oman or those found off Israel. Chemical evidence suggests a single source and technology for the Uluburun ingots sampled, without admixtures of recycled bronze. The microstructure and refining methods are consistent with copper from Cyprus. See Hauptmann et al., "On the Structure and Composition," 17–19. The bibliographic references in Hauptmann et al. are useful in reconstructing the positions taken by various academics in discussions, occasionally acrimonious, of the issues of the four-handled copper ingots.

14. Gale, *Bronze Age Trade*, 225–226.

15. Ibid., 201.

16. See M. Primas and E. Pernicka, "Der Depotfund von Oberwilfingen: Neue Ergebnisse zur Zirkulation von Metallbarren," *Germania* 76 (1998): 25–65.

17. I see little useful in the decades-old debate over whether the goods on the Uluburun ship were for trade or gifts between kings. Trade goods are generally defined as having extrinsic value when exchanged for some other commodity (some quantity of grain exchanged for some quantity of fish). It is argued that gifts, in contrast, have intrinsic value because they initiate and strengthen relationships and cannot readily be converted into other commodities. The distinction seems arbitrary and unsatisfactory. Many gift items, in fact, had intrinsic value. Thus, gold jewelry, once a gift, could be sold, melted, and reused. In similar fashion the gift of one king to another might well be quantified in terms of the projected benefits of a strengthened alliance. In the absence of any documentation referring directly to the Uluburun ship, we cannot know whether the objects were intended for trade, gift, or some blending of intrinsic and extrinsic value. See Christoph Bachhuber, "Aegean Interest on the Uluburun Ship," *American Journal of Archaeology* 110, no. 3 (July 2006): 345–363.

18. D. Rutter Symington, "Late Bronze Age Writing Boards and Their Uses: Textual Evidence from Anatolia and Syria," *Anatolian Studies* 41:111–123. See also E. Laroche, *Catalogue des textes Hittites* (Paris: Klencksieck, 1971).

19. See Dorothy G. Shephard, "Two Silver Rhyta," *Bulletin of the Cleveland Museum of Art*, October 1966. See also A. S. Melikian-Chirvani, "The Iranian Wine Horn from Pre-Achaemenid Antiquity to the Safavid Dynasty," *Bulletin of the Asian Institute* 10 (1996): 85–139.

20. C. Davaras, "A Minoan Beetle-Rhyton from Prinias Siteias," *Annual of the British School at Athens* 83 (1988): 45–46.

21. Susanne Ebbinghaus and J. Ellis Jones, "New Evidence on the Von Mercklin Class of Rhyta: A Black-Gloss Rhyton from Agrileza, Laureion, Attica," *Annual of the British School at Athens* 96 (2001): 381–394.

22. François Louis, "The Hejiacun Rhyton and the Chinese Wine Horn (Gong): Intoxicating Rarities and Their Antiquarian History," *Artibus Asiae* 67, no. 2 (2007): 201–242.

23. Pulak, "Cargo," 25.

24. See A. L. Oppenheim, "Towards a History of Glass in the Ancient Near East," *Journal of the American Oriental Society* 93 (1973): 259–263. See also Marco Beretta, *The Alchemy of Glass: Counterfeit, Imitation, and Transmutation in Ancient Glassmaking* (Chicago: University of Chicago Press, 2010), chap. 1.

25. The coastal areas of Palestine/Syria certainly produced glass, since its import is mentioned in Egyptian records. At roughly the same time Egypt was exporting glass ingots to Mesopotamia. These exports and imports hardly make sense unless various glassworks produced specialty colors. See Pulak, "Cargo," 27.

26. Thilo Rehren and Edgar B. Pusch, "Late Bronze Age Glass Production at Qantir-Piramesses, Egypt," *Science*, New Series, vol. 308, no. 5729 (June 17, 2005): 1756–1758.

27. Cheryl Haldane, "Direct Evidence for Organic Cargoes in the Late Bronze Age," *World Archaeology* 24, no. 3, Ancient Trade: New Perspectives (February 1993): 352.

28. My discussion of the pomegranate relies on Ward, "Pomegranates," 529–541.

29. Ibid., 529.

30. See Eric H. Cline, "Egyptian and Near Eastern Imports at Late Bronze Age Mycenae," in *Egypt, the Aegean and the Levant: Interconnections in the Second Millennium BC*, ed. W. Vivian Davies and Louise Schofield (London: British Museum Press, 1995), 91–115.

31. Some Baltic amber circulated in the world of the late Bronze Age Eastern Mediterranean, but the finds are rare, and the imports were probably occasional. All the finds of Baltic amber in the Eastern Mediterranean at the period of the Uluburun wreck could have been carried in a single backpack. See Anthony Harding, Helen Hughes-Brock, and Curt W. Beck, "Amber in the Mycenaean World," *Annual of the British School at Athens* 69 (1974): 145–172.

32. This period of decline has been termed the "Bronze Age collapse." The evidence was synthesized by Robert Drews, *The End of the Bronze Age: Changes in Warfare and the Catastrophe ca. 1200 B.C.* (Princeton, NJ: Princeton University Press, 1993). The theory has been criticized for lack of chronological accuracy and combining various local and regional factors into a single large pattern.

### 4. Sutton Hoo Burial

1. *Times* (London), Tuesday, August 15, 1939, p. 9. The Sutton Hoo find was also extensively covered in the *Guardian*, the *Scotsman*, and the *Observer*. See *Times of India*, August 19, 1939.

2. *Billings (MT) Gazette*, September 29, 1939; *Chester (PA) Times*, September 29; *Helena (MT) Independent*, September 29; *San Antonio (TX) Light*, September 24; *La Prensa*, San Antonio, November 12.

3. The only other ship burial in England is known as the Asthall barrow, near Snape, about ten miles north of Sutton Hoo. It was nowhere near as rich a find as Sutton Hoo, though it did yield a gold ring set with a Roman intaglio, in addition to the remains of a claw beaker (a drinking glass with hollow protrusions). The site differs in a significant way from Sutton Hoo in that everything at Asthall was burned at the time of the burial.

4. A sampling of ship burials, discovery dates, and approximate burial date is as follows: Valsgärde Gamla, Uppsala, Sweden, 1920s (sixth century); Vendel, Ottarshögen Uppland, Sweden, 1863 (early seventh century); Kallandsö Island, Lake Vänern, Sweden, 2009 (600–1000 CE); Sutton Hoo, Suffolk, England, 1939 (c. 645); Ladby, Denmark, 1937 (ninth–tenth centuries); Scar, Orkney Islands, 1985 (875–925 CE); Gokstad Farm, Vestfold, Norway, 1860 (c. 900 CE); Oseberg Farm Vestfold, Norway, 1904

(c. 900 CE); Haugen Farm, Tune, Østfold, Norway, discovery date unclear (c. 900 CE); Balladoole, Isle of Man, 1945, 1974 (850–950 CE); Port an Eilean Mhòir, Western Scotland, 2011 (tenth century). Research comparing Sutton Hoo and Scandinavian sites is ongoing. In 2009, Swedish archaeologists announced the find of a ship burial that dates from the period of Sutton Hoo. See coverage in the *Local,* an English-language Swedish newspaper, at http://www.thelocal.se/21716/20090827/#.uYz5hBwqmEM. See also, for example, "Sutton Hoo: A Swedish Perspective," a conference organized by the Sutton Hoo Society that brought Scandinavian archaeologists and historians to England in 2011. Summaries of the conference papers are at http://www.suttonhoo.org/conference -2011.asp.

5. See illustration in Owain T. P. Roberts, "Descendents of Viking Boats," in *Cogs, Caravels and Galleons: The Sailing Ship, 1000–1650,* ed. Robert Gardiner (London: Conway Maritime Press, 1994), 12.

6. The side rudder placed toward the stern has been independently discovered in a variety of times and places, including ancient Egypt, China, and North America.

7. The complexity of the political situation in England at the time and the few and limited nature of the sources are well covered in Pauline Stafford, ed., *A Companion to the Early Middle Ages: Britain and Ireland, c. 500–c. 1100* (Chichester, UK: Wiley-Blackwell, 2007).

8. Later Viking-period boats had lockers under the rowing benches, which provided some measure of protection for trade goods.

9. James E. McKeithen, "The Risalah of Ibn Fadlan: An Annotated Translation with Introduction," Dissertation Abstracts International (40 [10A], 5437, 1979), 25.

10. H. J. R. Murray, *A History of Chess* (Northampton, MA: Benjamin Press, 1985). For a less detailed and more readable history of chess see David Shenk, *The Immortal Game: A History of Chess or How 32 Carved Pieces on a Board Illuminated Our Understanding of War, Art, Science, and the Human Brain* (New York: Doubleday, 2006).

11. See the British Museum feature on the Lewis Chess pieces at https://www.british museum.org/explore/highlights/highlight_objects/pe_mla/t/the_lewis_chessmen .aspx.

12. For a discussion of the cardamom trade from the Malabar Coast to Aden and Cairo see Stewart Gordon, *When Asia Was the World* (Boston: Da Capo, 2008), chap. 5.

13. The spectrographic analysis of Middle East amber samples is covered in the *Journal of Baltic Studies,* Special Issue on Baltic Amber, no. 3, 1985.

14. The most complete discussion of the earlier finds at Sutton Hoo is in the three volumes published by the British Museum: Rupert Bruce-Mitford, *The Sutton Hoo Ship Burial* (London: British Museum, 1975). For a much shorter but thorough description of the find see Angela Care Evans, *The Sutton Hoo Ship Burial* (London: British Museum, 1986). Modern scholarship on Sutton Hoo has in various ways attempted to contextualize the burial and the hoard. See, for example, *The Age of Sutton Hoo: The Seventh Century in North-Western Europe* (Woodbridge, UK: Boydell Press, 1992);

Calvin B. Kendell and Peter S. Wells, eds., *Voyage to the Other World: The Legacy of Sutton Hoo* (Minneapolis: University of Minnesota Press, 1992); and Martin Carver, *Sutton Hoo: Burial Ground of Kings?* (London: British Museum, 1998).

15. The Digital Norseman, http://www.digitalnorseman.com.

16. Georgina R. Bowden, Patricia Balaresque, Turi E. King, et al., "Excavating Past Population Structures by Surname-Based Sampling: The Genetic Legacy of the Vikings in Northwest England," *Molecular Biology and Evolution* 25, no. 2 (2008): 301–309. See also S. Goodacre, A. Helgason, J. Nicholson, et al., "Genetic Evidence for a Family-Based Scandinavian Settlement of Shetland and Orkney during the Viking Periods," *Heredity* 95, no. 2: 129–135. For the general method see A. L. Topf, M. T. Gilbert, J. P. Dumbacher, and A. R. Hoelzel, "Tracing the Phylogeography of Human Populations in Britain Based on 4th–11th Century mtDNA Genotypes," *Molecular Biology and Evolution* 23, no. 1 (2006): 52–161.

17. See, for example, the coverage of the opening in the *Telegraph*, April 22, 2014, which includes video of the display space and an interview with the Early Medieval curator, at www.telegraph.co.uk.

## 5. Intan Shipwreck

1. Michael Flecker, "The Archaeological Excavation of the 10th Century Intan Shipwreck," British Archaeological Reports International Series, 1047 (Oxford: Archaeopress, 2002).

2. The history of ironworking in island Southeast Asia remains murky, at best. Ironworking developed early in Malaysia and southern Vietnam but does not seem to have spread to island Southeast Asia. See Nicholas Tarling, ed., *The Cambridge History of Southeast Asia: From Early Times to c. 1800* (Cambridge: Cambridge University Press, 1992), 131–132.

3. Flecker, "Archaeological Excavation," 22–24.

4. Ibid., 126–149. For a careful analysis of the archaeological data that comes to the same conclusions see Pierre-Yves Manguin, "Trading Ships of the South China Sea: Shipping Techniques and Their Role in the History of the Development of Asian Trade Networks," *Journal of the Economic and Social History of the Orient* 36 (1993): 256–265. See also Anthony Reid, *Charting the Shape of Early Modern Southeast Asia* (Chiang Mai, Thailand: Silkworm Books, 1999), 65–59.

5. Flecker, "Archaeological Excavation," 90.

6. Gerald R. Tibbetts, *A Study of the Arabic Texts Containing Material on South-East Asia* (Leiden: Brill, 1979), 39.

7. There is virtually no copper in South China. It is quite possible that the copper in the Chinese mirrors came from Japan. Swords and copper were prominent Japanese exports to much of East Asia at the time. See Bennett Bronson, "Patterns in the Early Southeast Asian Metals Trade," in *Early Metallurgy, Trade and Urban Centers*

*in Thailand and Southeast Asia*, ed. Ian Glover, Pornchai Suchitta, and John Villiers (Bangkok: White Lotus, 1992), 71–72. In Arab accounts of the ninth century, copper was prominently mentioned as a desirable item to trade to China: *Arab Classical Accounts of India and China*, trans. S. Maqbul Ahmad (Rddhi, India: Indian Institute of Advanced Study, 1979).

8. An excellent new study of the relations between the Malay Peninsula and southern China is Derek Heng, *Sino-Malay Trade and Diplomacy from the Tenth through the Fourteenth Century* (Athens: Ohio University Press, 2009).

9. The pattern of the rise and fall of these mainland kingdoms is explored in Victor Lieberman, *Strange Parallels: Southeast Asia in Global Context, c. 800–1830* (Cambridge: Cambridge University Press, 2003).

10. Kenneth R. Hall, "Eleventh-Century Commercial Developments in Angkor and Champa," *Journal of Southeast Asian Studies* 10, no. 2 (September 1979): 420–434.

11. Flecker, "Archaeological Excavation," 54–60. See also Ranabir Chakravarti, "Seafarings, Ships and Ship Owners: India and the Indian Ocean (AD 700–1500)," in *Ships and the Development of Maritime Technology on the Indian Ocean*, ed. Ruth Barnes and David Parkin (London: Routledge Curzon, 2002), 36–48.

12. The ceramics aboard reinforce the idea of differentiated markets, some more and some less expensive similar items. A relatively small number of fine Chinese domestic ceramics were found—jars, pots, and bowls. Their numbers are overwhelmed by seven thousand pieces of coarse domestic ceramics. Most of these were originally in closely nested and bound packages of bowls, ware now known as Yue, from a variety of kilns in the coastal province now known as Zhejiang.

13. Bronson, "Patterns," 65.

14. R. A. L. H. Gunawardana, "Cosmopolitan Buddhism on the Move: South India and Sri Lanka in the Early Expansion of Theravada in Southeast Asia," in *Fruits of Inspiration: Studies in Honour of Prof. J. G. de Marijke*, ed. J. Klokke and Karel R. van Kooij (Groningen, Holland: Egbert Forsten, 2001), 135–155. The definitive new work on the interconnectedness of China, India, and Southeast Asia in this period is Tansen Sen, *Buddhism, Diplomacy, and Trade: The Realignment of Sino-Indian Relations, 600–1400* (Honolulu: Association for Asian Studies and University of Hawai'i Press, 2003).

15. Kenneth R. Hall, "State and Statecraft in Early Srivijaya," in *Explorations in Early Southeast Asian History: The Origins of Southeast Asian Statecraft*, ed. Kenneth R. Hall and John K. Whitmore (Ann Arbor, MI: Center for South and Southeast Asian Studies, 1976), 92–93.

16. Northern Vietnam, for example, had been a province of the Tang Chinese empire, and its Buddhist institutions were closely tied to Chinese sects. Around the time of the shipwreck, Vietnam successfully rebelled from China and developed its own local variants of Buddhism. See Keith Taylor, "The Rise of Dai Viet and the Establishment of Thang-Long," in Hall and Whitmore, *Explorations*, 171–181.

17. Flecker, "Archaeological Excavation," 36–41. Recent research suggests that

Borobadur was primarily a Vajrayana monument. See Jeffery Roger Sundberg, "The Wilderness Monks of Abyayagirivihara and the Origins of Sino-Javanese Esoteric Buddhism," *Bijdragen tot de Taal-, Land-, en Volkenkunde* 160, no. 1 (2004): 95–123.

18. Flecker, "Archaeological Excavation," 53–54.

19. Ibid., 83. For use of silver coinage in Java and Bali see Jan W. Christie, "Asian Sea Trade between the Tenth and Thirteenth Centuries and Its Impact on the States of Java and Bali," in *Archaeology of Seafaring: The Indian Ocean in the Ancient Period*, ed. Himansahu P. Ray (Delhi: Pragati Publications, 1999), 237–238. Substantial quantities of both silver and gold appear in the scattering of inscriptions from eastern Java that are roughly contemporary with the shipwreck. See Antoinette M. Barrett Jones, "Early Tenth-Century Java from the Inscriptions," *Verhandelingen van het Koninklijk Instituut voor Taal-, Land-, en Volkenkunde* 107 (Dordrecht: Foris Publications, 1984): 32–34.

20. At the time of the shipwreck, the south of China was the political and economic center. The north had been generally ravaged by warfare and competing warlords. Unification came with the Song dynasty in late decades of the tenth century. For the development of the Chinese process of cast iron see Bronson, "Patterns," 71.

21. Bronson, "Patterns," 89–90.

22. Flecker, "Archaeological Excavation," 78–79.

23. Alastair Lamb, "Takupa: The Probable Site of a Pre-Malaccan Entrepot in the Malay Peninsula," in *Malayan and Indonesian Studies*, ed. John Bastin and Roelof Roolvink (Oxford: Oxford University Press, 1964), 81–82. See also Peter Francis Jr., *Beads and the Bead Trade in Southeast Asia: A Preliminary Report on Research into the Bead Trade of Southeast Asia as a Segment of the Indian Ocean Bead Trade* (Lake Placid, NY: Center for Bead Research, 1989). See also Peter Francis Jr., *Asia's Maritime Bead Trade from ca. 300 BC to the Present* (Honolulu: University of Hawai'i Press, 2002).

24. Himanshu P. Ray, *The Winds of Change: Buddhism and the Maritime Links of Early South Asia* (Delhi: Oxford University Press, 1994), 92–93, 118–119.

25. Taylor, "Rise of Dai Viet," 169. More than five centuries before the Intan shipwreck, piracy was already a problem. In 414 CE, the Chinese Buddhist pilgrim Fa Hien described the area near Java thusly: "On the sea (hereabouts) there are many pirates, to meet whom is speedy death": Fa-Hien, *A Record of Buddhistic Kingdoms: Being an Account by the Chinese Monk of His Travels in India and Ceylon (A.D. 399–414) in Search of the Buddhist Books of Discipline*, trans. James Legge (New York: Paragon Reprint Corp., 1965), 112.

26. Jan W. Christie, "Trade and Settlement in Early Java: Integrating the Epigraphic and Archaeological Data," in Glover, Suchitta, and Villiers, *Early Metallurgy*, 181–195.

27. Flecker, "Archaeological Excavation," 101–103. Early Arab traders knew incense was an important trade item in China. See Ahmad, *Arab Classical Accounts*, 46.

28. Flecker, "Archaeological Excavation," 96.

29. The farthest-traveled artifacts of the Intan wreck were a small group of ceramics,

all broken. The turquoise blue glaze and the incised patterns were certainly Islamic and could only have come from the Middle East, possibly Baghdad.

## 6. Maimonides Wreck

1. Buzurg ibn Shahriyar, *The Book of the Marvels of India*, trans. L. Marcel Devic (London: George Routledge & Sons, 1928), 141–144. Bracketed interpolations are translator's.

2. About two centuries later Ibn Battuta made the same crossing from the Nile to the Red Sea but found it "totally devoid of settlements but quite safe." See *The Travels of Ibn Battuta, A.D. 1325–1354*, trans. H. A. R. Gibb (New Delhi: Munshiram Manoharlal Publishers, reprinted ed., 1993), 1:68.

3. Aydhab flourished as a port for about three centuries. It was destroyed in warfare in the fifteenth century and never rebuilt. Aydhab is today a site of archaeological research.

4. Cambridge University Library Or.1081 J1. This translation is from S. D. Goitein, *Letters of Medieval Jewish Traders* (Princeton, NJ: Princeton University Press, 1973), 209–210.

5. Goitein, *Letters*, 207.

6. Some Jewish groups retain this belief today.

7. In the late nineteenth century scholars became aware of this uncataloged and untouched treasure. Several libraries bought large lots of the papers, by the pound, and the collection is now divided between Russia, England, and the United States. Recent scanning of thousands of documents and computer analysis of word frequency has at last allowed reassembling of family collections. In the last decade scholars have used this material for analysis of many historical subjects, such as Jewish family law, maritime law, the economic structures of Jewish traders, and the trading practices of individual cities. See, for example, Jessica L. Goldberg, *Trade and Institutions in the Medieval Mediterranean: The Geniza Merchants and Their Business World* (Cambridge: Cambridge University Press, 2012).

8. George F. Hourani, *Arab Seafaring in the Indian Ocean in Ancient and Medieval Times*, rev. and expanded by John Carswell (Princeton, NJ: Princeton University Press [1951], rev. ed. 1995), 88, 101–102. See also G. R. Tibbetts, *Arab Navigation in the Indian Ocean before the Coming of the Portuguese* (London: Royal Asiatic Society, 1971).

9. Hourani, *Arab Seafaring*, 89n.

10. The monsoon pattern made for predictable winds across a huge swath of coastal and island Asia, including the Bay of Bengal, the China Sea, and the Western Pacific. Traders used these winds for travel between large port cities centuries before David's voyage. A Greek captain described the pattern in the Indian Ocean in the first century. See *The Periplus of the Erythrean Sea* (London: printed by A. Strahan, for T. Cadell Jun. and W. Davies, 1800–1805). Also see Himansahu P. Ray, *Archaeology of Seafaring: The Indian Ocean in the Ancient Period* (Delhi: Pragati Publications, 1999). For the

monsoon in modern-day India see P. K. Das, *The Monsoons* (New Delhi: National Book Trust, 1968).

11. For an insular but interesting look at European use of and fascination with tropical spices see Paul Freedman, *Out of the East: Tropical Spices and the Medieval Imagination* (New Haven, CT: Yale University Press, 2008).

12. Maxime Rodinson, A. J. Arberry, and Charles Perry, *Medieval Arab Cookery* (Devon, UK: Prospect Books, 2001). See also David Waines, *In a Caliph's Kitchen* (London: Riad El-Rayyes Books, 1989). There has been steady publication of medieval European recipes in the last decade, now including more than two thousand of English provenance alone. Other than pepper, tropical spices, such as ginger, cardamom, mace, cloves, cinnamon, and cubeb, rarely seem to appear in England before the fourteenth century. See Constance B. Hieatt, "Making Sense of Medieval Culinary Records: Much Done, but Much to Do," in *Food and Eating in Medieval Europe*, ed. Martha Carlin and Joel T. Rosenthal (London: Hambledon Press, 1998), 101–116. See also *The Forme of Cury, a Roll of Ancient English Cookery; Compiled, about A.D. 1390, by the Master-Cooks of King Richard II, Presented Afterwards to Queen Elizabeth by Edward Lord Stafford and Now in the Possession of Gustavus Brander, Esq.* Text available online at www.gutenberg.org.

13. Ray, *Archaeology of Seafaring*, 55.

14. Kings across Asia, North Africa, and Spain used and stockpiled tropical spices and often tried to grow them. Most attempts failed because the plants grew only in specific tropical microclimates.

15. Jonathan M. Bloom, *Paper before Print: The History and Impact of Paper on the Islamic World* (New Haven, CT: Yale University Press, 2001), 47–50.

16. Fustat ("camp" in Arabic) was the armed camp built by the invading Muslim army in the seventh century. It developed into a large city and was the Egyptian capital until the Fatimid dynasty of the tenth century. Fustat was burned to avoid capture by a Crusader army in 1168 CE. Only the area along the river recovered, which included several Coptic churches and Jewish synagogues. Starting in the thirteenth century, most of old Fustat became a garbage dump for the developing city of Cairo to the north.

17. Quoted in Bloom, *Paper before Print*, 49.

18. See ibid., 68.

19. Letter from Khalaf bin Isaac bin Bundar to Ibrahin bin Yiju. Undated, but internal evidence assigns it to 1139 CE. Translated in Goitein, *Letters*, 187–192.

20. The nature of one-to-one partnerships among trades has been convincingly argued in Goldberg, *Trade and Institutions*, chap. 2.

21. Shlomo Goitein, *A Mediterranean Society: The Jewish Community of the Arab World as Portrayed in the Documents of the Cairo Geniza* (Berkeley: University of California Press, 1967), 203.

22. Gems were so small, light, and high value that David might have dispatched a

trusted slave with his goods for sale in Cairo. Nevertheless, he would have needed a partner/gem dealer in Cairo to receive the goods, sell them for him, and either dispatch the proceeds to Malabar or keep them until David's slave returned.

23. Amitav Ghosh, *In an Antique Land* (New York: Vintage Books, 1994), 267–268. Also see Yedida K. Stillman, "New Data on Islamic Textiles from the Cairo Geniza," in *Patterns of Everyday Life*, ed. David Waines (Aldershot, UK: Ashgate, 2002).

24. The letters of Abraham in Yiju are quite poignant on his attempts to find a Tunisian boy to marry his daughter. He turned down a marriage proposal from a wealthy non-Tunisian family.

25. See, for example, Avner Grief, *Institutions and the Path to the Modern Economy: Lessons from Medieval Trade* (Cambridge: Cambridge University Press, 2006).

26. See the crucial documents in Li Guo, *Commerce and Community in a Red Sea Port in the Thirteenth Century: The Arabic Documents from Quseir* (Leiden: Brill, 2004).

27. The emergence of a "head" of the Jewish community as a corporate entity was likely an organic and internal process driven by fragmentation of Jewish religious authority at the time. See Mark R. Cohen, *Jewish Self-Government in Medieval Egypt: The Origins of the Office of the Head of the Jews, ca. 1065–1126* (Princeton, NJ: Princeton University Press, 1980).

28. Shlomo Goitein, "Portrait of a Medieval Indian Trader: Three Letters from the Cairo Geniza," *Bulletin of the School of Oriental and African Studies* 50, no. 3 (1987): 449–450. See also Shlomo Goitein, *Studies in Islamic History and Institutions* (Leiden: Brill, 1966), 344.

29. Whole congregations sought to move away from fanaticism and warfare. Some sent travelers to explore possibilities in various Muslim cities. See, for example, *The Itinerary of Benjamin of Tudela: Travels in the Middle Ages*, intro. by Michael A. Signer (Malibu, CA: J. Simon, reprinted ed., 1983).

30. Goitein, *Letters*, 194. Metalworking and reworking were common industries and crafts that Jews engaged in. See Goitein, *Letters*, 17–18, 188–189. Madmun wrote to Abraham bin Yiju of the good market in Aden for Indian iron. Shlomo Goitein, "From Aden to India: Specimens of the Correspondence of India Traders in the Twelfth Century," *Journal of the Economic and Social History of the Orient* 23 (1980): 52–53.

31. See Abdul Sheriff, *Dhow Cultures of the Indian Ocean: Cosmopolitanism, Commerce and Islam* (New York: Columbia University Press, 2010). Also Michael M. Pearson, *Merchants and Rulers in Gujarat: The Response to the Portuguese in the Sixteenth Century* (Berkeley: University of California Press, 1976).

32. A few dhows are still made in Gujarat but no longer in Malabar. Some fishing craft are still sewn together rather than nailed. A decade ago the author had the good fortune to purchase a dhow model from a shipwright who had previously made full-size craft.

33. Goitein, *Letters*, 64–65.

## 7. Kublai Khan's Fleet

1. Hakata had, in fact, been built by Chinese traders in the late eleventh century and consisted of a town ringed by docks and warehouses. At first it was inhabited solely by Chinese, but many traders intermarried with local families and merged with the local society. See Bruce L. Batten, *Gateway to Japan: Hakata in War and Peace, 500–1300* (Honolulu: University of Hawai'i Press, 2006).

2. The repulsing of the first Mongol invasion fleet and the destruction by a typhoon has generated some recent historical writing. The most accessible account is by James P. Delgado, *Khubilai Khan's Lost Fleet: In Search of a Legendary Armada* (Vancouver, BC: Douglas & McIntyre, 2008), which accompanied the BBC documentary of the same title. A shorter summary of the invasion and the state of discoveries in Hakata Bay is James P. Delgado, Randall J. Sasaki, and Kenzo Hayashida, "The Lost Fleet of Kublai Khan: Mongol Invasions of Japan," in *Genghis Khan and the Mongol Empire*, ed. William W. Fitzhugh, Morris Rossabi, and William Honeychurch (Houston: Houston Museum of Natural Science, 2009).

3. See Timothy May, *The Mongol Art of War: Chinggis Khan and the Mongol Military System* (Barnesley, UK: Pen and Sword Military, 2007), 72–76. A tactical retreat was a typical maneuver for a Mongol army, especially when faced with rainy weather, which damaged the Mongol composite bows. It is thus no surprise that the first invasion fleet left Hakata Bay after destroying the port. See May, chap. 3.

4. An excellent biography is Morris Rossabi, *Khubilai Khan: His Life and Times* (Berkeley: University of California Press, 1988).

5. For the last days of the Southern Song dynasty see Richard L. Davis, *Wind against the Mountain: The Crisis of Politics and Culture in Thirteen-Century China* (Cambridge, MA: Council on East Asian Studies, Harvard University, 1996).

6. Kublai Khan's administration was a rather ungainly mix of Mongol and foreign talent. He surrounded himself with advisers from a variety of backgrounds—Nestorian Christian, Buddhist, and Chinese. He retained much of the Chinese bureaucracy but appointed a parallel Mongol provincial administration to oversee taxes and other crucial matters. See Rossabi, *Khubilai Khan*, 14–16.

7. Relations between the Mongols and Korea were, in fact, far more tangled and combative than their alliance to conquer Japan suggests. The Mongols repeatedly invaded Korea over the course of almost fifty years and eventually conquered it. Subordinate relations were solidified by marriages between the Mongol and Korean royal houses. See William E. Henthorn, *Korea: The Mongol Invasions* (Leiden: Brill, 1963).

8. The imperial Chinese annals of the failed invasion of Japan are translated in *Chinese Dynastic Histories: Later Han through Ming Dynasties*, trans. Ryusaku Tsunoda, ed. L. Carrington Goodrich (South Pasadena, CA: P. D. and Ione Perkins, 1951), 81–91.

9. May to October is considered the typhoon season, with the largest number of typhoons in August and September. Several typhoons typically hit the main islands of

Japan each year. A near contemporary, though heavily damaged, Japanese scroll depicts the battle. Unfortunately the sections that would have showed the Mongols retreating to their ships are missing. See http://www.bowdoin.edu/mongol-scrolls/.

10. In fairness to the Mongol leaders, they had, over time, frequently adapted to unknown strategies by opponents. Mongol armies fought successfully, for example, against the Jin forces, which mainly stayed in fortified cities, though the conquest of the Jin took twenty-five years. See May, *Mongol Art of War*, 101–104, and the remainder of chap. 7. In their defeat of the Song, the Mongols had learned how to conduct a campaign based on ships. See Peter Lorge, *War, Politics and Society in Early Modern China, 900–1795* (London: Routledge, 2005). It is possible that the planned third invasion of Japan would have conquered the island, though holding it would have been difficult. It is perhaps worth noting that the samurai's defense of Hakata was the origin of the notion of "kamikaze," a "divine wind" that aided the brave in defense of the homeland, an ideology promoted by the nationalists from the 1890s onward and at the heart of the Japanese suicide bombing missions of World War II.

11. For a thorough discussion of the Mongol "world conquering" ideology and its impact across a vast swath of Asia see Anne F. Broadbridge, *Kingship and Ideology in the Islamic and Mongol Worlds* (Cambridge: Cambridge University Press, 2008).

12. See *The Mongol Mission: Narratives and Letters of the Franciscan Missionaries in Mongolia and China in the Thirteenth and Fourteenth Centuries*, trans. by a Nun of the Stanbrook Abbey, ed. Christopher Dawson (London: Sheed and Ward, 1955), 85–86. After the death of Genghis Khan his sons moved quickly to convert conquest to administration, including taxation departments, an efficient post system, and hiring of competent bureaucrats. See Thomas T. Allsen, *Mongol Imperialism: The Politics of the Grand Qan Möngke in China, Russia, and the Islamic Lands, 1251–1259* (Berkeley: University of California Press, 1989). Also Peter Jackson, "From Ulus to Khanate: The Making of the Mongol States, c. 1220–c. 1290," in *The Mongol Empire and Its Legacy*, ed. Reuven Amital-Preiss and David O. Morgan (Leiden: Brill, 1999), 12–38.

13. 'Ala-ad-Din 'Ata-Malik Juvaini, *Genghis Khan: The History of the World Conqueror*, 2nd ed., trans. J. A. Boyle (Manchester: Manchester University Press, 1997), 80. For a detailed analysis of the full campaign, which stretched along the western Silk Road, see Richard A. Gabriel, *Subotai the Valiant: Genghis Khan's Greatest General* (Westport, CT: Praeger, 2004), 73–88.

14. Juvaini, *Genghis Khan*, 84.

15. Douglas S. Benson, *The Mongol Campaigns in Asia: A Summary History of Mongolian Warfare with the Governments of Eastern and Western Asia in the 13th Century* (Ashland, OH: Bookmasters, 1991), 19.

16. See Thomas T. Allsen's brilliant article, using both Chinese and Arabic sources, that traces the origins of the trebuchet and its subsequent "migrations": "The Circulation of Military Technology in the Mongolian Empire," in *Warfare in Inner Asian History (500–1800)*, ed. Nicola Dicosmo (Leiden: Brill, 2002), 265–294. Allsen thoroughly

debunks Marco Polo's claim that he introduced the weapon to the Mongols. The article makes a convincing argument for the centrality of the Mongol Empire in the spread of gunpowder and gunpowder weapons across Eurasia.

17. The Mongols used twenty catapults against a single gate of the Syrian city of Aleppo in 1259 and took it after a five-day siege.

18. Huang K'uan-chung, "Mountain Fortress Defense: The Experience of the Southern Sung and Korea in Resisting the Mongol Invasions," in *Warfare in Chinese History*, ed. Hans Van de Ven (Leiden: Brill, 2000), 233–234. It is important to remember that the Mongols were hardly the first steppe nomad group to attack and conquer agricultural regions north of the Yangtze River. Trade, war, tribute, and conquest typified relations between the steppe nomads and agricultural-based dynasties for more than a thousand years before the Mongols, with nomad-based dynasties sometimes ruling broad areas of the region. See Thomas Barfield, *The Perilous Frontier: Nomad Empires and China* (Cambridge, MA: Blackwell, 1989).

19. See May, *Mongol Art of War*, 109–114.

20. Balázs Szabó, "Initiation to the Art of War: A Preliminary Text of the Takenouchi School," *Acta Orientalia Academiae Scientiarum Hung.* 66, no. 1 (2013): 96.

21. Quoted ibid., 103.

22. See *In Little Need of Divine Intervention: Takezaki Suenaga's Scrolls of the Mongol Invasions of Japan*, trans. and an interpretive essay by Thomas D. Conlan (Ithaca, NY: East Asia Program, Cornell University, 2001).

23. Xu Jing, a Chinese emissary to the Korean court, noted that the Korean ships were different from contemporary Chinese craft.

24. See Christopher Wake, "The Great Ocean-Going Ships of Southern China in the Age of Chinese Maritime Voyaging to India, Twelfth to Fifteenth Centuries," *International Journal of Maritime History* 9, no. 2 (December 1997): 51–81.

25. See Fitzhugh, Rossabi, and Honeychurch, *Genghis Khan*, 250–251.

26. (*Daily*) *Mail Online*, "Divers Find 13th Century Wreck from Kublai Khan's Mongol Invasion Fleet That Was Destroyed by 'Divine' Typhoon," http://www.dailymail.co .uk/news/article-2053656/Divers-13th-century-wreck-Kublai-Kahns-Mongol-invasion -fleet-destroyed-divine-typhoon.html.

27. For example, three traditional routes connected the southern coast of Korea to China. One route went north and east to the tip of the Shandong Peninsula. A second went east and slightly south to a small port about two hundred miles north of Shanghai. The third route went to Shanghai at the mouth of the Yangtze River. See Choi Wan Ghee, *The Traditional Ships of Korea*, trans. Lee Jean Young (Seoul: Ewha Women's University Press, 2006), 66). The pattern of Korea, Japan, and China jockeying for power in East Asian waters, of course, continued through the twentieth century and continues today.

28. I am following the data and analysis in Hugh R. Clark, *Community, Trade, and Networks: Southern Fujian Province from the Third to the Thirteenth Century* (Cam-

bridge: Cambridge University Press, 1991). Equally useful is Billy K. S. So, *Prosperity, Region, and Institutions in Maritime China: The South Fukien Pattern, 946–1368* (Cambridge, MA: Harvard University Press, 2000).

29. The issue of trade and tribute is well considered in David C. Kang, *East Asia before the West: Five Centuries of Trade and Tribute* (New York: Columbia University Press, 2010). See also Stephen Tseng-Hsin Chang, "Commodities Imported into the Chang-chou Region of Fukien during the Late Ming Period: A Preliminary Analysis of Tax Lists Found in the Tung-hsi-yang k'ao," in *Emporia, Commodities and Entrepreneurs in Asian Maritime Trade, c. 1400–1740*, ed. Roderich Ptak and Dietmar Rothermund (Stuttgart: Franz Steiner Verlag, 1991), 166–186. In the same volume articles discuss the tortoiseshell trade and the use of cowry shells from the Maldive islands in the southern provinces of China.

30. Marco Polo visited Burma shortly after its conquest and left a short, not very helpful description of the capital. See *The Travels of Marco Polo: The Complete Yule-Cordier Edition* (New York: Dover Publications, 1993), 3:87. A worthy attempt to attach known historical places to Marco Polo's place names is Stephen G. Haw, *Marco Polo's China: A Venetian in the Realm of Khubilai Khan* (Abingdon, UK: Routledge, 2006).

31. As in Japan the Mongols demanded tribute and a full personal submission from the Tran dynasty of northern Vietnam and the Cham dynasty of central Vietnam. Both sent tribute but equivocated on personal submission.

32. It is perhaps worth noting that the same combination of watery coastal plain backed by mountains was instrumental in the defeat of the American forces in Vietnam in the 1970s.

33. For centuries Chinese writers have been unable to deal with China losing its position as the center of the world in this period. See T. H. Barrett, "Qubilai Qa'an and the Historians: Some Remarks on the Position of the Great Khan in Pre-Modern Chinese Historiography," in *The Mongol Empire and Its Legacy*, ed. Reuven Amitai-Preis and David O. Morgan (Leiden: Brill, 1999), 250–259. Even though Mongol rule in China lasted only a century and a half, it had profound effects. See Hidehiro Okada, "China as a Successor State to the Mongol Empire," in the same volume, 260–272. See also two important articles by Henry Serruys reprinted in *The Mongols and Ming China: Customs and History* (London: Variorum Reprints, 1987).

34. For Carpini's memoir see Friar Giovanni Di Plano Carpini, *The Story of the Mongols Whom We Call Tartars*, trans. Erik Hildinger (Boston: Branden Publishing Co., 1996).

## 8. Bremen Cog

1. The story of finding, identifying, and restoring the Bremen cog is told in Gabrielle Hoffmann and Per Hoffmann, "Sailing the Bremen Cog," *International Journal of Nautical Archaeology* 38, no. 2 (2009): 282–283.

2. Scholars have, for example, linked the cog to simple flat-bottomed boat models found in funerary urns in the Weser River area, which date to c. 200 BCE. Other scholars have argued for a Dutch origin for the cog based on medallions and coins minted by Dutch towns showing a flat-bottomed vessel, which date from 800 CE onward. See Owain T. P. Roerts, "Descendents of Viking Boats," in *Cogs, Caravels and Galleons: The Sailing Ship, 1000–1650*, ed. Robert Gardiner (London: Conway Maritime Press, 1994), 11.

3. Frederick M. Hocker, "Bottom-Based Shipbuilding in Northern Europe," in Frederick M. Hocker and Cheryl A. Ward, *The Philosophy of Shipbuilding: Conceptual Approaches to the Study of Wooden Ships* (College Station: Texas A&M University Press, 2005), 65–93.

4. Ole Crumlin-Pederson, "To Be or Not to Be a Cog: The Bremen Cog in Perspective," *International Journal of Nautical Archaeology* 29, no. 2 (2000): 239.

5. Timothy J. Runyan, "The Cog as Warship," in Gardiner, *Cogs, Caravels and Galleons*, 48.

6. Ibid.

7. Richard W. Unger, *The Ship in the Medieval Economy, 600–1600* (London: Croon Helm, 1980), 139.

8. Gardiner, *Cogs, Caravels and Galleons*, 48.

9. Ibid.

10. Ian Friel, *The Good Ship: Ships, Shipbuilding and Technology in England, 1200–1520* (London: British Museum Press, 1995), 95.

11. Ibid., 97.

12. Gillian Hutchinson, *Medieval Ships and Shipping* (London: Leicester University Press, 1997), 98.

13. Ibid., 84

14. Ibid., 66–168.

15. Gardiner, *Cogs, Caravels and Galleons*, 40.

16. Hutchinson, *Medieval Ships and Shipping*, 121.

17. Ibid., 104.

18. Gardiner, *Cogs, Caravels and Galleons*, 47.

19. Ibid.

20. Hutchinson, *Medieval Ships and Shipping*, 110.

21. Jan Bill, "The Cargo Vessels," in Lars Berggren, Nils Hybel, and Annette Landen, *Cogs, Cargoes, and Commerce: Maritime Bulk Trade in Northern Europe, 1150–1400* (Toronto: Pontifical Institute of Medieval Studies), 92–112.

22. Richard Unger, "Beer: A New Bulk Good of International Trade," in Berggren, Hybel, and Landen, *Cogs*, 113–127.

23. Wendy R. Childs, "Timber for Cloth: Changing Commodities in Anglo-Baltic Trade in the Fourteenth Century," in Berggren, Hybel, and Landen, *Cogs*, 181–211.

24. Gardiner, *Cogs, Caravels and Galleons*, 40.

25. Lars Berggren, "The Export of Limestone and Limestone Fonts from Gotland during the Thirteenth and Fourteenth Centuries," in Berggren, Hybel, and Landen, *Cogs*, 143–180.

26. Bjorn Poulson, "The Widening of Import Trade and Consumption around 1200 A.D.: A Danish Perspective," in Berggren, Hybel, and Landen, *Cogs*, 46.

27. Ibid., 40–44.

28. Rolf Hammel-Kiesow, "Lübeck and the Baltic Trade in Bulk Goods for the North Sea Region, 1150–1400," in Berggren, Hybel, and Landen, *Cogs*, 65.

29. Gardiner, *Cogs, Caravels and Galleons*, 41.

30. Friel, *Good Ship*, 134.

31. Ibid.

32. The description of the Hansa's development and export of hopped beer relies on Unger, "Beer," 112–127.

33. Gardiner, *Cogs, Caravels and Galleons*, 38. This partnership of sea-based trades and land-based producers is depicted on the seal of Lübeck (1294).

34. Ibid.

35. See Hutchinson, *Medieval Ships and Shipping*, 115.

36. Unger, *Ship in the Medieval Economy*, 246.

37. Ibid., 252. See also Hutchinson, *Medieval Ships and Shipping*, 154–156.

38. Gardiner, *Cogs, Caravels and Galleons*, 43.

39. *Froissart's Chronicles*, ed. and trans. John Joliffe (London: Penguin Books, 2001), xv–xviii.

40. Jean Froissart, *The Chronicles of Froissart*, trans. John Bourchier, Lord Berners, ed. G. C. Macaulay (London: Macmillan and Co., 1895), 61.

41. Susan Rose, "Battle of Sluys," in Eric Grove, *Great Battles of the Royal Navy* (London: Arms and Armour, c. 1994).

42. Gardiner, *Cogs, Caravels and Galleons*, 53.

43. Froissart, *Chronicles*, 62.

44. Hutchinson, *Medieval Ships and Shipping*, 255–256

45. Friel, *Good Ship*, 29. The uncertainties of commerce led to the first law of the sea in Atlantic waters, which was based on Mediterranean (and ultimately Roman) law as observed and promulgated by Eleanor of Aquitaine in 1159. Its fifty-two articles describe responsibility for many types of losses at sea, on entering and leaving harbors, and during ship repairs. See the text at http://www.admiraltylawguide.com.

46. Unger, *Ship in the Medieval Economy*, 129–132.

47. Ibid., 186–188.

48. Ibid.

49. Ibid., 169–171.

50. Hutchinson, *Medieval Ships and Shipping*, 160–162.

51. See Hoffmann and Hoffmann, "Sailing the Bremen Cog."

52. "The Pilgrims Sea-Voyage" (from a manuscript held by Trinity College, Cam-

bridge, MS. R, 3, 19, t. Hen. VI.), in *The Stacions of Rome*, ed. Frederick J. Furnivall (New York: Greenwood Press, reprinted ed., 1969).

## 9. Barbary War Galley

1. Richard Hasleton, *The Strange and Wonderful Things That Happened to Rd. Hasleton. . . .* (London, 1595). Reprinted in Edward Arber, *An English Garner: Ingatherings from Our History and Literature* (London: Archibald Constable and Co. [c. 1910]).

2. Longer galleys tended to droop both fore and aft. In maritime terminology this problem is known as "hogging." The solution was to anchor a heavy rope at each end of the boat and to tighten it, thereby raising the ends. This rope was an essential piece of equipment prominently mentioned for each vessel of the "Naval Inventories" inscription of a fourth-century BCE fleet.

3. For a general description of Barbary galleys see James L. George, *History of Warships: From Ancient Times to the Twenty-First Century* (Annapolis, MD: Naval Institute Press, 1998), chap. 2.

4. The painting can be viewed online at http://www.bbc.co.uk/arts/yourpaintings /paintings/action-between-the-dutch-fleet-and-barbary-pirates-175922.

5. Stephen Clissold, *The Barbary Slaves* (London: P. Elek, 1977), 34.

6. A document of criminals condemned to slavery by Spanish courts, 1586–1589, lists sixty-five hundred men. See Henry Kamen, "Galley Service and Crime in Sixteenth-Century Spain," *Economic History Review*, New Series, vol. 22, no. 2 (August 1969): 304.

7. Robert C. Davis, *Christian Slaves, Muslim Masters* (New York: Palgrave, 2003), 13.

8. Ibid., 23.

9. Patrick Manning, *The African Diaspora: A History through Culture* (New York: Columbia University Press, 2009), 23.

10. A single bank of rowers allowed for considerable storage in lockers under the rowing benches. A second tier of rowers consumed all this storage space.

11. John Morrison, "The Trireme," in *Age of the Galley*, ed. Robert Gardiner (London: Conway Maritime Press, 1995), 63. The most thorough documentation about triremes is found in fragments of a large inscription found at Piraeus, which details a fleet of the fourth century.

12. Ibid., 64.

13. Ibid., 57–58.

14. Thus, Brutus's flagship in the battle of Massalia in 49 BCE was a six.

15. In the later period of the Roman Empire actual use of ships in warfare was mainly confined to transporting legions on the Rhine and Danube to battles with various "barbarian" opponents. In the larger picture the broad retreat of Rome from all these provinces around 300 CE meant the disappearance of Roman fleets.

16. Lionel Casson, "Merchant Galleys," in Gardiner, *Age of the Galley*, 121. These big Roman merchant galleys had thirty or even fifty oarsmen.

17. Nikolaos Kaltsas, Elena Vlachogianni, Polyxeni Bouyia, eds., *The Antikythera Shipwreck: The Ship, the Treasures, the Mechanism* (Athens: Kapon, 2012).

18. Hocker, "Bottom-Based Shipbuilding," 96.

19. Greek fire seems endlessly fascinating to popular audiences. See, for example, the National Geographic special at http://channel.nationalgeographic.com/channel/the -link/videos/greek-fire/.

20. See F. Foerster, "The Warships of the Kings of Aragon and Their Fighting Tactics during the 13th and 14th Centuries AD," *International Journal of Nautical Archaeology and Underwater Exploration* 16 (1987): 19–29. Venetian galleys put three rowers on the same bench. An outrigger pivot point allowed each oar to contact the water at slightly different distances from the hull. The longest oar, at 32 feet, operated by the innermost rower, was quite heavy and had to be counterweighted to be rowed at all. The middle oar was 30.5 feet, and the shortest oar was 29.5 feet. See Casson, "Merchant Galleys," 125, 149.

21. John H. Pryor, *Geography, Technology, and War: Studies in the Maritime History on the Mediterranean, 649–1571* (Cambridge: Cambridge University Press, 1988), 116.

22. Hasleton, *Strange and Wonderful Things*, 162.

23. Ibid., 166.

24. Ibid., 168–170

25. Ibid., 175.

26. Ibid., 180.

27. See Gardiner, *Age of the Galley*, chap. 12, for a dense technical discussion of the various parameters and limits of human rowing on galleys.

28. America has its own history of enslavement at the hands of Barbary corsairs. The first colonial ship was captured in 1640, only two decades after the founding of Plymouth. Ships were occasionally taken through the seventeenth and eighteenth centuries, but colonial shipping was generally protected by treaties between England and the Barbary states. The American Revolution changed all that. American shipping was no longer protected by British treaties, and the Barbary states immediately captured American ships and enslaved American sailors. All the United States could do was pay a huge ransom for the return of its sailors. Naval campaigns of 1803 and 1815 invaded the kingdom of Algeria and eventually forced a treaty freeing all American sailors. This invasion is celebrated in the Marine Corp Hymn's line "to the shores of Tripoli."

## 10. *Los Tres Reyes*

1. The story of the wreck and the salvage is told in Carla Rahn Phillips, *Los Tres Reyes: The Short Life of an Unlucky Spanish Galleon, 1628–1634* (Minneapolis: University of Minnesota Press, 1990), 54–57.

2. Ibid.

3. The story of the capture of the Spanish treasure fleet has been told many times. See, for example, the short version in Timothy R. Walton, *The Spanish Treasure Fleets* (Sarasota, FL: Pineapple Press, 1994), 121–122. A considerably longer version appears in Carla Rahn Phillips, *Six Galleons for the King of Spain: Imperial Defense in the Early Seventeenth Century* (Baltimore: Johns Hopkins University Press, 1986).

4. No illustrations of *Los Tres Reyes* exist, but this is hardly surprising. Ship paintings of the period generally displayed a battle, a landing party, or the ceremonial review of a fleet. *Los Tres Reyes* did not happen to be present at one of these paintable occasions. Small drawings of ships also filled empty spaces in maps, but these illustrations were generic and typically did not portray a particular ship.

5. Carla Rahn Phillips, "The Caravel and the Galleon," in *Cogs, Caravels and Galleons: The Sailing Ship, 1000–1650*, ed. Robert Gardiner (London: Conway Maritime Press, 1994), 100–101. For a comprehensive discussion of the variations in early fully rigged ships see Phillips, *Six Galleons*, 32–40.

6. The word "galleon" is derived from the Venetian *gallioni*, a rowed river patrol boat. Early versions in other parts of Europe retained the oars. Later ships called galleons dropped the oars, changed the design, but retained the name. See Phillips, "Caravel and the Galleon," 91–144.

7. See Phillips, *Six Galleons*, 229. Also Walton, *Spanish Treasure Fleets*, 57–59.

8. Phillips, *Los Tres Reyes*, 10.

9. Phillips, "Caravel and the Galleon," 102.

10. Phillips, *Six Galleons*, 48.

11. Ibid., 97–98.

12. Ibid., 99.

13. William D. Phillips and Carla Rahn Phillips, *A Concise History of Spain* (Cambridge: Cambridge University Press, 2010), 158–159. For more detail see Phillips, *Six Galleons*, 62–63.

14. Tonnage was basically a matter of the relation between length and beam. The master shipbuilder had to get the arc of the ribs right to get the beam correct and hit the specified tonnage.

15. Philips, *Los Tres Reyes*, 8.

16. Phillips, *Six Galleons*, 66–68. Arana may have broken even on the construction of the six galleons, though the documents suggest not. He was, however, rewarded by the crown with the office of superintendent of war over the one hundred or so soldiers stationed at Santander, presumably an ongoing source on income. See Phillips, *Six Galleons*, 89.

17. A modern scholar has speculated that the crown decided that the ships would not be ready for the seasonal sailing to the Indies in 1727 and found ways to delay them until the following year. See Phillips, *Six Galleons*, 65.

18. Ibid., 104–105.

19. Ibid.

20. This is not to deny that pirates were many in the Caribbean in the seventeenth century. Their main prey was local shipping. The most lucrative venture for pirates was contraband items needed in Spanish colonies and only legally available at high tariff. See John Lynch, *Spain under the Hapsburgs*, vol. 2, 2nd ed. (Oxford: Blackwell, 1981), 190.

21. Ibid., 187–188.

22. At that time only two other mercury mines existed in the European world, one in Spain and one in Slovenia, both under Hapsburg authority.

23. See Walton, *Spanish Treasure Fleets*, 37–42.

24. There was also a major gold strike in New Granada, but most of the gold shipped to Spain from the New World came from panning rivers in the region. This was brutal work, as brutal as the mines. Impressed locals quickly died, and the Spanish soon turned to African slave labor for all these ventures.

25. Lynch, *Spain under the Hapsburgs*, 167.

26. Phillips, *Los Tres Reyes*, 35.

27. The ducat was originally minted in Venice but became so successful as an international currency that by the seventeenth century similar coins were minted in other countries of Italy, the Low Countries (called a guilder), France (the livre), and Germany (gulden).

28. Lynch, *Spain under the Hapsburgs*, 90.

29. Ibid., 89.

30. Ibid., 170–171.

31. Lincoln P. Paine, *Ships of Discovery and Exploration* (Boston: Mariner Books/Houghton Mifflin, 2000), 47.

32. Jacques de Coutre, *The Memoirs and Memorials of Jacques de Couture: Security, Trade and Society in 16th and 17th-Century Southeast Asia*, ed. and intro. by Peter Borscberg, trans. Roopanji Roy (Singapore: NUS Press), 158–162.

33. Ibid., 242–271.

34. Lynch, *Spain under the Hapsburgs*, 187.

35. Ibid., 122.

36. Ibid., 76.

37. Ibid., 182.


## 11. HMS *Victory*

1. *Old England or the Constitutional Journal* (London), Saturday, October 20, 1744, issue 80. Gale/Cengage Burney Collection of 17th–18th Century Newspapers.

2. W. L. Clowes, *A History of the Royal Navy from the Earliest Time to the Present*, vol. 3 (London: Chatham Publishing, reprinted ed., 1996), 107–108.

3. Neil Cunningham Dobson and Sean Kingsley, "HMS *Victory*, a First-Rate Royal Navy Warship Lost in the English Channel, 1744: Preliminary Survey and Identifica-

tion," Odyssey Papers 2 (Tampa, FL: Odyssey Marine Exploration, 2009), 7, http://www.shipwreck.net/pdf/OMEPapers2-HMS_victory.pdf.

4. Ibid., 8.

5. See Brian Lavery, *The Arming and Fitting of English Ships of War: 1600–1815* (Annapolis, MD: Conway Maritime Press, 1987), 9–22. Also Brian Lavery, *Building the Wooden Walls: The Design and Construction of the 74-Gun Ship* Valiant (London: Conway Maritime Press, 1991).

6. Brian Lavery, *The Ship-of-the-Line*, vol. 1, *The Development of the Battlefleet, 1650–1850* (Annapolis, MD: Conway Maritime Press, 1983), 78.

7. During the war a policy of continuing the British blockade of the French coast into the winter was instituted. It resulted in major victories, such as Quiberon Bay at the end of November 1759. The officers and men suffered during this service, as E. Hawke wrote: "Thank God. I am very well tho' almost starved with Cold; I hope to be allow'd to go home soon, for I have a long and tiresome service of it." Quoted in G. J. Marcus, *Heart of Oak: A Survey of the British Sea Power in the Georgian Era* (London: Oxford University Press, 1975), 235.

8. Naval budgets remained essentially flat in the long period of peace between 1715 and 1745. This meant not only that few new ships were constructed but also that ships received less maintenance. See Clowes, *History of the Royal Navy*, 5.

9. The politics of British naval acquisition is considered in detail in Clive Wilkinson, *The British Navy and the State in the 18th Century* (Woodbridge, UK: Boydell Press, 2004). See also Lavery, *Ship-of-the-Line*, 68.

10. For construction methods and details of ship design see Peter Goodwin, *The Construction and Fitting of the English Man of War: 1650–1850* (Annapolis, MD: Naval Institute Press, 1987).

11. Lavery, *Ship-of-the-Line*, 64. For an interesting musing on what sorts of governments were capable of sustaining a naval fleet see "The Military Revolution at Sea," in N. A. M. Rodger, *Essays in Naval History, from Medieval to Modern* (Farham, UK: Ashgate Variorum, 2009).

12. The standardization of naval ordnance proceeded throughout the eighteenth century. See, for example, Spencer Tucker, *Arming the Fleet: U.S. Navy Ordnance in the Muzzle-Loading Era* (Annapolis, MD: Naval Institute Press, 1989).

13. Lavery, *Ship-of-the-Line*, 70.

14. Robert Gardiner, ed., *The Line of Battle: The Sailing Warships, 1650–1840* (London: Conway Maritime Press, 1992), chaps. 2–5.

15. Clowes, *History of the Royal Navy*, 13–14. Much more detail and context are found in Gloria Clifton, "The London Instrument Makers and the British Navy, 1700–1800," in *Science and the French and British Navies, 1700–1850*, ed. Pieter van der Merwe (Greenwich: National Maritime Museum, 2003), 24–33.

16. Lavery, *Ship-of-the-Line*, 93–97.

17. Ibid., 96–97.

18. N. A. M. Rodger, *The Wood World: An Anatomy of the Georgian Navy* (Annapolis, MD: Naval Institute Press, 1986), 162. The figures suggest a typical ship's turnover rate was 20–80 percent per year. Not all of these men left to return to land-based jobs. Many simply shifted to another ship. The desertion rate was highest in the first year of service and generally declined thereafter. See Rodger, *Wood World*, 196–197.

19. Marcus, *Heart of Oak*, 62–64.

20. Ibid., 71.

21. Ibid., 195–196.

22. Lavery, *Ship-of-the-Line*, 80.

23. Lavery, *Arming and Fitting*, 151.

24. See David J. Hepper, *British Warship Losses in the Age of Sail, 1650–1859* (Rotherfield, UK: Jean Boudriot Publications, 1994), 212–213. Only one mid-eighteenth-century ship-of-the-line remains today, Nelson's flagship at the battle of Trafalgar, the justly famous *Victory*, which was built in 1759 and was the next (and last) in line of Royal Navy ships to use the name *Victory*. Nelson's *Victory* is in a permanent historic dockyard at Portsmouth, England.

25. Michael Duffy, ed., *Parameters of British Naval Power: 1650–1850* (Exeter: University of Exeter Press, 1992), 6.

26. Sean A. Kingsley, Neil Cunningham Dobson, and Frederick Van de Wall, "Balchin's Victory (Site 25C): Shipwreck Monitoring and Cannon Impacts, 2008–2012," Odyssey Papers 24 (Tampa, FL: Odyssey Marine Exploration, 2012), http://shipwreck .net/.

27. Odyssey Marine Exploration press release February 2, 2012, http://shipwreck .net. The firm also produced a recent scientific paper on the movement of sediments and the formation of large-scale sediment waveforms in the region of the *Victory* wreck, suggesting that much of the wreck is still buried.


### 12. *Lucy Walker*

1. There are two main digitally available collections of nineteenth-century American newspapers, a free one compiled by the Library of Congress at http://chroniclingamerica.loc.gov and a much larger subscription one at http://infoweb.newsbank.com. I have searched both in the relevant years with the tag "Lucy Walker" and "disaster."

2. This section draws heavily from Richard R. John, *Spreading the News: The American Postal System from Franklin to Morse* (Cambridge, MA: Harvard University Press, 1995), esp. chaps. 1–3.

3. W. C. Redfield, *Letter to the Secretary of the Treasury on the History and Causes of Steamboat Explosions*, rev. ed. (New York: William Osborn, 1839), 4.

4. Report no. 478, "Steamboats," May 18, 1832, in Reports of the Committees of the House of Representatives at the First Session of the Twenty-Second Congress, Begun and Held at the City of Washington, December 7, 1831, p. 3.

5. See James T. Lloyd, *Steamboat Directory, and Disasters on the Western Waters* (Cincinnati: James T. Lloyd & Co., 1856), 89–93.

6. See Doc. no. 24, House of Representatives, Twenty-Ninth Congress, First Session (December 11, 1846), "Relative to Steamboat Explosions."

7. *Report of the Proceedings and Testimony at the Coroner's Inquest in the Case of the Explosion of the Steamboat Empire State on the Night of July 26, 1856* (Fall River, MA: Almay & Milne, Printers, 1856), 5.

8. J. H. Kavanach, "Sweet Mississippi" (1853). Available at the American Memory Project of the Library of Congress, original bound volumes, Ma A12v vd.53. Folk music, written by those who worked and lived along the river, presented rather earthier viewpoints. Titles included "Mississippi Baby," "Mississippi Bottom Blues," "Mississippi Boll Weevil Blues," "Mississippi Flood," "Mississippi Heavy Water Blues," "Mississippi Moan," "Mississippi Mud," "Mississippi Snag," "The Flood of 1927," and "Mississippi River Man." See www.ibiblio.org/folkindex/kwframe.htm.

9. See Timothy Flint, *Recollections of the Last Ten Years*, ed. C. Hartley Grattan (New York: Knopf, 1932), 20–22. The author was on the Mississippi River and its tributaries, from Pittsburgh to the Missouri River, from 1815 to 1825.

10. Ibid., 26.

11. See R. John Brockman, *Exploding Steamboats, Senate Debates, and Technical Reports: The Convergence of Technology, Politics, and Rhetoric in the Steamboat Bill of 1838* (Amityville, NY: Baywood Publishing Co., 2002).

12. *Arkansas State Gazette*, February 8, 1843, 3.

13. *New Orleans Daily Picayune*, February 10, 1843, 2.

14. *Arkansas State Gazette*, March 15, 1843, 2.

15. The commitment of crucial information to memory is one of the most universal features of professionals who live by navigating routes. For example, traditional sailors on the east coast of Africa chanted their landmarks and star headings in rhymed verses. Today, apprentice truck drivers learn how to move through cities from more experienced drivers.

16. Mark Twain, *Life on the Mississippi* (New York: Harper and Brothers, 1901), 50.

17. Doc. no. 24, House of Representatives, p. 2.

18. Edwin J. Clapp, *The Navigable Rhine: The Development of Its Shipping, the Basis of the Prosperity of Its Commerce and Its Traffic in 1907* (Boston: Houghton Mifflin, 1911), 16–17.

19. For a bibliography of this Rhine-based genre see Michael Schmitt, *Die Illustrierten Rhein-Beschreibungen: Dokumentation der Werke und Ansichten von der Romantik bis zun ende des 19. Jahrhunders* (Cologne: Böhlau Verlag GmbH & Cie, 1996).

20. George S. Pabis, *Daily Life along the Mississippi* (Westport, CT, 2007), 78.

21. Ibid., 112–113, 148–149.

22. *Wilson's History and Directory of Southeastern Missouri Southern Illinois* (St. Louis, 1876).

23. Joe Kelsey and Charley Straight, *See Those Mississippi Steamboats on Parade* (New York: Jerome H. Remick & Co., 1916).

24. Early coal transport on the Mississippi River system was rather more exciting than today's barge traffic. In the last three decades of the nineteenth century coal from the hills of western Pennsylvania moved on barges, which could clear the rocks on the Ohio River only for a few days in the spring. The boats waited in Pittsburgh, their captains watching for a rise in the Ohio River. The moment the water was deep enough, the coal fleet of several thousand boats raced downriver to deliver the year's coal to downstream cities and towns. The fleet also restocked coaling stations throughout the Mississippi system, which fueled the steamboats.

## 13. *Flying Cloud*

1. A search of various databases of newspapers of the time yielded not a single story of the wreck of the *Flying Cloud*. For the details of its loss see David W. Shaw, *Flying Cloud: The True Story of America's Most Famous Clipper Ship and the Woman Who Guided Her* (New York: William Morrow, 2000), 263–264.

2. This argument is developed in the magisterial work on clipper ships by Carl C. Cutler, *Greyhounds of the Sea: The Story of the American Clipper Ship* (Annapolis, MD: Naval Institute Press, 1930). The argument is not entirely persuasive, since the majority of the ships built were not built for speed but for specific tasks, such as fishing or carrying sugar from the Caribbean.

3. Shaw, *Flying Cloud*, 40.

4. See Diana Fontaine (Maury) Corbin, *A Life of Matthew Fontaine Maury* (London: Sampson, Low Marston, Searle & Rivington, 1888), 24. Maury, as founder of modern ocean cartography and navigational charts, is a fascinating character, actively participating in several scientific fields, such as magnetism. He was a founding member of the American Academy of Sciences. The biography by his daughter is available at https://archive.org.

5. These instruments, broadly known as the octant, had substantially improved in the second half of the eighteenth century. Though claimed as an invention, the new device was actually the product of the concentration of instrument making and metal skill in London. The new octant was in common use by 1800. See Gloria Clifton, "The London Instrument Makers and the British Navy, 1700–1850," in *Science and the British and French Navies, 1700–1850*, ed. Pieter van der Merwe (Greenwich: National Maritime Museum, 2003), 24–33.

6. For the full story of Harrison and his chronometer see Dava Sobel, *Longitude: The True Story of a Lone Genius Who Solved the Greatest Scientific Problem of His Time* (New York: Walker & Co., 1995).

7. The author learned and sang this chantey in the 1960s. It turns out that there are several more verses whose lyrics are readily available on the Internet. See http://www.jsward.com/shanty/BlowYeWinds/.

8. "On the Expediency of Authorizing an Exploring Expedition, by Vessels of the Navy, to the Pacific Ocean and South Seas," Twenty-Fourth Congress, First Session, no. 620, March 21, 1836, 867.

9. An unlikely export of New England was ice, cut from ponds in winter and shipped as a luxury item to the American South, the Caribbean, South American ports, and all the way to India. Eventually the ice trade also included England. Faster passage was obviously important to this trade. At each destination local investors built an insulated ice building to keep the ice.

10. See, for example, Basil Greenhill, *The Merchant Schooners* (Annapolis, MD: Naval Institute Press, 1951).

11. The overall number of clipper ships produced will vary with each author's definition of a fast merchant vessel of the period. One list of such ships and their records is Octavius T. Howe and Frederick C. Matthews, *American Clipper Ships: 1833–1858* (Salem, MA: Marine Research Society, Publication 13, 1926–1927).

12. See Cutler, *Greyhounds of the Sea*, chaps. 7 and 8.

13. Ibid., 561–568.

14. Shaw, *Flying Cloud*, 3.

15. Ibid., 23.

16. Ibid., 49.

17. See Robert Coupe, *Australia's Gold Rushes* (Sydney: New Holland, 2000).

18. "The Disappointed Girl," by Thatcher, in *The Victoria Songster Containing Various New and Original Colonial Songs together with a Choice Selection of Most Popular Songs of the Day*, 2nd ed. (Melbourne: Charlwood & Son, 1860), 170, www.nia.gov/apps/doview/nla-aus.

19. For a sense of the British competition to American clipper ships see David R. MacGregor, *British and American Clippers: A Comparison of Their Design, Construction and Performance in the 1850s* (London: Conway Maritime Press, 1993).

20. On the reasons for the abrupt decline of the clipper ships I have mainly followed Cutler. He not only reviewed the testimony at several congressional hearings in the later decades of the nineteenth century, but because he wrote in the 1930s he had access to a few remaining men who had served on clipper ships and personally observed the decline.

21. By the time that the *Flying Cloud* foundered in the Bay of Fundy, the whole process of building a ship had become an industrial enterprise, both in Britain and in the United States. See William H. Theissen, *Industrializing American Shipbuilding: The Transformation of Ship Design and Construction, 1820–1920* (Gainesville: University Press of Florida, 2006).

22. The highest London insurance rating (based on the best materials and construction methods) earned a sixteen-year rating, that is, a good likelihood of lasting sixteen years. See B. C. Whipple, ed., *The Clipper Ships* (Alexandria, VA: Time-Life Books), 143.

23. For clipper-type ships that survived into the twentieth century see the photographs in Robin Knox-Johnson, *The Twilight of Sail* (London: Sidgwick & Jackson Ltd., 1978). For the last of the tall ships carrying grain to Australia see Eric Newby, *Windjammer: Pictures of Life before the Mast in the Last Grain Race* (New York: Dutton, 1968).

## 14. *Lusitania*

1. See Thomas A. Bailey, "The Sinking of the *Lusitania*," *American Historical Review* 42, no. 1: 54 and 54n.

2. Quoted in Neil McCart, *Atlantic Liners of the Cunard Line: From 1884 to the Present Day* (Wellingborough, UK: Patrick Stephens Ltd., 1990), 66.

3. Quoted ibid., 57. Many more stories of people aboard the *Lusitania* are gathered in Sean Molony, *Lusitania: An Irish Tragedy* (Douglas Village, Cork, Ireland: Mercier Press, 2004).

4. A. A. Hoehling and Mary Hoehling, *The Last Voyage of the Lusitania* (New York: Henry Holt, 1956), 27.

5. The details of the *Lusitania*'s passengers and crew on its last voyage are available at http://www.rmsLusitania.info/people. The last voyage was somewhat understaffed, and four of the *Lusitania*'s boilers were cold as an economy measure. The stoker crew was therefore smaller than typical, which might have been around three hundred men for a normal crossing.

6. The successful conversion to steam-powered riverboats had come earlier and faster. Recall from chapter 13 that before steam power, the only way to move cargo and passengers upstream on rivers had been to drag the vessel, a brutal, slow, and expensive process. Downstream transport was equally primitive, as the pilots had very limited means of avoiding shallows or moving the craft to speedier channels of the river. In contrast, sailing ships were well suited to the seas they traversed. They benefited from long experience with the seasonal wind patterns and an equally long history of technological refinements in design and navigation tools. The very decades (1830–1850) when steam power profoundly changed river transport saw shipyards producing the fastest, most sophisticated sailing ships in man's history.

7. Many of these interiors are pictured in William H. Miller Jr., *The First Great Ocean Liners in Photographs* (New York: Dover Publications, 1984), 1–71.

8. A recent book gives a thorough analysis of how crucial immigrant passengers were to the transatlantic liner companies. See Drew Keeling, *The Business of Transatlantic Migration between Europe and the United States, 1900–1914* (Zurich: Chronos, 2012). The price of steerage passage is discussed in appendix 7, 298–299.

9. Sixty-First Congress, Third Session, Senate, Reports of the Immigrations Commission, "Steerage," Doc. no. 753 (Washington, DC: Government Printing Office, 1911), 7.

10. Ibid., 21.

11. Francis E. Hyde, *Cunard and the North Atlantic: 1840–1973* (London: Macmillan, 1973), 1–3.

12. See Miller, *First Great Ocean Liners*, 1–4.

13. The size of the German ships trended steadily upward, from the 14,200 tons of the *Kaiser Wilhelm* to the 19,360 tons of the *Kronprinzessin Cecilie*, launched in 1906.

14. A useful summary of the P&O Line's history is found at http://www.poheritage .com/our-history/timeline.

15. Its rival transatlantic line, the White Star Lines, had recently been purchased by J. P. Morgan and a combine of American investors, though it continued to fly the British flag.

16. Thomas A. Bailey and Paul Ryan, *The Lusitania Disaster: An Episode in Modern Warfare and Diplomacy* (New York: Free Press, 1975), 5.

17. At the time of the sinking of the *Lusitania* in 1915, the Admiralty, because of the subsidized building loan, still owned more than half the ship. It was also listed as an Admiralty ship in numerous government documents. See Bailey and Ryan, *Lusitania Disaster*, 6.

18. The story of the battleship arms race and the role of battleships in World War I has been told many times, usually from the viewpoint of one or another of the major protagonists. A more balanced worldwide perspective is Paul Halpern, *A Naval History of World War I* (Annapolis, MD: Naval Institute Press, 2012). See also Tim Benbow, *History of World War I: Naval Warfare, 1914–1918* (Newbury, UK: Amber, 2008). For a sense of how rapidly naval technology developed during World War I see Norman Friedman, *Naval Weapons of World War One: Guns, Torpedoes, Mines, and ASW Weapons of All Nations; An Illustrated Directory* (Annapolis, MD: Naval Institute Press, 2011).

19. Only weeks before the *Lusitania* was sunk and in the same area in which it was intercepted, the ship had hoisted an American flag and the hovering submarine did not fire. America was, of course, furious at this wholly illegal act, which put all American shipping at risk.

20. Patrick O'Sullivan, *Lusitania: Unraveling the Mysteries* (Wilton, Ireland: Collins Press), 62.

21. A complete list of British ships sunk month by month in the early years of World War I is available at http://www.naval-history.net/WW1LossesBrMS1914–16.htm.

22. O'Sullivan, *Lusitania*, 68. The range of submarines was considerably enhanced by 1917. Some subs operated off South America, and others entered the Pacific.

23. The German worry about armed merchant shipping was hardly idle speculation. In the months after the sinking of the *Lusitania*, the Admiralty in great secrecy took ordinary freighters, changed their name, perhaps added a funnel to make their identity unclear, flagged them from neutral countries, and installed disguised guns. Q-boats (after the port of Queenstown, where the conversion took place) lured submarines intending to capture them to the surface, hoisted a white flag, put out phony lifeboats, then opened fire and engaged the sub. At least a dozen German submarines were sunk by Q-boats in

the second year of war, after which the submarines struck without warning. See O'Sullivan, *Lusitania*, 32–37.

24. Colin Simpson, *Lusitania* (London: Longman, 1974), 41–42. The head of Cunard stated that he would prefer to lay up the *Lusitania* for the remainder of the war. Passenger traffic was considerably down, and much of the crew had joined the navy. He was told to continue the ship's regular runs.

25. See U.S. Department of State, Senate doc. no. 176 of the Sixty-Seventh Congress, "Lusitania Claims," 1922. This document includes the German response to the assertion of claims by families of American victims. It is perhaps worth noting that there were no American casualties on American ships until America entered the war.

26. See Diana Preston, *Wilful Murder: The Sinking of the Lusitania* (London: Doubleday, 2002).

27. David Ramsey, *Lusitania: Saga and Myth* (London: Chatham Publishing, 2001).

28. See McCart, *Atlantic Liners*, 93–168. See also John Maxtone-Graham, *The Only Way to Cross* (New York: Macmillan, 1972), chaps. 6 and 7.

29. These trends have been extracted from the raw data in Frederick Emmons, *The Atlantic Liners, 1925–70* (New York: Drake Publishers, 1972).

30. See, for example, the extensive photographs in John H. Shaum and William H. Flayhart III, *Majesty at Sea: The Four-Stackers* (New York: W. W. Norton, 1981).

### 15. *Exxon Valdez*

1. Front page, *Seattle Times*, March 24, 1989 (accessed at ProQuest Newspapers).

2. "Grounded Tanker Gushes Oil into Alaskan Waters," *Seattle Times*, March 25, 1989 (accessed at ProQuest Newspapers). For human stories of the days and weeks after the spill see John Keeble, *Out of the Channel: The Exxon Valdez Oil Spill in Prince William Sound* (Cheney: Eastern Washington University Press, 1999). Also see Art Davidson, *In the Wake of the Exxon Valdez: The Devastating Impact of the Alaska Oil Spill* (San Francisco: Sierra Club Books, 1990).

3. Accessed at ProQuest Newspapers.

4. Ibid.

5. It was in this early period that the standard barrel of oil was set at forty-two gallons, a standard that remains today.

6. See Walter W. Jaffee, *The Tankers* (Palo Alto, CA: Glencannon Press, 2008), 4–5. These tankers were far slower than the liners of the time. The fastest tanker took eleven days to cross the Atlantic. Liners did the run in four to five days. For a more thorough discussion of the variety and functions of early tankers see Laurence Dunn, *The World's Tankers* (London: Adlard Coles, 1956).

7. Philippe Valois, *Tankers: An Introduction to the Transport of Oil by Sea* (London: Witherby & Co., 1997), 6.

8. A few of the ships failed, most spectacularly two splitting in half on the same night.

A subsequent investigation concluded that the ship's high-sulfur-content steel became brittle in very cold conditions. There were also allegations that many of the T2s, as they were termed, were shoddily made, though the long subsequent civilian service of many of the vessels suggests otherwise. See http://www.maritimeprofessional.com.

9. The scale of the tanks is about the same as a good-size cathedral; they have been aptly termed "steel cathedrals."

10. See Valois, *Tankers*, 23–36.

11. More accurately there are currently three types of tanker: a smaller size, which operates only within a defined region, such as the Gulf of Mexico; a larger size, which operates in the middle distances between sources and markets; and supertankers, which move oil across vast distances between sources and refining destinations. Nevertheless, all vessels of each size look virtually identical.

12. See Michael Chanpness and Gilbert Jenkins, *Oil Tanker Handbook: 1985* (London: Elsevier Applied Science Publishers, 1985), 1–19.

13. Ibid., 124–125.

14. Ibid., 272.

15. Valois, *Tankers*, 133.

16. Patrick Barkham, "Oil Spills: Legacy of the *Torrey Canyon*," *Guardian*, June 23, 2010 (accessed at ProQuest Newspapers).

17. Report by the Joyce Research Group, University of Georgia, Department of Marine Sciences, http://www.joyeresearchgroup.uga.edu.

18. Joshua Ashenmiller, "The Alaska Pipeline as an Internal Improvement, 1969–1973," *Pacific Historical Review* 75, no. 3 (August 2006): 461–490.

19. See Nancy Lord, *Troubled Waters: A Review of the History, Science, and Technology Associated with the Exxon Valdez Oil Spill and Cleanup* (Homer, AK: Pratt Museum, 1992), 1–5.

20. See the EPA summary of the 1990 act at http://www.epa.gov.

21. "1990 State/Federal Natural Resource Damage Assessment and Restoration Plan for the *Exxon Valdez* Oil Spill," reviewer copy of reproduced typescript, accessed at the University of Michigan Museums Library / Bird Collection.

22. "Prince William Sound after the Exxon Valdez Spill," hearing before the Committee on Merchant Marine and Fisheries, House of Representatives, 103rd Congress, First Session, March 24, 1993 (Washington, DC: Government Printing Office, 1993), 44–45.

23. See *Proceedings of the Exxon Valdez Oil Spill Symposium*, ed. Stanley D. Rice et al. (Bethesda, MD: American Fisheries Society, 1996). Another collection of scientific papers is *Exxon Valdez Oil Spill: Fate and Effects in Alaskan Waters*, ed. Peter G. Wells, James N. Butler, and Jane S. Hughes (Philadelphia: ASTM, 1995). Yet a third group of scholarly studies is *Marine Mammals and the Exxon Valdez*, ed. Thomas R. Loughlin (San Diego: Academic Press, 1994).

24. See Joan F. Braddock et al., "Patterns of Microbial Activity in Oiled and Unoiled Sediments in Prince William Sound," in Rice et al., *Spill Symposium*, 94–107.

25. R. T. Paine, Jennifer L. Ruesink, Adrian Sun, et al., "Trouble on Oiled Waters: Lessons from the *Exxon Valdez* Oil Spill," *Annual Review of Ecology and Systematics* 27 (November 1996).

26. Lord, *Troubled Waters*, 12–14.

27. See the photographs of the embedded boulders and the essentially missing bottom of the *Exxon Valdez* in G. S. Martin, *Tanker Operations: A Handbook for the Ship's Officers*, 3rd ed. (Centerville, MD: Cornell Maritime Press, 1992), 228, 250.

28. Dennis Geogatos, "Repairs on Tanker Valdez Nearing Completion," Associated Press, *Anchorage Daily News*, March 19, 1990, B2, http://www.adn.com.

29. Martin, *Tanker Operations*, 229–230.

30. Mother Nature Network, http://www.mnn.com.

31. For tanker operations before the *Exxon Valdez* disaster see Alex Marks, *Elements of Oil-Tanker Transportation* (Tulsa, OK: PennWell Books, 1982). For a sense of the changed oil tanker world after the wreck see the chapters on design, regulations, insurance, and risk management in Kenneth Rawson, ed., *The Carriage of Bulk Oil and Chemicals at Sea* (Rugby, UK: Institution of Chemical Engineers, 1994).

## 16. *Costa Concordia*

1. "Several Killed in Ship Crash," *Detroit Free Press*, January 14, 2012 (accessed at ProQuest Newspapers).

2. John Hopperstad, "Puyallup Woman Who Survived Cruise Disaster Describes 'Unbelievable' Scene," *McClatchy-Tribune Business News*, January 14, 2012 (accessed at ProQuest Newspapers).

3. "Witnesses, Authorities: Captain Left Ship," *Detroit Free Press*, January 16, 2012, A8.

4. See, for example, the newspapers *Alarabiya* and *Seven Days in Dubai*, the Xinhua News Agency in China, and Asian News International in New Delhi.

5. A few lines already went places that could reasonably be developed for tourism. The Matson Line, for example, mainly shipped produce from Hawaii to the mainland and returned with manufactured goods needed in the islands, but in the 1920s added two ships to take vacationers to Hawaii. These ships might be thought of as passenger ships with cargo rather than cargo ships with passengers.

6. "The State of the Cruise Industry in Passenger Numbers and Product Offerings," Cruise Lines International Association (CLIA), 2014, http://www.cruising.org/vacation/news/press_releases/2014/01/.

7. There are good reasons for dividing the market into ethnic segments. International hotels, which cater to customers of a variety of ethnic backgrounds, have discovered that meeting their food expectations requires Herculean efforts. Breakfast typically consists of several buffets featuring utterly different items: smoked fish in one, noodles and broth in another.

8. See Cruise Lines International Association (CLIA), 2013 North America Cruise Industry Update, at http://www.cruising.org/.

9. Ibid., 3–4.

10. Ibid.

11. Jane Archer, "So Will This Sink the Cruise Industry?," *Daily Telegraph* (London), January 17, 2012, 19 (accessed at ProQuest Newspapers).

12. Ashley Post, "Plaintiffs Firms Prepare to Sue Carnival on Behalf of Cruise Ship Passengers," *Inside Counsel*, March 2012 (accessed at ProQuest Newspapers).

13. "Marine Insurers Assess Costa Concordia Loss," *Reactions*, 2012 (accessed at ProQuest Newspapers).

14. "Union Airs Concerns after Grounding," *BreakingNews.ie*, January 14, 2012 (accessed at ProQuest Newspapers).

15. "Report on the Investigation of Heavy Weather Encountered by the Cruise Ship *Pacific Sun* 200 Miles North North East of North Cape, New Zealand, on 30 July 2008 Resulting in Injuries to 77 Passengers and Crew," Marine Accident Investigation Branch, Carlton House, Southampton, UK, Report no. 14/2009, June 2009, http://www.maib.gov.uk/.

16. For a full list of cruise ship accidents such as grounding, serious listing, dock collisions, etc., see http://www.cruiseshipsinking.com/.

17. See "Outbreak Updates for International Cruise Ships," http://www.cdc.gov/.

18. See Anders Björkman, "Costa Concordia Incidents in January 13–14, 2012 Caused by Ship Not Being Seaworthy," http://heiwaco.tripod.com/news8.htm.

19. Laurel Brubaker Calkins, "Carnival Cruise Ship Ordered Held in Texas Shipwreck Suit," Bloomberg News, March 31, 2012, http://www.bloomberg.com/news/2012–03-31/texas-judge-orders-cruise-ship-seizure-in-costa-concordia-suit.html.

20. Laurel Brubaker Calkins, "Carnival Ship Released from Texas Port after Deal Is Struck," Bloomberg BusinessWeek, April 1, 2012, http://www.businessweek.com/news/2012–03-31/carnival-triumph-released-to-sail-after-deal-struck-lawyer-says.

21. One can even locate cruise ships for sale on the Internet.

22. See www.atlantis.com for the rooms and facilities.

# INDEX

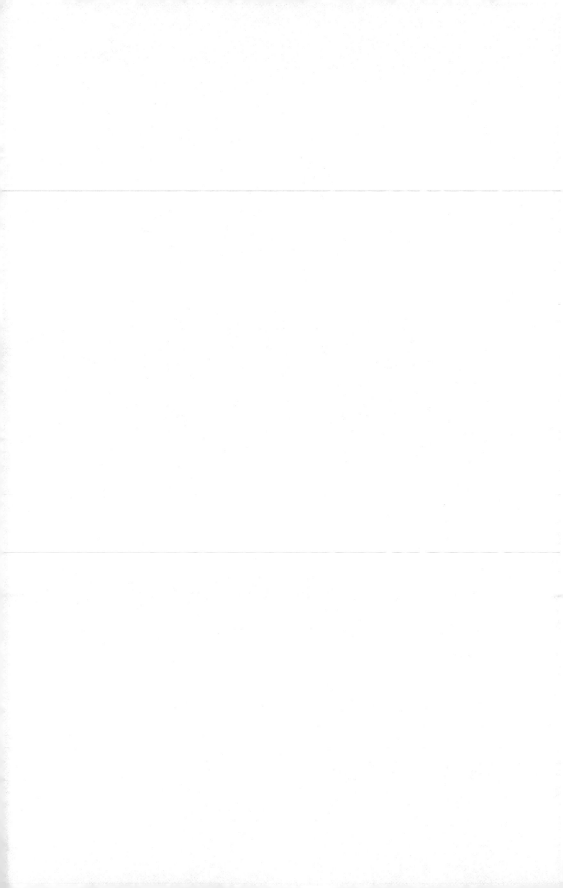